GOOGLE AND DEMOCRACY

For the first time in human history, access to information on almost any topic is accessible through the Internet. A powerful extraction system is needed to disseminate this knowledge, which for most users is Google. Google Search is an extremely powerful and important component to American political life in the twenty-first century, yet its influence is poorly researched or understood.

Sean Richey and J. Benjamin Taylor explore for the first time the influence of Google on American politics, specifically on direct democracy. Using original experiments and nationally representative cross-sectional data, Richey and Taylor show how Google Search returns quality information, that users click on quality information, and gain political knowledge and other contingent benefits. Additionally, they correlate Google usage with real-world voting behavior on direct democracy.

Building a theory of Google Search use for ballot measures, *Google and Democracy* is an original addition to the literature on the direct democracy, Internet politics, and information technology. An indispensable read to all those wishing to gain new insights on how the Internet has the power to be a normatively valuable resource for citizens.

Sean Richey is Associate Professor of Political Science at Georgia State University, U.S.A. He was a Fulbright Fellow from 2013–2014 at the University of Tokyo. He was a Japan Society for the Promotion of Science Post-Doctoral Fellow at the University of Tokyo between 2004 and 2006. He researches American politics with a specialization in elections, voting behavior, public opinion, and quantitative methodology. His research has appeared in two peer-reviewed books and in academic journals articles in *Political Research Quarterly*, the *British Journal of Political Science*, *Political Communication*, *Political Behavior*, *International Studies Quarterly*, and others.

J. Benjamin Taylor is Assistant Professor of Political Science at the University of North Carolina Wilmington, U.S.A. He researches and teaches courses on American political behavior with a focus on the effect of media on political behavior and attitudes. He has published a peer-reviewed book, *Extreme Media and American Politics: In Defense of Extremity* (Palgrave Macmillan, 2017) and has published articles in *Political Communication*, *State Politics & Policy Quarterly*, *American Politics Research*, *Politics & Religion*, and *Presidential Studies Quarterly*.

'The most recent US presidential election showed that voting behavior is far more complicated than expected; this book helps us to understand the digital tools citizens use to frame their vote decision.'

'The radical change in citizens' access to specific and relevant information has profound implications for democracy. Soon, we may well feel that voting without searching for information on the Internet is as irresponsible as making a major purchase without comparison shopping, or signing a binding contract without reading it. *Google and Democracy* makes a compelling, and reassuring, case for that future.'

GOOGLE AND DEMOCRACY

Politics and the Power of the Internet

Sean Richey and
J. Benjamin Taylor

NEW YORK AND LONDON

First published 2018
by Routledge
711 Third Avenue, New York, NY 10017

and by Routledge
2 Park Square, Milton Park, Abingdon, Oxon, OX14 4RN

*Routledge is an imprint of the Taylor & Francis Group, an informa
business*

Library of Congress Cataloging-in-Publication Data
A catalog record for this book has been requested

ISBN: 978-1-138-06643-4 (hbk)
ISBN: 978-1-138-06645-8 (pbk)
ISBN: 978-1-315-15915-7 (ebk)

Typeset in Times New Roman
by Apex CoVantage, LLC

CONTENTS

TABLES

FIGURES

ACKNOWLEDGMENTS

This project began in conversations about the amazing nature of Google in the first decade of the twenty-first century. As we discussed the potential for the Internet to revolutionize the way people got information, we realized we were making empirically testable observations and raising empirical questions. There was one problem: very few—if any—scholars were doing work along the lines of inquiry we were going in 2010 and 2011. Thus, this idea for this project was born. This book represents what we believe is the first of many steps toward understanding what Google means for American democracy. There is much more to uncover, and we discuss this at length throughout the book. Fundamentally, this book was a labor of love—love of the research process, love of direct democracy and state politics, and a deep and abiding sense that there is much more good than bad about the Internet's potential. We are not crazy; we know there are reasons to be concerned about malfeasance and ne'er-do-wells online. However, given the enormous upside, we owe it to ourselves to cast a more nuanced view about the effects of Internet use and Internet politics in the United States.

As with any project that has gone on for as long as ours has, we owe a debt of gratitude to many people. Surely, someone will be left out. For that, we apologize. However, we do want to take some space and thank several people without whom this book might have never been written. First, we want to thank Shauna Reilly. Shauna is an excellent scholar, and a contributor to this book. Her work with us on aspects of Chapter 7 is instrumental to helping us close the loop on how Google Search behavior affects roll-off. Additionally, we would like to thank Thomas Carsey who, as the editor at *State Politics & Policy Quarterly* in 2011, gave us immensely helpful and constructive comments about aspects of this research. Without his direction and the excellent reviews from our anonymous reviewers we might have given up on aspects of this project without seeing through to this end. Furthermore, we owe a hearty "thank you" to the anonymous reviewers of this book, and to all of the conference discussants and fellow panelists who have seen and commented on aspects of this book over the last five years. We cannot possibly name them all here, but they helped guide this work as well.

Doing the experiments for this book was difficult, to say the least. It is incredibly difficult to convince someone to take time out of their day walking down the streets of Atlanta to answer questions about a ballot measure they have never heard of. However, besides ourselves, Junyan Zhu became an expert at doing just that during her time as Sean's research assistant. Junyan was dedicated and dependable for the weeks our experiments were in the field. Similarly, it is difficult to have good experiments if you do not have willing and able subjects. We would like to thank all those students, non-students, and MTurkers who gave their time for little compensation to help us answer the questions we pose in this book. We also appreciate the ANES principle investigators for doing an outstanding survey in 2012 concerning direct democracy. The ANES contributions to this book make it a much better study, and help make our experimental findings generalizable. Finally, we appreciate Natalja Mortensen at Routledge for guiding us and this book through the review process. This has been an incredibly smooth process, and for that, we will be forever grateful to Natalja. Last but not least, we want to thank our families for their love and support. Working on a book means that you do not get to spend time with others in your life who deserve your time, so for their patience and understanding, we are very grateful.

There is no doubt that many people have had a hand in making this book what it is now. We are, as we state above, very thankful for the help, guidance, and critique we have received. This has, no doubt, made this book better. Regardless, this is our book, so whatever errors exist are ours and ours alone. Our names are listed alphabetically signifying the equal and collaborate authorship we share for this book. We did not receive any funding from outside sources to conduct this research, including Google. We feel that this book is an important contribution, but it is just a first step. The stage is now set for more scholars to replicate our findings, and make better, deeper, and more conclusive findings about the impact of Internet politics in American politics and direct democracy.

1

INTRODUCTION

Direct Democracy, Political Knowledge, and the Internet

For the first time in human history, citizens have instant access to all the information they need to make wise choices—thanks to the Internet. This access radically challenges basic assumptions in democratic theory, which has assumed mass ignorance since Plato. While access to the sum of human knowledge is a significant event for politics in general, this is a particularly important development for direct democracy in the United States. Direct democracy is the one place where citizens get to actually make policy for themselves, and—as democratic theory suggests—having the requisite knowledge to make informed choices is a crucial aspect for citizen participation in these elections. The Internet has the potential to profoundly alter the capacity for citizens to make choices, but for the Internet to distribute almost all of the world's knowledge requires a formidable information extraction system, and for most users Google serves this propose (Sullivan 2013).

If Google is the conduit through which millions of people now access information, then a question quickly arises as to the influence of Google on information provision. The "filter bubble" theory (Pariser 2011) states that Google has a deleterious effect on knowledge among Internet users because people create ideological and informational cocoons in which only the information and perspectives that they seek out enter their information patterns. Others suggest that the Internet offers a great opportunity but only if it is handled properly (Sunstein 2009). More recently, some research purports to show how Internet search engines can be "gamed" to produce biased results (Epstein and Robertson 2015). Problematically, these theories and studies do not consider the economic incentives and computer science underlying Google, nor do they actually include any empirical tests of whether Google behaves as they suggest. Thus, an important gap exists between their hypotheses about how the Internet affects political behavior and empirical evidence of such behavior.

In the chapters that follow, we highlight several critiques explored in the current Internet politics literature and expand this research to show the utility of Google, particularly concerning the impact of the Internet on direct democracy. Almost all of the concerns about the Internet revolve around its lack of a formal editorial gatekeeper to sort through the vast information and efficiently present a palatable selection of the most important stories. Because mass media has editors, information is controlled and bias is limited. Without an editor, a dual concern is that there is both too much information to sort through efficiently and no limits on misinformation or manipulation.

We show that the computer science underlying Google functions as a *de facto* editorial gatekeeper, delivering a limited selection of the most important information from the Internet without bias and removing conspiracy websites and sites explicitly created to manipulate information when searching for information related to direct democracy. The system accomplishes this selection without an active editor simply as a result of how the search algorithm sorts information. We readily admit (and outline in Chapter 2) there are certainly pertinent concerns about Google, but much of the debate is not based on how the algorithm works, nor is there any scientific empirical test of the search engine using real-world information for real-world political purposes.

In this book, we create the first experimental tests of Google's search provision on political knowledge, and they clearly show uniformly high-quality search results using three ballot measures in various election contexts. Furthermore, we show that beyond knowledge, Google Search creates confidence in one's choices, which is the mechanism for decreasing roll-off in direct democracy elections. These findings are important because direct democracy is difficult for average citizens because they have to decide far more than in a usual election, but they do not have the usual heuristics that assist with voting decisions. They vote not on party and politician but rather the expected outcome of entirety of the policy. Even in this manipulative, complex environment, our results consistently show that Google provides almost exclusively mainstream and informative sites to searchers. Our results also show that people usually follow Google's guidance and click on highly ranked sites. This pattern holds true even when participants' cookies have created a filter bubble for them. Across all topics, we confirm that the searchers learn from the sites that they click on by having them complete open-ended knowledge tests about the most important aspects of the topics. The results show that randomly assigned searchers who used Google are far more knowledgeable about the topics than those who did not use it. In sum, Google improves the quality of civic competence in theoretically expected and empirically validated ways in direct democracy.

At the end of this chapter, we provide a more detailed outline of these findings, as well as those from other empirical tests of Google Search. However, before we move to the empirical tests, it is important to outline the current state of scholarly work on both political knowledge as direct democracy as well as their intersection. These two fields of American politics are vast, but they speak to each other in important ways. One of the ways they meet—and the place we find fruitful in this book—is at the intersection of political knowledge, direct democracy, and the utility of technology.

The Path to Citizen Action: Political Knowledge and Direct Democracy

A Quintessential American Debate

Political knowledge is an essential characteristic of good citizens in a democracy (Dalton 2013; Kuklinski and Quirk 2001; Milner 2002), yet research on civic literacy shows that most citizens lack knowledge about politics (Delli Carpini and Keeter 1996). Concerns about civic competence or political knowledge are not new. In fact, concerns about civic and political knowledge, or the lack thereof, have animated Western political thought for millennia. The debate generally focuses on two aspects; first, are citizens capable of learning, and, second, in what ways can technology assist citizens in their quest to become the knowledgeable civic participants much of democratic theory requires them to be?

In terms of capacity, scholars have generally been ambivalent about the extent to which the masses can learn about politics. As far back as Plato, there has been a vein of thought considering human cognition and the maintenance of political knowledge to be the fundamental stumbling block for democracy government. For instance, Plato's "Allegory of the Cave" (2004, 514a-20d) is a warning about the persistence of ignorance among the general public. Plato suggests that even if one—as a philosopher—understands the truth or true nature of a thing, when one tries to inform other citizens, those who are being informed about true reality would ignore the truth-teller out of their lack of interest in acquiring knowledge.[1] This lack of interest in acquiring knowledge is the basis for Plato's argument for philosopher-kings in the Republic, and was used by the framers of the U.S. Constitution as a legitimating reason for republican government at the national level in the United States (Markovitz 2012). Furthermore, as Carr (2008) points out, not only was the lack of capacity a problem in Plato's Socratic dialogues, but the use of technology (i.e., writing) itself was a harbinger of a less educated, less intelligent public.[2]

Concern about levels of political knowledge and the degree to which the public can make good decisions is constant in American politics. Since the Progressive Era, there has been a steady march toward more popular democratic governance in the United States at the state level (Johnston 2003). This movement toward popular democracy coincides with the onset of rapid technological innovation at the beginning of the twentieth century. Like the ancients before them, some American thinkers hoped these changes would usher in an era of enlightened citizens making wise choices for the United States, while others doubted that this development would be the case.

In the 1920s, a fascinating public debate on this crucial question occurred between Walter Lippmann and John Dewey. Lippmann argued that the public was incapable of making good political choices because it was broadly limited in two critical areas: accurate dissemination of information (i.e., technology, but—specifically—the press) and general capacity to understand information at all (Lippmann 1922). His concern about the public's capacity to make sense of political and social events is well taken as even modern empirical research clearly supports his assertion that general political knowledge is quite low in the mass public (i.e., see Delli Carpini and Keeter 1996). Lippmann was particularly concerned about the ability for citizens to overcome bias to accurately understand information they were given. Lippmann writes,

> For the troubles of the press, like the troubles of representative government, be it territorial or functional, like the troubles of industry, be it capitalists, cooperative, or communist, go back to a common source: the failure of a self-governing people to transcend their casual experience and their prejudice, by inventing, creating, and organizing a machinery of knowledge. It is possible they are compelled to act without a reliable picture of the world, that governments, schools, newspapers, and churches make such small headway against the more obvious failings of democracy, against violent prejudice, apathy, preferences for the curious trivial as against the dull important, and the hunger for sideshows and three-legged calves. This is the primary defect of popular government, a defect inherent in its traditions, and all other defects can, I believe, be traced to this one.
>
> *(1922, 364–5)*

Lippmann's fundamental critique is what we now understand as "motivated reasoning," which is to say that people seek out information that confirms their previous held beliefs and reject information that is counter to those prior attitudes (Kunda 1990; Lodge and Taber 2000).

While we now understand the cognitively powerful effects of motivated reasoning (i.e., see Nyhan and Reifler 2010; Redlawsk, Civettini, and Emmerson 2010), one of Lippmann's highlighted proposed methods of overcoming the biases citizens have is to provide them with better information through the press. However, he regards this proposed solution as a non-starter. He pointed out that most people did not have the means to obtain information through the news media—such as those who were isolated on farms or those in urban tenement slums who were illiterate—and that the media were not capable of providing quality information. He states,

> The press, in other words, has come to be regarded as an organ of direct democracy. . . . It is not workable. And when you consider the nature of

news, it is not even thinkable. . . . Unless the event is capable of being named, measured, given shape, made specific, it either fails to take the character of news, or it is subject to the accidents and prejudices of observation. . . . At its best the press is a servant guardian of institutions; at its worst it is a means by which the few exploit social disorganization to their own ends.

(1922, 363–4)

Dewey (1927), conversely, contended that the public could be educated and that new technology would readily permit dissemination of information. The future Dewey depicted involved technological progress that would grant greater access to information, facilitating better choices by the masses. In *The Public and Its Problems*, Dewey says,

It has been implied throughout that knowledge is communication as well as understanding. . . . Record and communication are indispensable to knowledge. Knowledge cooped up in private consciousness is a myth, and knowledge of social phenomenon is primarily dependent upon dissemination, for only by distribution can such knowledge be either obtained or tested.

(1927, 176–7)

Dewey saw a twentieth century full of rapid technological progress that would facilitate increased sharing of information and knowledge. This process would result in a more informed public, which would result in a more democratic United States. Information and its dissemination were the foundations upon which a new American politics could be developed.

Dewey's hopes for technology and information were predicated on the assumption that citizens *wanted* information and *wanted* to be involved. Lippmann took a darker view. Lippmann saw Americans' reactions to rapid technological change, and his concerns centered on the inability and unwillingness for citizens to utilize technology for civic reasons rather than leisurely pastimes and entertainment. Moreover, Lippmann (1922) points out that apathetic citizens would not seek out information even if it was easy to obtain. In his view, entertainment would be too irresistible for these new technologies and their civic functionality would be wasted or not utilized at all. Thus, the key question to explore—and still unanswered part of the debate over civic competence—is this: if citizens use new technologies, does it improve their civic competence, and does this lead to more participation in difficult areas of American politics? There is a robust literature on the impact of the Big Three media (i.e., newspapers, radio, and television), and we provide answers toward settling this debate by analyzing objective Internet search data on direct democracy in the twenty-first century.

Empirical Research on Political Knowledge

As highlighted by Plato's writings and the Lippmann-Dewey debate, political knowledge is the fundamental concept at work when trying to explain how technology can improve citizen engagement. Technology is the tool that leads to competence, so understanding "competence" is fundamentally important. Scholarship shows there is difficulty in deciding exactly what knowledge *is* and how it is *used*. For some, political knowledge is a construct that can be ascertained by fact-based questions about civics or current events (Delli Carpini and Keeter 1996), while others focus on the specifics of policy outcomes associated with items in public opinion polls to denote knowledge among the public (i.e., see Bartels 1996; 2005; 2007). Civics-based knowledge is generally considered a robust measure because it is indicative of other, deeper levels and types of political information (Delli Carpini and Keeter 1996). Others suggest that, in some circumstances, researchers want to be able to understand how citizens encounter and organize political knowledge from the world around them or "surveillance" political knowledge (i.e., see Jerit, Barabas, and Bolsen 2006). However, regardless of the type of information involved, both of these recall measures (Lodge, McGraw, and Stroh 1989; Popkin and Dimock 1999) are indicative of normatively beneficial political knowledge.

Of course, there are some who question the relevance of facts based on political knowledge. Facts are generally colored to some degree by the cognitive and affective biases held by the person interpreting the fact or political event (Sniderman, Brody, and Tetlock 1993). Heuristics are deployed in a number of scenarios that help citizens make decisions in limited information environments (Popkin 1991; Lau and Redlawsk 2006). Yet, even when using cognitive shortcuts, those who are able to use heuristics most efficiently are those with more fact-based political knowledge (Lau and Redlawsk 1997). Even proxies for the effects of political knowledge—such as political sophistication (i.e., see Luskin 1990)—cannot completely mute the effects of fact-based political knowledge in multivariate studies (Popkin and Dimock 1999). Regardless of the debates about the conceptualization of knowledge and measurement, the level of political knowledge in the mass public does ebb and flow with the salience of issues (Stimson 2015). Yet, when we look at aggregate knowledge and opinion, the most important, salient political topics over the course of modern American politics research shows that opinion and levels of knowledge are quite stable (Page and Shapiro 1992).

One of the reasons we focus on political knowledge in this book—beyond reasons pertaining to democratic theory—is that political knowledge is one of the most robust predictors of political participation in American politics (Delli Carpini and Keeter 1996; Galston 2001). Political knowledge is a significant predictor for turning out to vote (Delli Carpini and Keeter 1996), discussing politics (Eveland 2004), advocating for preferred candidates (Richey and Taylor 2012), being active in campaigns more generally (Rosenstone and Hansen 1993), and is an important component in political social networks (Huckfeldt and Sprague 1995). Thus, the empirical effects of political knowledge match the normative aspirations: political knowledge is a normatively good quality because it produces citizen engagement and activity, and we can measure these effects through citizen behavior. The question then becomes: how does one acquire political knowledge?

A prerequisite for political knowledge is political interest (Campbell et al. 1960; Converse 1964; Luskin 1990), and we know that social capital has a reciprocal relationship with political knowledge (Putnam 2001). Somewhat obvious attributes like increased levels of education, socioeconomic status, and age also predict increased levels of political knowledge (Delli Carpini and Keeter 1996; Galston 2001). Beyond these attitudinal and demographic predictors, we also know that media play an important role giving Americans the information they need to understand and learn about politics (Graber 1988; 2001; 2004).

Mass Media and Political Knowledge

Until the advent of the Internet, media communication was a one-way transmission model. Citizens got their news by listening to the radio, reading a newspaper, or watching television. The minimal effect hypothesis (Berelson, Lazarsfeld, and McPhee 1954; Lazarsfeld, Berelson, and Gaudet 1948) arose during this time. Minimal effects posited that media have little effects over the choices and attitudes of citizens because they rely mainly on attitudinally congruent information and partisan identification for their choices. This theory mainly applies to attitude change, but it also specified expectations for political knowledge. As voters were not reading much information that was counter to their prior opinions, they did not have much need to learn more about politics beyond rudimentary information. However, as researchers began to use more sophisticated techniques, the ways in which media teach and help citizens learn became more apparent.

Television is the medium most people use to access political news (Graber 2004). Learning about politics happens when citizens watch traditional television news (Graber 1990), but it also occurs through "soft news" such as *Oprah* or *The Daily Show* (Baum 2003) and even through extreme, partisan television content (Taylor 2017). Learning through television is often described as shallow given the nature of the medium and its reliance on short, framed content that eschews deeper levels of information and contextual information like one finds in newspapers (Clarke and Fredin 1978). However, newspapers are not uniformly better for generating knowledge. Typically, citizens with greater levels of prior political knowledge, interest, and education are best at getting political knowledge from newspapers (De Vreese and Boomgaarden 2006; Jerit, Barabas, and Bolsen 2006). Citizens with the lowest levels of prior knowledge or interest actually see the biggest gains in knowledge from television (Chaffee and Frank 1996; Jerit, Barabas, and Bolsen 2006; Prior 2005). The Internet represents a hybridization of these media, which is coupled with the capacity for the user to generate as well as consume content (December 1996; Morris and Ogan 1996). As a result, the Internet creates a unique opportunity for scholars of political knowledge and its effects to expand our understanding about how political information is obtained.

Direct Democracy: Its Role in American Politics

What we call "direct democracy" in the United States is an outgrowth of the Progressive Movement from the late nineteenth and early twentieth centuries (Goebel 2003; Piott 2003; National Conference of State Legislatures 2012). In this book, we focus on ballot measures—specifically referendums—because they are the most common form of direct democracy in the United States today (see Ballotpedia 2014; National Conference of State Legislatures 2012). Intiatives, referendums, and recall were first used at the state level in South Dakota and quickly moved into use in most western states' politics and legal systems, but now every state in the Union has some aspect of direct democracy incorporated into their government (Cronin 1989; National Conference of State Legislatures 2015). Progressives sought direct democracy reforms to combat the powers of state legislatures particularly as a method to break the link between monopoly-based corporate culture and state political power brokers (Goebel 2003). Furthermore, reformers believed that one of the reasons for citizen apathy was their lack of agency through the political institutions of the day, so direct democracy was promoted as a method to encourage more citizen engagement and activism (Smith and Tolbert 2004). Despite the best hopes of Progressive Era reformers, empirical evidence suggests direct democracy has its own set of issues for citizens.

Ballot questions often feature obscure language that is difficult to comprehend, and voters are typically not familiar with the issues in question (Reilly 2010; Reilly and Richey 2011; Seabrook, Dyck, and Lascher 2015). This reality is a motivating concern for this book. The complexity of ballot questions generates questions about voter competence when answering them. One often-discussed solution to alleviate voter incompetence is the Internet (Bennett 2008; Boulianne 2009; Cantijoch, Jorba, and San Martin 2008; Chadwick 2006; Davis 2005; Hardy and Scheufele 2005; Kenski and Stroud 2006; Price and Cappella 2002; Stromer-Galley 2003; Wellman et al. 2001; Wojcieszak and Mutz 2009). Easy access to information through the Internet may improve voter knowledge about ballot measures. While the beneficial impact of Internet usage is intuitive, the current research[3] is highly skeptical of the Internet's ability to improve citizen competencies because of worries about selective exposure and the creation of online news enclaves.

As we highlighted in the previous section, political knowledge is both an intrinsic and extrinsic good in American politics. The extrinsic value of knowledge is pronounced in direct democracy in particular because these elections allow citizens to bypass their elected representatives and make policy themselves. If the limited political knowledge in the general public extends to ballot measures and the issues at stake on those measures, then citizens could be making (or not making) laws without any legitimate basis for their decisions. A contributing factor to these concerns is that limited knowledge on ballot measures is predictable because ballot measures often have low salience (Kenski and Stroud 2006). This lack of salience results in problematically low contextual knowledge (Schlozman and Yohai 2008) about ballot measures in many elections, but when there are environmental factors increasing salience, voters learn more and are more likely to participate in other elections as well (Burnett and Kogan 2012; Nicholson 2003).

Even though research shows citizens are often uninformed about most ballot measures, mounting evidence suggests that voters are not completely ignorant of facts about ballot measures (Bowler, Donovan, and Tolbert 1998; Gibson and Caldeira 2009; Lupia 1994; Soltan 1999), which indicates voters may doing research on ballot measures prior to arriving at the polls. Bowler and Donovan (2000) find that despite limited information, citizens are making "thoughtful responses" to referendum questions, and Smith and Tolbert (2004) suggest that the use of initiatives actually increases citizen competence within a state because it increases voting, civic engagement, and confidence in government. Further, Nicholson (2005) reports that ballot initiatives can affect the information and discourse on up-ticket races, demonstrating that citizens do seek out some information about these types of elections.

As awareness about ballot measures increases, scholars point out that—as with general political knowledge—voters use heuristics and other cognitive shortcuts to decrease the costs of learning about this relatively opaque area of politics. Lupia (1994) shows that citizens use endorsements from interest groups, politicians, and other opinion leaders to make reasonable choices on ballot questions, and—crucially—he finds these choices are consistent with their preferences when voters have full information. However, citizens must access the heuristics outside the ballot booth for Lupia's (2001) model to hold, and Internet searching makes such access more likely. Thus, Internet searches may possibly facilitate the civic competence needed for direct democracy by providing easy access to valuable information and heuristics.

Details About the Ballot Measures in This Book

Given the preceding discussion about the importance of ballot measures in American politics, it is important to detail the facts surrounding each of the questions used in the parts of the book discussing the experiments. There are relatively few examples of ballot measures being used to generate elevated levels of attention, or at least enough attention and publicity that they may affect voter behavior. Some notable exceptions to this norm include California's Prop. 187 in 1994 (Nicholson 2005) and Prop. 8 in 2008 (Abrajano 2010) as well as the raft of same-sex marriage ballot measures across the states in 2004 (Biggers 2011). As Nicholson (2003) demonstrates, when ballot measures do affect awareness or interest the effects are often quite subtle. Recently, high salience ballot measures typically deal with social issues like same-sex marriage or state-level concerns about undocumented immigrants. These are the types of "wedge issues" (see Hillygus and Shields 2014) specifically designed to motivate one side of the partisan spectrum while simultaneously dividing the other side of the aisle.

The capacity for ballot measures to be used as motivation for voters is most clearly demonstrated with the eleven states proposing same-sex marriage bans in 2004.[4] Many of these states with ballot measures were solidly Republican (i.e., Arkansas, Georgia, Kentucky, and Oklahoma to name a few), but the purpose of measures in these states was to energize the socially conservative, more religious base of the 2004 Bush reelection coalition while perhaps making some would-be Democratic voters think twice about their position on this or other similar social issues (Dao 2004). Social issue ballot measures are generally easier for voters because they can clearly identify supporters and opponents. Thus, social issue ballot measures could conceivably be an easier case for showing how research can produce learning; high salience would beget media coverage, and the nature of the issues would allow subjects to align the issues with their prior attitudes. While these are empirical claims worth scrutiny, they represent an iteration beyond our study, which is the first of its kind ever done on Internet search behavior in politics.

For the purposes of this study, we chose ballot measures that would present a hard case for citizen knowledge acquisition and partisan heuristics. Unlike social issue ballot measures, the three ballot measures used in this book's experiments have direct policy implications, which also make them more complex and "hard" in the Carmines and Stimson (1980) definition of issue type. Carmines and Stimson (1980; 1989) note that issue voting takes place among "hard" issues and "easy" issues. Hard issues are those where the details are often technical, relatively new to the political agenda, and the means of policymaking are at issue rather than simply the ends (see Carmines and Stimson 1980, 80). Furthermore, two of the three ballot measures we study experimentally are clearly "valance" issues, whereas the third measure is somewhere between a valance and "positional" issue (Stokes 1963). Valance issues are those where there is general agreement that something should be done about an issue, but the specific steps to alleviate the policy concern are in question. For instance, everyone agrees that education is important, and that every child should have access to some basic level of education. However, deciding how to provide that education creates conflict; there is agreement that the issue is important and deserves attention, but the resolution for the policy is not clear. Positional issues are more clearly aligned with ideological or partisan issue dimensions, and are therefore easier to understand and easier for parties to agree on their preferred policy outcome. It may not be the case that the differing sides agree with each other, but at least they understand their relative positions. Using these theoretical constructs, we now explain our reasons behind our experimental ballot measures.

Transportation Special Purpose Local Option Sales Tax, Georgia Summer 2012

The first ballot question we test is the Georgia transportation Special Purpose Local Option Sales Tax (T-SPLOST) from July of 2012. In an effort to specify and fund transportation projects around the state simultaneously, the Georgia General Assembly approved a referendum allowing the state's citizens to vote by sub-region on a 1% sales tax increase for a period of ten years. The funds from this 1% tax would be spent on a pre-approved list of projects that was created locally by a commission of local mayors and a few other local politicians in each of the various sub-regions.[5] The election was held during the general primary on July 31, 2012—not to be confused with the presidential primary of the same year.

This ballot measure makes for a unique test because it is a "hard" issue, a valance issue, and cuts across ideological and other traditional heuristics in Georgia politics. Public debate on the measure was rancorous with a coalition of T.E.A. Party,[6] Black Nationalist, and environmental groups opposing the bill for differing reasons, and most centrist organizations such as the Chamber of Commerce supporting it. The most highly watched and anticipated list of projects belonged to the Atlanta region, where almost half the population of Georgia resides and where some of the worst traffic in the nation occurs on a daily basis (Caldwell 2013; Toone 2016).

Arguably considered the most important policy-related ballot question in Georgia politics in decades, we chose this ballot measure to examine whether the Internet would allow voters to gain more knowledge and be more involved on this complicated and vexing issue specifically because there was so much already known and understood about the measure in general. Furthermore, given the complex nature of the support and opposition groups, we maintain this measure is a likely candidate for misinformation and misleading claims about the policy on the ballot or its intended effects. Basically, the July 2012 T-SPLOST vote exhibits all of the traits that make ballot measures difficult for Americans, and a good test for ascertaining the utility of Internet search engines for knowledge acquisition in complex areas.

In the end, the measure passed in just three of the twelve districts. In the Atlanta region, the measure was defeated 63% to 37%.

Charter Schools, Amendment 1, Georgia Fall 2012

The second ballot measure we test deals with the creation and administration of charter schools in Georgia. Nathan (1997), a charter school advocate, describes charter schools as "public, non-sectarian schools that operate under a written contract from a local school board or other organization." Finn and colleagues outline the five fundamental aspects of charter schools as,

> 1) they can be created by almost anyone, 2) they are exempt from most state and local regulations, essentially autonomous in their operations, 3) they are attended by youngsters whose families choose them, 4) they are staffed by educators who are also there by choice, and 5) they are liable to be closed for not producing satisfactory results.
>
> *(2001, 15)*

The first charter school started in Minnesota in 1991, and within the first decade of the charter school movement more than 2,500 charter schools were established across the United States (Finnaga et al. 2004).

Charter schools got their start in Georgia shortly after the Minnesota start in 1991. Georgia passed a law enabling local school boards to convert existing schools into charter schools following specific guidelines passed by the General Assembly in 1994, and start-up charters were allowed in 1998 (Georgia Department of Education 2016). Until 2008, regardless of the conversion or start-up nature of the charter school, the charter "authorizer" was the local board of education. However, in 2008, the Georgia General Assembly created the Georgia Charter School Commission (Georgia Department of Education 2016), which was found unconstitutional by the Georgia Supreme Court in 2011 for overriding the constitutional role of local boards of education (Touchton 2011). Thus, before the ballot measure, charter schools in Georgia had been established only through local school boards and only for a short, three-year period by the Georgia Charter Schools Commission. To overcome this legal obstacle the political leadership in Georgia decided to place a measure on the ballot to make the Commission constitutional. This ballot measure amends the state's constitution to allow the state legislature to set up a commissioning board that could override the wishes of local school boards and establish charter schools anyway.

Like the T-SPLOST before it, Georgia's 2012 Amendment 1 is a classic hard, valance issue with complex cross-cutting heuristics. Key executive level figures like Republican State School Superintendent John Barge came out against the measure as well as organizations such as the Georgia School Boards Association. Meanwhile, unlikely partners Republican Governor Nathan Deal and Democratic Atlanta Mayor Kasim Reid were strong supporters as were organizations like the Georgia Charter Schools Association. As Washington (2012) reports, this ballot measure cut across discernible voting patterns in Georgia with African Americans in south metro Atlanta and social conservatives in the northern Atlanta suburbs being two of the more supportive voting blocs. Thus, as with transportation in the T-SPLOST measure, this ballot measure deals with policy process and institutional arrangements rather than the specifics ends of a policy. Furthermore, as no one in the debate was particularly opposed to innovation in education, this measure is clearly a hard, valance issue. Once again, this makes a hard case to test our theory and hypotheses.

Minimum Wage Increase Amendment, Public Question 2 (SCR 1), New Jersey Fall 2013

Finally, the third ballot measure we test is the 2013 New Jersey minimum wage increase. At first look, a ballot measure on the minimum wage may not seem to fit into the hard, valance issue category as with T-SPLOST and the charter school amendment, but the details of the minimum wage battle in New Jersey illustrate how it does fit into these categories for our purposes.

In January 2013, Governor Chris Christie vetoed a bill that would raise the New Jersey minimum wage by $1.25, and would tie the minimum wage to the Consumer Price Index (Portnoy 2013). In response to this veto, Democrats in the state legislature voted to put the issue to the voters through a ballot measure. This ballot measure received national attention because of the national minimum wage debate, but also because Gov. Christie was widely seen as a legitimate 2016 Republican presidential contender. At the national level, increasing the minimum wage is a largely partisan issue. However, because New Jersey is a generally more Democratic state, attitudes on this ballot measure cut a more pro-business and pro-worker divide. Some Democrats were opposed because it did not go far enough, in their mind, and some business groups—such as the New Jersey Main Street Alliance—were actually actively in favor of the measure for quality-of-life reasons (Livio 2013a; 2013b). Polling near Election Day showed that almost two-thirds of voters in the Garden State supported the measure (Verndon 2013). Those groups and politicians who opposed the measure claimed they opposed it not for ideological or partisan reasons, but because they did not want minimum wage policy attached to the state constitution (Verndon 2013).

This ballot measure makes a good, final test because this issue would generally be considered an easy issue that could—under the right circumstances—be a positional issue. In this case, however, it is a hard issue because the details of the measure are not just about raising the minimum wage, but about attaching the increase to a specific economic measure for future increases. This makes for a more complex decision that also makes the choice somewhat less distinctly partisan.[7] Furthermore, although minimum wage debates can often seem positional at the national level, Gov. Christie proposed a revised, more scaled-down minimum wage increase of his own (Farrell 2013; Portnoy 2013). Thus, while Gov. Christie's critics and proponents of the ballot measure presented the issue as a simple choice, the reality is that the minimum wage debate in New Jersey in 2013 was a classic valence issue where both sides wanted a similar outcome (i.e., increased minimum wage), but differed on the details of the policy and the process on how to get to their preferred end-goal. These contextual factors make this ballot measure—like the T-SPLOST and charter school amendments—a hard, valance issue. To conclude this introductory chapter, we close with an outline of the book.

A Roadmap for the Book

Summary for Chapter 1

In this chapter, we outlined the basics of our theory about how information technology can assist voters in direct democracy. To make the case about why this is important, we outlined the normative positions and empirical findings concerning political knowledge in the United States. Basically, citizens do not know much in general, but there is evidence that when it matters, they know just enough. More to the point, we know that citizens *learn* about politics in multiple ways, but the primary way is through media. Information technology is an extension of media at this time. Furthermore, we established the need for this research in the direct democracy literature. In the one area of politics where citizens are actually making policy for themselves, knowledge is a premium component to qualitatively valuable citizen action. We conclude with specific details about the ballot measures we test and why they make good test cases for our theory.

Chapter 2—Internet Politics and the Computer Science of Google

In Chapter 2, we provide an in-depth theory of how Google can create more knowledgeable citizens. We focus on Google because of staggering usage figures showing Google is by far the dominant platform for accessing news. We explain how the computer science underlying Google ensures that accurate information will be provided even when users' personal information is included. The computer science shows that the filter bubble is not likely to be a problem. Thus, the negative potential effects of usage that pundits and scholars worry about will not be an issue for most users. Understanding how the search algorithm works explains a significant portion of the effect of the Internet on political behavior because Google is not only the dominant search provider, but also the largest news provider, with 50% of all news consumed coming through Google links. Crucially, we situate this book in the wider literature on Internet politics describing both the merits of our unique and heretofore original study as well as the limits of our claims.

Chapter 3—Google Search Returns on Ballot Measures

Here, we empirically show what Google returns to users for three policy areas (i.e., transportation funding, charter schools, and minimum wage) and three direct democracy ballot measures. Using three experiments, with different samples and different ballot measures, we show that Google provides accurate information and primarily links to mainstream news sources and informative websites. This chapter establishes the baseline for information provision through Google on questions that might be found on ballot measures. We highlight that these questions present a hard case given the ideological nature of the policies involved, but—even here—we find that Google searches provide normatively and substantively good information.

Chapter 4—Click Behavior and Direct Democracy

Beyond simply showing that Google provides beneficial information, we find that users effectively navigate the links that Google returns to them. The evidence derives from two factors related to how Google displays links. First, the top-listed links dominate all other links. Thus, understanding which site Google links to first is paramount. Second, 90% of users do not go past the first page of returned results, which are typically the top-ten suggested links. Thus, the information overload thesis, whereby users are overwhelmed by too much online content, is eliminated by Google's search display, which narrows the billions of websites down to a concise top-ten list. We show that concerns over clustering within ideologically similar websites is overblown, at least for direct democracy, because most of the results listed on the top of the page are mainstream media and other non-ideological sites. Since only a few users bother to dig deeper than the first page, searches are effectively limited to mainstream sites. Beyond the experiments, we use 2012 American National Election Study data to get a better sense of the predictors of using Internet research on direct democracy in the first place. By coupling these two sets of empirical findings, we are able to create a robust picture of Internet search behavior on direct democracy.

Chapter 5—Learning Happens: Political Knowledge and Three Ballot Measures

In Chapter 5, we examine the outcomes of searching Google for political information. We find a consistent positive effect from information searches. Users are able to extract valuable information from the websites that Google suggests to them, and thus, we can expect improved civic competence from using Google.

We also show that this effect endures for at least one week, suggesting that the learning is long term. Our findings are unexpected and robust, and they are generated through a completely original series of experiments that have yet to be performed in political science for other research questions.

Chapter 6—Internet Research and Intellectually Secure Decisions in Direct Democracy

What is the value of political knowledge if one is not secure enough to have confidence in the decisions one makes as a result of that knowledge? In this chapter, we examine this question with evidence from T-SPLOST and the charter school amendment as well as the 2012 ANES. We show that treatment group subjects exhibit positive effects on vote confidence from their search activity, which is to say, they are more secure in their decisions as the amount of time spent searching increases. We then show how respondents in the 2012 ANES who used Internet research to learn about ballot measures reported that their ballot measures were easier to understand compared to respondents who did not use the Internet for research and that they enjoy voting on ballot measures more than those who do not use the Internet for research. These sets of results create the mechanism that transitions political knowledge into a motivational impetus for participating in direct democracy. As citizens learn they become more confident, and this confidence should lead to positive effects on behavior like decreased "roll-off," or not voting, down the ballot.

Chapter 7—Real-World Applications: Does Google Use Correlate With Real-World Political Behavior?

We use a combination of nationally representative survey data and observational data from Google Trends to examine how search behavior predicts real-world behavior. First, we find that those who use the Internet report rolling-off less on ballot measures with 2012 ANES data. Then, we validate this with a series of models using Google Trends data finding that states exhibiting a higher density of Google searches for ballot measure names are states where citizens are less likely to roll-off. This chapter lends external validity to aspects of our experimental results showing that Google Search behavior has real-world implications. The fundamental point is that Google Search activity is a proxy for increasing interest in the population, which leads to a more knowledgeable and active voting public. Most importantly, it means that voters continue to vote down their ballot, which—as highlighted from previous chapters' empirical results—is likely due to the increased knowledge and confidence citizens get from doing research on Google.

Chapter 8—Conclusions and Directions for Future Research

We conclude the book by summarizing our arguments and results. We suggest ways in which computer science and political science can be jointly and success-fully analyzed by future researchers. We also examine some policy proposals to help citizens make better decisions on ballot measures. During an age when eve-ryone has a computer in their pocket (i.e., cell phone) that is more complex than those aboard the Apollo spaceships sending astronauts to the moon, it seems both short-sighted and uninformed to assume that the worst possible outcomes will nec-essarily come to pass. The likelihood that any one individual or group may use the Internet or search returns to bias political information in their favor is remote. However, holding a Pollyanna-like view that all will be well and nothing bad can happen from Internet searches for political information is equally problematic. A middle ground exists. In some areas of democracy, where a need for information is present and malfeasance and conspiracy theories are unlikely, it makes sense both theoretically and practically that the Internet can be a valuable resource and improve the quality of citizens' behaviors and participation in government. This book shows one such area—direct democracy. Appropriately, it is the oldest, truest form of democracy.

Notes

1 More to the point, the cave-dwellers would rather beat the philosopher to death than accept that their reality consists of shadows on the wall, not the Form of the images they see.
2 To see the original discussion in the Platonic dialogues, see Hackforth's (1952, 274c–275b) translation of *Phaedrus*.
3 We explore this literature at length in the next chapter.
4 The states were Mississippi, Georgia, Oklahoma, Kentucky, Arkansas, North Dakota, Montana, Utah, Ohio, Michigan, and Oregon.
5 There were twelve sub-regions: N.W. Georgia, GA Mountains, Atlanta, Three Rivers, N.E. Georgia, Middle Georgia, Central Savannah River, River Valley, Heart of Georgia, S.W. Georgia, South Georgia, and Coastal. The ballot measure only passed in three— Central Savannah River, River Valley, and Heart of Georgia—of the twelve regions.
6 T.E.A. is actually an acronym for "taxed enough already" (Schroeder 2009).
7 As told by former Speaker of the House Tip O'Neill (1988) and his former Chief of Staff Chris Matthews (1999), one of the main reasons members of Congress resisted any automatic increases in social security benefits until 1982 was because they wanted to be able to take credit for the increases and make it a politically useful issue during elections. Pegging benefits to complex economic indicators makes the decision more complex and technocratic.

References

Abrajano, Marisa. 2010. "Are Blacks and Latinos Responsible for the Passage of Propo-sition 8? Analyzing Voter Attitudes on California's Proposal to Ban Same-Sex Mar-riage in 2008." *Political Research Quarterly* 63 (4): 922–32.

Ballotpedia. 2014. "Forms of Direct Democracy in the American States." Information. *Ballotpedia.org*. https://ballotpedia.org/Forms_of_direct_democracy_in_the_American_states.

Bartels, Larry M. 1996. "Uninformed Votes: Information Effects in Presidential Elections." *American Journal of Political Science* 40 (1): 194–230.

———. 2005. "Homer Gets a Tax Cut: Inequality and Public Policy in the American Mind." *Perspectives on Politics* 3: 15–31.

———. 2007. "Homer Gets a Warm Hug: A Note on Ignorance and Extenuation." *Perspectives on Politics* 5: 785–90.

Baum, Matthew A. 2003. "Soft News and Political Knowledge: Evidence of Absence or Absence of Evidence?" *Political Communication* 20: 173–90. http://dx.doi.org/10.1080/10584600390211181.

Bennett, W. Lance. 2008. "Changing Citizenship in a Digital Age." In *Civic Life Online: Learning How Digital Media Can Engage Youth*, edited by W. Lance Bennett, 1–24. Cambridge: MIT Press.

Berelson, Bernard, Paul F. Lazarsfeld, and William N. McPhee. 1954. *Voting: A Study of Opinion Formation in a Presidential Campaign*. Chicago, IL: University of Chicago Press.

Biggers, Daniel R. 2011. "When Ballot Issues Matter: Social Issue Ballot Measures and Their Impact on Turnout." *Political Behavior* 33 (1): 3–25. doi:10.1007/s11109-010-9113-1.

Boulianne, Shelley. 2009. "Does Internet Use Affect Engagement? A Meta-Analysis of Research." *Political Communication* 26 (2): 193–211. doi:10.1080/1058460 0902854363.

Bowler, Shaun and Todd Donovan. 2000. *Demanding Choices: Opinion, Voting, and Direct Democracy*. Ann Arbor: University of Michigan Press.

Bowler, Shaun, Todd Donovan, and Caroline J. Tolbert. 1998. *Citizens as Legislators: Direct Democracy in the United States*. Columbus: Ohio State University Press.

Burnett, Craig M. and Vladimir Kogan. 2012. "Familiar Choices: Reconsidering the Institutional Effects of the Direct Initiative." *State Politics & Policy Quarterly* 12 (2): 204–24. doi:10.1177/1532440012442912.

Caldwell, Clara. 2013. "Study: Atlanta, Chicago Tie for 7th Worst Commute." *Atlanta Business Chronicle*. February 5. www.bizjournals.com/atlanta/morning_call/2013/02/study-atlanta-chicago-tie-for-7th.html.

Campbell, Angus, Philip E. Converse, Warren E. Miller, and Donald E. Stokes. 1960. *The American Voter*. Chicago, IL: University of Chicago Press.

Cantijoch, Marta, Laia Jorba, and Josep San Martin. 2008. "Exposure to Political Information in New and Old Media: Which Impact on Political Participation." Paper presented at the annual meeting of the APSA 2008 Annual Meeting, Hynes Convention Center, Boston, Massachusetts, August 28.

Carmines, Edward G. and James A. Stimson. 1980. "The Two Faces of Issue Voting." *American Political Science Review* 74 (1): 78–91. doi:10.2307/1955648.

———. 1989. *Issue Evolution: Race and the Transformation of American Politics*. Princeton: Princeton University Press.

Carr, Nicholas. 2008. "Is Google Making Us Stupid?" *Yearbook of the National Society for the Study of Education* 107 (2): 89–94. doi:10.1111/j.1744–7984.2008.00172.x.

Chadwick, Andrew. 2006. *Internet Politics: States, Citizens, and New Communication Technologies*. New York: Oxford University Press.

Chaffee, Steven and Stacey Frank. 1996. "How Americans Get Political Information: Print Versus Broadcast News." *The Annals of the American Academy of Political and Social Science* 546 (1): 48–58. doi:10.1177/0002716296546001005.

Clarke, Peter and Eric Fredin. 1978. "Newspapers, Television and Political Reasoning." *Public Opinion Quarterly* 42 (2): 143–60. doi:10.1086/268439.

Converse, Philip E. 1964. "The Nature of Belief Systems in Mass Publics." In *Ideology and Discontent*, edited by David Apter. New York: Free Press.

Cronin, Thomas E. 1989. *Direct Democracy: The Politics of Initiative, Referendum and Recall*. Cambridge, MA: Harvard University Press.

Dalton, Russell J. 2013. *Citizen Politics: Public Opinion and Political Parties in Advanced Industrial Democracies*. 6th ed. Washington, D.C.: CQ Press.

Dao, James. 2004. "Same-Sex Marriage Issue Key to Some G.O.P. Races." *The New York Times*. November 4. www.nytimes.com/2004/11/04/politics/campaign/samesex-marriage-issue-key-to-some-gop-races.html.

Davis, Richard. 2005. *Politics Online: Blogs, Chatrooms, and Discussion Groups in American Democracy*. New York: Routledge.

December, John. 1996. "Units of Analysis for Internet Communication." *Journal of Computer-Mediated Communication* 1 (4): 14–37. doi:10.1111/j.1083–6101.1996. tb00173.x.

Delli Carpini, Michael X. and Scott Keeter. 1996. *What Americans Know About Politics and Why It Matters*. New Haven, NY: Yale University Press.

Dewey, John. 1927. *The Public and Its Problems*. New York, NY: Holt Press.

Epstein, Robert and Ronald E. Robertson. 2015. "The Search Engine Manipulation Effect (SEME) and Its Possible Impact on the Outcomes of Elections." *Proceedings of the National Academy of Sciences* 112 (33): E4512–21. doi:10.1073/pnas.1419828112.

Eveland, Jr., William P. 2004. "The Effect of Political Discussion in Producing Informed Citizens: The Roles of Information, Motivation, and Elaboration." *Political Communication* 21: 177–93. doi:10.1080/10584600490443877.

Farrell, Joelle. 2013. "Christie Conditionally Vetoes Minimum-Wage Hike." News Blog. *Philly.com*. January 29. http://articles.philly.com/2013-01-29/news/36638066_1_vetoes-minimum-wage-hike-christie-senate-president-stephen-sweeney.

Finn, Jr., Chester E., Bruno V. Manno, and Gregg Vanourek. 2001. *Charter Schools in Action: Renewing Public Education*. Princeton, NJ: Princeton University Press.

Finnaga, Kara, Nancy Adleman, Lee Anderson, Lynyonne Cotton, Mary Beth Donnelly, and Tiffany Price. 2004. "Evaluation of the Public Charter Schools Program." Final Report 2004–08. *Policy and Program Studies Service*. Washington, D.C.: Department of Education. www2.ed.gov/rschstat/eval/choice/pcsp-final/finalreport.pdf.

Galston, William A. 2001. "Political Knowledge, Political Engagement, and Civic Education." *Annual Review of Political Science* 4 (1): 217–34. doi:10.1146/annurev. polisci.4.1.217.

Georgia Department of Education. 2016. "General Frequently Asked Questions." Government Information. *GADOE.gov*. December. www.gadoe.org/External-Affairs-and-Policy/Charter-Schools/Pages/General-Frequently-Asked-Questions.aspx.

Gibson, James L. and Gregory A. Caldeira. 2009. *Citizens, Courts, and Confirmations: Positivity Theory and the Judgments of the American People*. Princeton: Princeton University Press.

Goebel, Thomas. 2003. *A Government by the People: Direct Democracy in America, 1890–1940*. Chapel Hill, NC: University of North Carolina Press.

Graber, Doris. 1988. *Processing the News: How People Tame the Information Tide*. New York, NY: Longman Press.

———. 1990. "Seeing Is Remembering: How Visuals Contribute to Learning from Television News." *Journal of Communication* 40 (3): 134–56. doi:10.1111/j.1460–2466.1990. tb02275.x.

———. 2001. *Processing Politics: Learning from Television in the Internet Age*. Chicago, IL: University of Chicago Press.

———. 2004. "Mediated Politics and Citizenship in the Twenty-First Century." *Annual Review of Psychology* 55: 545–71.

Hardy, Bruce W. and Dietram A. Scheufele. 2005. "Examining Differential Gains from Internet Use: Comparing the Moderating Role of Talk and Online Interactions." *Journal of Communication* 55 (1): 71–84. doi:10.1111/j.1460–2466.2005.tb02659.x.

Hillygus, D. Sunshine and Todd G. Shields. 2014. *The Persuadable Voter: Wedge Issues in Presidential Campaigns*. Princeton: Princeton University Press.

Huckfeldt, Robert and John Sprague. 1995. *Citizens, Politics and Social Communication: Information and Influence in an Election Campaign*. Cambridge, UK: Cambridge University Press.

Jerit, Jennifer, Jason Barabas, and Toby Bolsen. 2006. "Citizens, Knowledge, and the Information Environment." *American Journal of Political Science* 50: 266–82.

Johnston, Robert D. 2003. *The Radical Middle Class: Populist Democracy and the Question of Capitalism in Progressive Era Portland, Oregon*. Princeton, NJ: Princeton University Press.

Kenski, Kate and Natalie Jomini Stroud. 2006. "Connections Between Internet Use and Political Efficacy, Knowledge, and Participation." *Journal of Broadcasting & Electronic Media* 50 (2): 173–92. doi:10.1207/s15506878jobem5002_1.

Kuklinski, James H. and Paul J. Quirk. 2001. "Conceptual Foundations of Citizen Competence." *Political Behavior* 23 (3): 285–311. doi:10.1023/A:1015063108221.

Kunda, Ziva. 1990. "The Case for Motivated Reasoning." *Psychological Bulletin* 108 (3): 480–98. doi:10.1037/0033–2909.108.3.480.

Lau, Richard R. and David P. Redlawsk. 1997. "Voting Correctly." *American Political Science Review* 91 (3): 585–98. doi:10.2307/2952076.

———. 2006. *How Voters Decide: Information Processing During Election Campaigns*. Cambridge, UK: Cambridge University Press.

Lazarsfeld, Paul F., Bernard Berelson, and Hazel Gaudet. 1948. *The People's Choice: How the Voter Makes Up His Mind in a Presidential Campaign*. New York, NY: Columbia University Press.

Lippmann, Walter. 1922. *Public Opinion*. New York, NY: Free Press.

———. 1925. *The Phantom Public*. New York, NY: Macmillan.

Livio, Susan K. 2013a. "N.J. Ballot Question Tying Minimum Wage Increases to Constitution Sparks Expensive Battle." News Blog. *NJ.com*. November 4. www.nj.com/politics/index.ssf/2013/11/nj_ballot_question_tying_minimum_wage_increases_to_constitution_sparking_expensive_battle.html.

———. 2013b. "N.J. Voters Approve Constitutional Amendment Raising Minimum Wage." News Blog. *NJ.com*. November 5. www.nj.com/politics/index.ssf/2013/11/nj_voters_approve_constitutional_amendment_raising_minimum_wage.html.

Lodge, Milton and Charles Taber. 2000. "Three Steps Toward a Theory of Motivated Political Reasoning." In *Elements of Reason: Cognition, Choice, and the Bounds of Rationality*, edited by Arthur Lupia, Mathew D. McCubbins, and Samuel L. Popkin, 183–213. New York, NY: Cambridge University Press.

Lodge, Milton, Katheleen M. McGraw, and Patrick Stroh. 1989. "An Impression-Driven Model of Candidate Evaluation." *American Political Science Review* 83 (2): 399–419.

Lupia, Arthur. 1994. "Shortcuts Versus Encyclopedias: Information and Voting Behavior in California Insurance Reform Elections." *American Political Science Review* 88 (1): 63–76. doi:10.2307/2944882.

———. 2001. "Dumber than Chimps? An Assessment of Direct Democracy Voters." In *Dangerous Democracy? The Battle Over Ballot Initiatives in America*, edited by Larry Sabato, Bruce A. Larson, and Howard R. Ernst, 66–70. Lanham: Rowman & Littlefield.

Luskin, Robert C. 1990. "Explaining Political Sophistication." *Political Behavior* 12: 331–61.

Markovitz, Irving Leonard. 2012. "Constitutions, The Federalist Papers, and the Transition to Democracy." In *Transitions to Democracy*, edited by Lisa Anderson, 42–71. New York, NY: Columbia University Press.

Matthews, Chris. 1999. *Hardball: How Politics Is Played, Told by One Who Knows the Game*. Revised and updated edition. New York, NY: Simon & Schuster.

Milner, Henry. 2002. *Civic Literacy: How Informed Citizens Make Democracy Work.* Hanover: University Press of New England.

Morris, Merrill and Christine Ogan. 1996. "The Internet as Mass Medium." *Journal of Computer-Mediated Communication* 1 (4): 39–50. doi:10.1111/j.1083–6101.1996. tb00174.x.

Nathan, Joe. 1997. *Charter Schools: Creating Hope and Opportunity for American Education: The Jossey-Bass Education Series*. San Francisco, CA: Jossey-Bass Inc. https://eric.ed.gov/?id=ED410657.

National Conference of State Legislatures. 2012. "Initiative, Referendum and Recall." Professional Organization. *NCSL.org*. September 20. www.ncsl.org/research/elections-and-campaigns/initiative-referendum-and-recall-overview.aspx.

———. 2015. "Chart of the Initiative States." Professional Organization. *NCSL.org*. December. www.ncsl.org/research/elections-and-campaigns/chart-of-the-initiative-states.aspx.

Nicholson, Stephen P. 2003. "The Political Environment and Ballot Proposition Awareness." *American Journal of Political Science* 47 (3): 403–10. doi:10.1111/1540–5907.00029.

———. 2005. *Voting the Agenda: Candidates, Elections, and Ballot Propositions.* Princeton: Princeton University Press.

Nyhan, Brendan and Jason Reifler. 2010. "When Corrections Fail: The Persistence of Political Misperceptions." *Political Behavior* 32: 303–30.

O'Neill, Tip. 1988. *Man of the House: The Life and Political Memoirs of Speaker Tip O'Neill*. New York: St. Martins Mass Market Paper.

Page, Benjamin I. and Robert Y. Shapiro. 1992. *The Rational Public: Fifty Years of Trends in Americans' Policy Preferences*. Chicago, IL: University of Chicago Press.

Pariser, Eli. 2011. *The Filter Bubble: How the New Personalized Web Is Changing What We Read and How We Think*. London, UK: Penguin.

Piott, Steven L. 2003. *Giving Voters a Voice: The Origins of the Initiative and Referendum in America*. Columbia, MO: University of Missouri Press.

Plato. 1952. *Plato: Phaedrus*. Translated by R. Hackforth. Cambridge, UK: Cambridge University Press.

———. 2004. *Republic*. Translated by C.D.C. Reeve. 3rd Edition. Indianapolis: Hackett Publishing Company, Inc.

Popkin, Samuel L. 1991. *The Reasoning Voter: Communication and Persuasion in Presidential Campaigns*. Chicago: University of Chicago Press.

Popkin, Samuel L. and Michael A. Dimock. 1999. "Political Knowledge and Citizen Competence." In *Citizen Competence and Democratic Institutions*, edited by Stephen L. Elkin and Karol Edward Soltan. University Park, PA: Pennsylvania State University Press.

Portnoy, Jenna. 2013. "Christie Vetoes Minimum Wage Bill, Democrats Vow to Put Measure on Ballot." Newspaper. *NJ.com*. January 28. www.nj.com/politics/index.ssf/2013/01/christie_minimum_wage.html.

Price, Vincent and Joseph N. Cappella. 2002. "Online Deliberation and Its Influence: The Electronic Dialogue Project in Campaign 2000." *IT & Society* 1 (1): 303–29.

Prior, Markus. 2005. "News vs. Entertainment: How Increasing Media Choice Widens Gaps in Political Knowledge and Turnout." *American Journal of Political Science* 49 (3): 577–92. doi:10.1111/j.1540–5907.2005.00143.x.

Putnam, Robert D. 2001. *Bowling Alone: The Collapse and Revival of American Community*. New York, NY: Simon and Schuster.

Redlawsk, David P., Andrew J. W. Civettini, and Karen M. Emmerson. 2010. "The Affective Tipping Point: Do Motivated Reasoners Ever 'Get It?'" *Political Psychology* 31 (4): 563–93.

Reilly, Shauna. 2010. *Design, Meaning and Choice in Direct Democracy: The Influences of Petitioners and Voters*. Burlington, VT: Ashgate Publishing.

Reilly, Shauna and Sean Richey. 2011. "Ballot Question Readability and Roll-Off: The Impact of Language Complexity." *Political Research Quarterly* 64 (1): 59–67. doi:10.1177/1065912909349629.

Richey, Sean and J. Benjamin Taylor. 2012. "Who Advocates? Determinants of Political Advocacy in Presidential Election Years." *Political Communication* 29 (4): 414–27. doi:10.1080/10584609.2012.721869.

Rosenstone, Steven J. and John Mark Hansen. 1993. *Mobilization, Participation, and Democracy in America*. New York, NY: Macmillan.

Schlozman, Daniel and Ian Yohai. 2008. "How Initiatives Don't Always Make Citizens: Ballot Initiatives in the American States, 1978–2004." *Political Behavior* 30 (4): 469–89. doi:10.1007/s11109-008-9062-0.

Schroeder, Anne. 2009. "T.E.A. = Taxed Enough Already: POLITICO.com." *Politico.com*. April 9. www.politico.com/blogs/anneschroeder/0409/TEA__Taxed_Enough_Already.html.

Seabrook, Nicholas R., Joshua J. Dyck, and Edward L. Lascher. 2015. "Do Ballot Initiatives Increase General Political Knowledge?" *Political Behavior* 37 (2): 279–307. doi:10.1007/s11109-014-9273-5.

Smith, Daniel A. and Caroline Tolbert. 2004. *Educated by Initiative: The Effects of Direct Democracy on Citizens and Political Organizations in the American States*. Ann Arbor: University of Michigan Press.

Sniderman, Paul M., Richard A. Brody, and Phillip E. Tetlock. 1993. *Reasoning and Choice: Explorations in Political Psychology*. New York, NY: Cambridge University Press.

Soltan, Karol Edward. 1999. "Introduction: Civic Competence, Democracy, and the Good Society." In *Citizen Competence and Democratic Institutions*, edited by Stephen L. Elkin and Karol Edward Soltan, 1–17. University Park: Pennsylvania State University Press.

Stimson, James A. 2015. *Tides of Consent: How Public Opinion Shapes American Politics.* 2nd Edition. New York, NY: Cambridge University Press.

Stokes, Donald E. 1963. "Spatial Models of Party Competition." *American Political Science Review* 57 (2): 368–77. doi:10.2307/1952828.

Stromer-Galley, Jennifer. 2003. "Diversity of Political Conversation on the Internet: Users' Perspectives." *Journal of Computer-Mediated Communication* 8 (3). doi:10.1111/j.1083–6101.2003.tb00215.x.

Sullivan, Danny. 2013. "Google Still World's Most Popular Search Engine by Far, but Share of Unique Searchers Dips Slightly." Industry Blog. *Search Engine Land.* February 11. http://searchengineland.com/google-worlds-most-popular-search-engine-148089.

Sunstein, Cass R. 2009. *Republic.com 2.0.* Princeton, NJ: Princeton University Press.

Taylor, J. Benjamin. 2017. "The Educative Effects of Extreme Television Media." *American Politics Research* 45 (1): 3–32. doi:10.1177/1532673X15600516.

Toone, Stephanie. 2016. "Worst Traffic Cities in America." Newspaper. *AJC.com.* March 15. www.myajc.com/news/local/how-much-time-metro-atlantans-waste-traffic/W5neMc6ISKOdQ1u5rzUdSP/.

Touchton, James R. 2011. "A Supreme Decision: The Next Steps for Charter Schools in Georgia." *Legislative Analysis: At Issue.* Atlanta, GA: Senate Research Office. www.senate.ga.gov/sro/Documents/AtIssue/atissue_nov11.pdf.

Verndon, Joan. 2013. "New Jersey Minimum Wage Ballot Fight Heats up." News Blog. *NorthJersey.com.* September 29. http://archive.northjersey.com/cm/2.1593/news/minimum-wage-ballot-fight-heats-up-1.692536.

Vreese, Claes H. de, and Hajo Boomgaarden. 2006. "News, Political Knowledge and Participation: The Differential Effects of News Media Exposure on Political Knowledge and Participation." *Acta Politica* 41 (4): 317–41. doi:10.1057/palgrave.ap.5500164.

Washington, Wayne. 2012. "State's Voters Approve Charter Amendment." Newspaper. *Ajc.com.* November 6. www.ajc.com/news/news/charter-school-amendment-heading-toward-passage/nSy2J/.

Wellman, Barry, Anabel Quan Haase, James Witte, and Keith Hampton. 2001. "Does the Internet Increase, Decrease, or Supplement Social Capital? Social Networks, Participation, and Community Commitment." *American Behavioral Scientist* 45 (3): 436–55. doi:10.1177/00027640121957286.

Wojcieszak, Magdalena E. and Diana C. Mutz. 2009. "Online Groups and Political Discourse: Do Online Discussion Spaces Facilitate Exposure to Political Disagreement?" *Journal of Communication* 59 (1): 40–56. doi:10.1111/j.1460–2466.2008.01403.x.

2

INTERNET POLITICS AND THE COMPUTER SCIENCE OF GOOGLE

In this chapter, we focus our attention squarely on Google and Internet politics. In the sections that follow, we lay out our theory for Google's impact on direct democracy knowledge acquisition, and examine how our expectations fit within the larger literature on Internet politics. The previous chapter established political knowledge and direct democracy are the political components of this book, but there is more than simply understanding how citizens gain knowledge on ballot measures in a general sense. We specifically care about how citizens gain knowledge on ballot measures *using the Internet*—in this case, Google. Before we can fully examine the impact of Google, we first need to explore three important questions: What aspects of the Internet's development led to it being a fertile place for politics and political behavior? In what ways do Internet politics inform American politics at present? Finally, what is "under the hood" with Google, and can we trust the returns it brings for users? The answers to these questions animate this chapter, and provide the avenue for placing this book in the larger discussion about Internet politics in the United States.

Why the Hope for Technology?

Thinking back to the Lippmann-Dewey debate, we can see that the Internet represents something like the pinnacle of information-driven society. Lippmann and Dewey could have never imagined the volume, speed, or accuracy with which people could locate information they need on any topic. We might also imagine that both thinkers would point out that the Internet is exactly the reason they take their respective positions: Lippmann foresaw the entertainment-drive in media even at the height of the newspaper era, and Dewey understood that information was going to be the hallmark of twentieth-century life. Yet, who was correct in their assumptions about the value of this information? We may not be able to answer that question conclusively in this book, but we believe our evidence demonstrates the validity of Dewey's positions. Access to information can improve the knowledge about the choices citizens have to make.

In general, many reasons exist to believe that Internet research will inform voters, rather than confuse or mislead them. We know that the Internet is broadly helpful in spreading accurate information, despite concerns about the influence of misinformation, propaganda, and extremism (Buddenbrock 2016; N. Lee 2016). Google's Bayesian "PageRank" algorithm is explicitly designed to and regularly returns valuable information (Arasu et al. 2001; Brin and Page 1998). As we outline in later chapters, subjects using Google searches for ballot measure information consistently returned informationally and normatively valuable websites, such as for the state Office of Elections or other government information pages. Another common search result in our experiments was Ballotpedia,[1] which is a nonprofit foundation website specializing in verified, accurate information about politics—particularly state politics.

An additional consideration is that the sheer amount of information on the Internet facilitates exposure to broader perspectives than can be accessed through broadcast media. Crucially, the interactive nature of the Internet allows the receiver to ask questions through posts on blogs or message boards, something that is impossible with unidirectional broadcast media. The interactivity should allow Internet users to clarify their misunderstandings and obtain more precise knowledge. Most importantly, the user can access the Internet's information whenever they want and not have to wait for the broadcast medium or printed page to be produced. Thus, through 24-hours-a-day, 365-days-a-year access, the Internet provides near unlimited provision of almost the entirety of human knowledge. Important gaps remain in personal Internet access, but these are rapidly diminishing, and the national government aims to be providing 100% access by 2020 or 2025 (Federal Communications Commission 2010).

The Development of the Internet and Internet Politics

To fully understand the ways this book matters, it is important to understand the history of the Internet and Internet politics. While this history is certainly not exhaustive, it is illustrative of the evolution of the Internet from both theoretical and practical points of view.[2] The most important point—for our purposes—is developers' focus on the Internet as a tool for good in the world. Regardless of our current dilemmas in the present (i.e., filter bubbles, flaming, "fake" news, etc.), there is no doubt that at each step in the evolution of the Internet, those who were building the infrastructure genuinely thought they were doing something normatively valuable for society. As such, there has always been an implicit political aspect to the Internet, which—at times—has become quite explicit.

Origins of the "Internet"

What we now know as the "Internet" began as a project in the 1960s called the Advanced Research Projects Agency network, or "ARPAnet" (Hafner and Lyon 1998). The goal of this network was to make communication between defense agencies, contractors, and military personal faster and more efficient. By the 1980s, universities and more government agencies had joined in on the program, and—by 1994—the Internet was available for public use as well (Hafner and Lyon 1998). For the first time, anyone with a computer that had access to this network of connected machines could access information stored on servers and other machines around the world with just a few clicks of a mouse.

Initially, the expectations for how the Internet might affect human behavior and politics were theoretical or, at best, aspirational. Curran et al. (2016) point out that the initial focus for Internet advocates was the democratization of information, just as Dewey had claimed nearly a century earlier. However, these hopes did not take into account the very real discrepancies between those who had access initially and those who did not. Socioeconomic, educational, and social position were early indicators of Internet access, so the capacity for broad citizen engagement through the Internet was quite limited (Curran, Fenton, and Freedman 2016). These limitations coupled with the lack of a robust way to interact with other users—beyond chat rooms or other thin types of participation— Internet politics was fundamentally unrealized potential until the dawn of the twenty-first century (Chadwick and Howard 2010).

The first truly political purposes of the Internet developed as part of Web 2.0 (Chadwick and Howard 2010; O'Reilly 2010). According to O'Reilly, Web 2.0 marks a turn from the Internet as a depository of information to a dynamic system where users are part of the creation process (O'Reilly 2010). Rather than simply accessing information in a virtual portal, users' access to information and their use of it makes that information more important in the system (i.e., Google's PageRank process for search results). Users can create content and interact with each other (i.e., Wikipedia or social media). This dynamic environment means that the Internet is ripe with potential for uses in politics and political behavior.

Internet Politics and Political Behavior

The Internet has become an important place for American citizens to engage in politics (Adamic and Glance 2005; Chadwick 2006; Drezner and Farrell 2007; Smith 2009). In 2008, more than 50% of Americans said they used the Internet as a way to engage politically (Smith 2009). As of 2016, nearly 66% of Americans use Facebook with almost one-third of those frequently engaging on political topics (Duggan and Smith 2016). It is important to note that while "The

Internet" is generally discussed as single thing, it is actually a complex ecosystem (i.e., thus, why the term "web" was first brought into use). Online activity includes commenting on blogs, using micro-blogs and social media, as well as using Internet search engines to access more content and information. The exact effects of these various political activities are not completely clear at this time, but research suggests that blogging can be effective for spurring political action among the most engaged (Kahn and Kellner 2004). In a large study on the effect of blogs, Pole (2010) shows blogs increase political knowledge, activism, and salience among key groups in American politics. However, online activity is always impacted by the density of Internet usage, and access to the Internet generally (Farrell 2012). It should be noted, too, that the Internet is not a panacea for political knowledge and engagement (Richey and Zhu 2015), which is why activity online is a key behavior of interest. It is behavior that impacts politics in the United States rather than Internet access alone.

For social media, Facebook activity is generally associated with increased offline political activity. Research shows Facebook has promise as a tool motivating voter turnout (Bond et al. 2012; Teresi and Michelson 2015), and the use of social media generally generates an accurate representation of citizens' ideologies and belief systems (Bond and Messing 2015). Twitter—a micro-blogging site— shows positive effects mobilizing users into political action using private messages, but public messages and tweets have no significant effects (Coppock, Guess, and Ternovski 2015).

It is becoming increasingly apparent that Internet politics will be crucial in the twenty-first century. Facebook and YouTube are increasingly places for political expression and organizing (Halpern and Gibbs 2013), and some of the most impactful events of this young century involve Internet politics. For instance, social media and other forms of Internet politics have been identified as influential on the Arab Spring in 2011 (Khondker 2011). Specifically, Wael Ghonim—an Egyptian-born Google employee—started a Facebook page to protest the death of Khaled Said who was killed at the hands of Hosni Mubarak's Egyptian government early in the spring of 2011 (Ghonim 2012). Within weeks of its creation, the Facebook page had over 250,000 "likes" and was used as a hub for others who organized through Facebook and Twitter beyond the reach of the traditional security apparatus in Egypt contributing to the overthrow of the Mubarak regime (Ghonim 2012; Vargas 2012). In a similar vein, "hacktivists"— like Edward Snowden—use Internet politics as a method to shine a light on government Internet and communication-gathering activities under the guise of an open information environment (Benkler 2013).

All of this strongly suggests that the Internet will be used politically, and that knowing the process that information is disseminated is crucial to understanding the impact of the Internet. Now, we turn to examining the possible political impacts of the most used tool for information gathering, Google.

Examining the Computer Science of Google

Google as Gatekeeper

There are five main concerns about the Internet as a source for political information:

1. Fallacious, superfluous, and malicious information is commonly available.
2. Millions of websites make it difficult to find information.
3. Manipulative people can easily create misleading websites.
4. Conspiracy theory websites are left unchecked.
5. Ideological clustering and cocooning occur more readily than in the past.

All of these potential problems stem from the notion that there is no gatekeeper, editor, or editorial board for the Internet (Carr 2011; Hindman 2009; Shirky 2008). Fundamentally, news editors try to sort through information to present an optimal selection on what consumers want to know, while eliminating badly written or overtly manipulative stories. Editors act as agenda-setters (McCombs and Shaw 1972). Typically, editors[3] select information based on the quality of the sources, thoroughness of the reporting, and—in some cases—the ideological match of the frame and organization (Deuze 2005; Entman 2004). Editors decide what should be on the agenda and establish issue salience, which affects the way the public evaluates issues and political actors (McCombs 1997). Although ideology plays a role in some of these processes, the norm of objectivity gives editors gravitas with readers and viewers, and curtails possibly extreme ideological behavior (Page 1996; Schudson 2001). Information on the Internet lacks this explicit control, so it is legitimate that scholars are suspicious of the Internet as a beneficial tool for democracy.

The computer science behind Google's search algorithm suggests the search engine does some of the tasks we expect of good editors (N. Lee 2016). With this "PageRank" system (Brin and Page 1998), Google provides a rank-ordering system that highlights websites with a lot of previous links, which tend to be mainstream media websites. This creates an Internet version of the "Matthew Effect" (Merton 1968) by bringing websites that are popular to the forefront and thereby lowering the profile of websites that have few links. Thus, Google reduces the amount of fallacious, superfluous, and malicious information in search results by ranking highly mainstream sites, which are often those published by the mass media or the government. Google prevents information overload by showing only the top-ten results on the first page, beyond which 90% of users never go (J. Lee 2013). Google also lessens exposure to manipulative and conspiracy websites by down-ranking them as a function of their relatively low number of links. Finally, Google includes all sides of stories because it only uses quantitative analysis of *the number of incoming links*; consequently, it does not overtly promote any ideology or belief system.

Notably, up-ranked mainstream media sites already have editorial control. For example, when searching for political information, Google often ranks links to *The New York Times* near or at the top of the first page. This happens not because Google privileges *The New York Times*, but because of the *Times's* extremely high PageRank due to having millions of incoming links from other websites. Despite Google not having a human gatekeeper or editor, the gatekeeping function of mainstream media is still being accomplished allowing Google to serve as a validated "secondary" gatekeeper (Singer 1997; Singer 2014). The reason for this book is that—to this point—there is no empirical work on this secondary process and political information.

It is important to note that all the traditional complaints about editorial gate-keeping—such as marginalizing outsider voices (Bennett 2004)—will hold with Google. Assuming that the online communications of marginalized populations will not have as many prior links as mainstream sites (which may not always be true), then Google will continue to marginalize these voices by pushing their websites and blogs lower in the rankings, making these sites less likely to be clicked. Thus, the understanding how the Google algorithm works also suggests this potential negative aspect of gatekeeping will also influence online information acquisition with Google searches. Our predictions are strictly about a main-streaming effect, with all the advantages and disadvantages that that entails.

The Algorithm

The Google Search algorithm is proprietary. Neither we nor any other researchers who do work on Google can know with 100% accuracy exactly what constitutes the model for search returns. However, because Google began as an academic exercise (N. Lee 2016), there are papers demonstrating the Google Search algorithm is explicitly designed to maximize access to accurate information (Arasu et al. 2001; Brin and Page 1998). The computer science underlying how Google handles the trillion webpages that it indexes is simple yet extremely elegant. The PageRank system (Brin and Page 1998) assigns a score to each website based on the number of websites that link to it (Page et al. 1999). The system first creates a distributed graph of every link on the Internet and then counts the number of links between pages.

For example, if one searched for information regarding the newest trends in food, a recent article from *The New York Times* on that very topic will likely be one of the first few links available. This is because *The New York Times* has been linked millions of times and would thus have a higher PageRank score than a newly created BlogSpot on the same subject that may have only a few links. As such, Google greatly up-ranks an article from *The New York Times* and down-ranks one from BlogSpot (if there are no other sites linking to the BlogSpot post). Thus, when someone searches for information on the topic, because the article from *The New York Times* is more highly ranked than other sites, it will be presented to searchers earlier in the returns.

Previous research states—and we also find in Chapter 4—that almost all searchers click the top-ranked sites first, and very few go beyond the first page of results (about ten URLs) (J. Lee 2013; Buddenbrock 2016). Through this process, Google suggests mainstream websites on the first page of results based on the number of prior links, and searchers click on those sites. According to Google's brief definition,

> PageRank works by counting the number and quality of links to a page to determine a rough estimate of how important the website is. The underlying assumption is that more important websites are likely to receive more links from other websites.
>
> *(Rombough 2013)*

Given its importance to our hypothesis, a deeper explanation of PageRank is in order. The algorithm starts by locating all sites that contain the search words contained in any given search. If a site lacks these words, then it obviously will not appear on the results page. The algorithm then applies a PageRank, which has been predetermined for all webpages, to each of the sites that contain the search words. PageRank is determined by counting the links leading to the page, which serve as a measure of popularity and mainstream status. These links are in turn weighted by the PageRank of the sites that link to the page from which a link arises and the distance in the network from other high-ranked sites.

Google can process billions of webpages almost instantly because the Page-Rank has been previously assigned. Manipulating the system is exceedingly difficult without having millions of different sites link to a particular site.[4] Because it penalizes multiple links from the same site or links from newly created sites, PageRank avoids "content farms" and other methods for achieving higher rankings.[5] For example, if site A is linked by site B, which is linked to by site C with a high PageRank, then site A will have a higher PageRank than if site C did not have a high PageRank.

Thus, the resulting PageRank system can be thought of as a network web graph, weighted by the density of the unidirectional links (Rieder 2012; Rogers 2002; Rombough 2013). As Rombough (2013) demonstrates, we can formally write this as:

$$PR(u) = \sum_{v \in B_u} \frac{PR(v)}{L(v)} \tag{1}$$

Where the PageRank (*PR*) of webpage u is equal to the sum of the PageRank of each linking webpage v in the set of all websites that link to u, divided by the number of links from the linking page $L(v)$. The more often a site has been linked raises its PageRank, but the more often sites that link to that site have been linked to will also raise its PageRank.[6] Consequently, the most important factor in being listed highly—and thus being clicked—is the number of incoming links from highly ranked websites, $\sum_{v \in B_u}$.

This system creates a *de facto* editorial process because the sites with the highest PageRank will be top-listed and will by definition be popular mainstream sites. The effectiveness of Google in providing information is due to the *wisdom of the crowds*, who have selectively linked to information they perceive to be valuable. As long as the sites getting the most links are mainstream reputable sites, then we should expect searchers to see them first and access reputable information.

Sub-Aspects Added After PageRank

Google has gradually added sub-aspects to the PageRank algorithm. Google does not list them in their entirety, but it maintains a blog that regularly explains them. Google has also patented nearly 100 of these sub-aspects. Furthermore, the company's employees have described dozens more in interviews. Based on these public facts, we can construct a detailed look at "what's under the hood." To validate our understanding, we compared our results with those from a survey of 120 search-engine experts (including many former Google employees) and found near-perfect overlap (see MOZ.com 2013). We believe this accurately represents what Google is doing, and it certainly matches what the company describes in general terms in stock filings, white papers, and other materials (see Google 2014a).

Although Google claims that two hundred sub-aspects influence the final rank of links, almost all of them fit into four very basic categories. First, by "crawling and indexing" (Google 2014b) the web, Google tries to combat trickery and Internet scams, so many of the filters pertain to things such as redirects. Google—and everyone else—can view the HTML coding of a website. So, if a webpage instantly redirects to another site, that site is heavily down-ranked. Further, if too many pop-ups or other telltale signs of scams are present, Google down-ranks and perhaps even removes the website from its index. These filters account for about sixty of the two hundred sub-aspects. They do not have political consequences other than increasing users' trust in Google because they do not experience a lot of scams. Another forty or so sub-aspects are related to the quality of the HTML coding. If the coding for a site contains numerous errors or scores of broken links, the algorithm down-ranks the site. This action again does not have much political impact, but it may lead to more mainstream sites being listed at the top, given the assumption that they probably have better HTML coding.

The remaining one hundred sub-algorithms are based on two key design factors for improving the quality of information that Google delivers. One set of factors involves newer forms of links, such as "likes" on Twitter, Facebook, and other social media, which are treated similarly to links from webpages and can basically be considered types of links. The remaining factors are associated with the development of Chrome, from which usage statistics can easily be collected and folded into the algorithm. Across about forty aspects, Google considers how often a site is clicked, how long before customers leave, whether users block the website using Chrome's blocking tool, and so on. Basically, as traffic and the number of links to a site increase, the more Google up-ranks it, and this process generally favors more mainstream sites.

Alongside software additions, the algorithm itself is not static (Gillespie 2014). Starting in 2009, further information was added to the rank of each website based on personal information of searchers, such as cookies or prior Google searches, among other changes (Gillespie 2014; Schwartz 2009). Other updates in 2012 and 2013 have made the search returns more robust and protect against spam-filled sites (Gesenhues 2013; Sullivan 2012).

Given these basic realities about the PageRank algorithm, evidence clearly indicates that Google research will be legitimate over time. However, as we detail below, market incentives are also at work, which similarly make the likelihood of nefarious manipulation less probable. Being sure that that we can trust search results—and that the results are efficiently provided—is crucial because of the overwhelming nature of information on ballot measures and direct democracy.

The Theory

Our theory is simple: Google provides beneficial information because of the way the search algorithm is designed, which then makes it so that those who use Google for complex areas of policy and politics will be able to get high-quality information. Google acts as a secondary gatekeeper providing high-quality information near the top of their search results, users click on these results, and users learn from this information in practically effective and normatively beneficial ways. Increases in political knowledge result in positive externalities such as increased confidence in vote choice, and increases in search activity can indicate a more active, engaged citizenry. While much of the work on Internet politics has been focused on large questions about how the Internet could change the nature of democratic activity on a mass scale (see Chadwick 2008), we suggest that an equally relevant aspect to the Internet politics debate has been overlooked: empirically testing hypotheses related to the way real Internet use affects real political behaviors and attitudes.

Expectations

Given the preceding literature review and theory, we use a series of experiments to test the main components of our Google-as-gatekeeper theory. We posit that subjects will be shown and then click on mainstream media websites more often. Mainstream sites will be ranked higher than other types of websites, and since mainstream media contains pertinent valid information, subjects who click on these sites will learn more than those who do not or those without Internet access. Formally, we make the following three specific hypotheses:

Hypothesis 1: Google will present mainstream media (newspaper and TV) websites higher in the rank order than other websites.

Hypothesis 2: Subjects will click on mainstream media websites more often than other websites.

Hypothesis 3: Subjects randomly assigned to have Google access will have significant increases in political knowledge.

Hypotheses 1 and 2 concern the *opportunity* to gain political knowledge, as it tests whether Google provides mainstream sites and whether the participant clicks on them. Hypothesis 3 concerns the *ability* of participants to actually learn from usage. Assuming people looking for information on the Internet have the capacity to learn new information, Google provides a cost-reducing forum where they can use their skills to acquire knowledge.

Importantly, the null hypothesis—that there is no educational effect from Google searches on ballot measures—is a real and distinct possibility. As the prior pessimistic scholarship outlines (see Carr 2011; DiMaggio et al. 2004; Zillien and Hargittai 2009), there are significant reasons to suggest the Internet and search returns generally may actually inhibit learning in any substantive way. Additionally, subjects may not click top-ranked sites, or it could be that no pertinent, valuable content exists online on a given area of dense political information. A likely scenario is that good information becomes obscured by poor information, or simply that learning is difficult. Finally, each of the ballot measures we test has very high salience given the high levels of knowledge in the control groups in experiments 1 and 2, making this a hard case for our theory.[7]

Note that Hypotheses 1 and 2 are based on the Google results and the behavior of treatment groups in our experiment. There are no possible results to examine for the control groups. As these are essentially observational data based on non-representative samples, we should be cautious in interpreting their broad generalizability. However, it would be nearly impossible to get a nationally representative sample of participants to enter a lab and allow us to monitor their Google results and click behavior. As such, it is worthwhile to examine the behavior of the diverse and multiple samples that we evaluate below.

These hypotheses represent the main test of our theory, but we also derive other important empirical tests in Chapters 6 and 7 related to the down-the-line implications for increases in political knowledge. Specifically, we expect Google use to be associated with increases in vote confidence, which should then lead to decreases in roll-off on ballot questions in elections. The fundamental starting place for all the benefits of Google Search activity is increased political knowledge, which is only possible if Google returns and subjects utilize good information from the engine.

Research Design and Three Ballot Questions

Experimental Procedures

To test our hypotheses, we use three samples to account for possible internal and external validity issues arising from studying the Internet. The aspects and research goals of the three experiments are shown in Table 2.1. Our three sets of subjects and experiments give us the chance to allow for a re-test, to get a non-"Internet-savvy" sample, to get participants from more than one state, and get participants inside their filter bubble. To the extent people are successfully able to use the Internet for information gathering at all, we know that those in higher socioeconomic groups and certain demographic groups (i.e., Whites) are typically better to extract information (DiMaggio et al. 2004, 2001; Zillien and Hargittai 2009), so experiments are the most appropriate methods to test our theory.

First, to account for knowledge decay, we use a student sample from a mandatory introductory course in American government class at a large public university in the southeastern United States. The ballot measure in question was a "transportation special purpose local option sales tax" (T-SPLOST) referendum.[8] Subjects were incentivized to participate, but *not* to answer correctly. Subjects came to a lab where they were randomly assigned into the treatment (Google access) or the control (no Google access) condition. In both conditions, subjects answered a pre-test questionnaire on demographics, political beliefs, generalized political participation and interest, and Internet usage. Treatment subjects were sent to a computer that defaulted to Google as the homepage, and used Chrome as the default browser. They were asked to research the T-SPLOST ballot measure, but were not told they would answer a follow-up quiz. They were also not told to research any specific phrase or wording—they chose their own way to research this topic—but most simply inputted "T-SPLOST ballot measure" into Google. We captured their search history to ensure compliance

TABLE 2.1 Research Goals of Three Studies

	Transportation	Charter Schools	Minimum Wage
Sample	Student	Adult	MTurk
Knowledge Decay	One-week re-test	No	No
Filter Bubble	No	No	Yes
State	GA	GA	NJ
Recruitment Site	On campus	On the street	Online
N	241	102	219

with the instructions and monitor their searches. We also captured their Google Search return[9] pages up to the tenth page, and we found that every participant did use Google to research T-SPLOST.

After searching, they were removed from the computer and given a post-test questionnaire without computer access. The control condition only filled out the pre- and post-test questionnaires without Internet access, and was also not allowed to use any web-enabled device. To escape Internet-savvy participants—an important consideration for research of this type (Zillien and Hargittai 2009)—we use an "on-the-street, in-person," non-student sample for the charter schools ballot measure. Interviewers walked around the streets of Atlanta asking adult, non-students if they wanted to participate in research for two dollars, not mentioning it was Internet research. While both college students and Amazon Mechanical Turk workers are valid pools of subjects for convenience samples with results generally reflecting larger, more representative samples (Berinsky, Huber, and Lenz 2012; Druckman and Kam 2011), these sets of individuals may more likely to be able to extract beneficial information from the Internet. By getting a non-student sample, we are able to overcome this external validity complaint often invoked against student samples. The first question asked of potential subjects was the screener question: "Are you a college student?" Only those that were currently not students were allowed to join. The distribution of education matches that of Georgia, and contains about 40% who do not have any college education. Once the adult non-students agreed to participate, they were randomly assigned into the treatment group—where they had access to a laptop computer with a clean version of Google's Chrome web browser available (i.e., no 'cookies'), but where they had no external help of any kind or the control group. The rest of the procedures were similar to those described above.

Finally, to get participants inside their filter bubble, and to broaden participants' geographic diversity, we use an Amazon Mechanical Turk worker sample incentivized with one dollar. Once in the experiment, the subjects were randomly assigned to the treatment where they were asked to use Google to search for information on New Jersey's Minimum Wage ballot measure, or the control where they were simply instructed to answer questions to the best of their ability. Through each of these experiments, we obtained the search histories for all of the treatment subjects during the experiment,[10] and we find that all three samples performed similarly. If we find similar treatment effects across multiple samples in multiple elections in two states, we can safely conclude that Google is an effective educational tool for political knowledge in direct democracy.

The Limits of Google Search

Research is not without examples of serious potential problems with the Internet as a resource for average citizens (see DiMaggio et al. 2001; DiMaggio et al. 2004). Being able to trust the Google Search results is crucial not just for this research, but for the millions of Americans who rely on Google to give them answers for their questions. If people were only using Google searches to find new recipes for their dinner parties, perhaps we would not concern ourselves with the overall quality of search results. However, people use Google for important questions regarding their life decisions. Even if Google is used as a starting place, it is a worthwhile empirical question to ask if Google is accurate in the new era of "fake news."[11]

The 2016 presidential election saw an unprecedented amount of attention on fake news. Fake news is false information put into the news environment as if it were accurate content with the goal of getting clicks and shares on social media or up-ranked in Google (see Hunt 2016). While some may consider satire websites like *The Onion* "fake news," *The Onion* does not pretend to be a legitimate news source. They present themselves as satire. If the reader does not understand their satirical point of view, then the reader has actually helped make their point.[12]

Fake news is specifically designed to look and feel like a truthful news story or event, and—at least in high-profile cases—is generally done for some monetary purpose. For instance, during the 2016 presidential campaign, Cameron Harris wrote a completely fictitious story on his website, *ChristianTimesNewspaper.com*, claiming there were thousands of pre-filled ballots for Hillary Clinton stuffed in boxes in an Ohio warehouse (Shane 2017). Although Harris is a Republican, his stated reason for creating his viral fake news story was so that he could make money from advertisers who pay by the click when Internet users access his website. While Harris's story did show up in Google Search results, it was primarily passed from person to person via social media.

Passing fake news via social media is not new to the 2016 presidential election. In fact, the winner of the 2016 race, Donald J. Trump, has a long history using social media to spread fake news-based conspiracy theories. Trump's promotion of "birther-ism," anti-vaccination positions, and questions on official government data (i.e., U.S. Department of Labor employment and GDP reports) has generally relied on fake news sources well before 2016 (Maheshwari 2017). Social media seems to have a particularly problematic relationship with fake news given the network nature of the information dissemination. That is not a problem for our theory. We cannot—and do not—speak to how citizens may learn from social media about politics. However, when social media fake news stories become prevalent in Google because of the way PageRank presents information, then we have concerns.

To the extent fake news is a problem for Google, they are actively fighting to keep their search results accurate. Google's commodity is accuracy. When one uses Google Search, there is an expectation the information is relevant and truthful. If Google is no longer trusted to bring back relevant and truthful results, perhaps searchers will use another search engine in the future. Thus, there is a pronounced market incentive for Google—and to a lesser extent, Facebook—to lead the charge against fake news and inaccurate search results.

In early 2017, both Google and Facebook outlined steps to make fake news less common on their sites (Wakabayashi and Isaac 2017). Google no longer allows companies with dubious content to use AdWords for revenue, and Facebook is ramping up their editorial functionality for their "Trending Stories" sidebar (Wingfield, Isaac, and Benner 2016). Despite these two companies being the main public faces of the twenty-first century "fake news" phenomenon, there is a fundamental difference that should be highlighted between Google and Facebook. Facebook is a social network, which means that the self-selection of information is more pronounced and is—in fact—part of the reason to use the network. The user chooses their "friends," and we know that most people choose networks that reflect their prior attitudes (Bond and Messing 2015). Google, conversely, is not a social network, but a type of utility. They use certain aspects of previous behaviors, which they measure using cookies and search history from users logged into their Google accounts, to generate results their algorithm estimates the user will find more to their liking. Is this a type of *de facto* information segregation? Most certainly; but, is this a dagger to the heart for Google's usefulness for politics? Perhaps not.

Beyond fake news, some research suggests that Google—or any search engine—could game their results to shift public opinion or behavior in such a way that it would affect the outcome of an election (Epstein and Robertson 2015). These startling findings are the result of a series of experiments where researchers created their own Google-like search engine and manipulated the results to see how subjects responded in both search activity and political behaviors (Epstein 2016). The researchers biased the search results in their experimental search-engine environment to see how changes in link rank, content, and page position affected subjects' attitudes and behaviors within their mock search-engine environment. They demonstrated that—in fact—bias *can* be introduced into the system, but they never established that Google Search *is* biased.

Once again, the issue for us is that Google's commodity is its users. Users only come to Google because it brings them information they can trust regardless of the search terms they use. Evidence that Google privileges their products (i.e., Gmail over Yahoo!) and partners (Google Play over Amazon or iTunes) over others when searching for specific products should not surprise us, as private label brands and related products are often sold as competition to other brands in traditional retail environments. Moreover, concerns that Google would give prime website real estate to sponsors and AdWords users are much ado about little—Google clearly labels these as advertisements with a green notation. The only fundamental critique to our theory based on Google is if Google's results that were systemically biased bring information for or against one side or the other on the ballot measures in our study. To some degree, we have to have confidence in the evidence we have laid out and research produced concerning Google's PageRank algorithm.

Similarly, this is an empirical question because we assume Google will bring forward useful and relevant results, but there is no evidence this happens to this point in politics. Furthermore, our claims are specifically limited to direct democracy. While we hope—and expect—our findings could and would be extended to other areas of politics, the specific expectations we have are based on how information about ballot measures makes its way to citizens. Anything beyond this will have to be decided by other researchers in future projects. Understanding the ways and extent Google Search can be useful to direct democracy is the first step in unlocking the heretofore black box that is Google and politics.

Perhaps the most difficult critique for Internet politics moving forward are issues with the "filter bubble." Filter bubbles occur because of the ways people search for information (i.e., motivated reasoning and cognitive dissonance) as well as the practices Internet companies use to gain information about their users. For example, because of Google's use of cookies in search results, some researchers suggest that Google is creating "filter bubbles" that limit users to only getting information that is predicted by their search behavior and—as a result—prior beliefs (Pariser 2011). This is a serious concern because as traditional gatekeepers have been replaced or augmented by Google (or other search engines), if one's Internet activities create an echo chamber this may have deleterious effects on the individual in question as well as society in the aggregate over time (Shirky 2008; Sunstein 2009). Moreover, once these filter bubbles come into place, Carr (2011) suggests because Internet searches incentivize shallow, quick information, the quality of the information could be problematic and the behavioral patterns will make it less likely Internet searchers will get better information in the future. Carr claims that rather than true knowledge—understanding concepts deeply and over time as one might in 300 pages of a book—the Internet incentivizes skimming and sampling pieces of information many of which may reinforce attitudinal priors, which means that "knowledge" is more difficult to acquire (see Carr 2011, Ch. 7).

Conclusions

Internet politics are already transforming the way Americans understand and participate in politics. While research is providing a better understanding about social media and their effects, much less research has been done to detail the impact of the most commonplace for Internet-citizen interaction: search queries. Scholars note there are certainly reasons to be concerned, but there is also reason to be hopeful. Google's economic incentives and corporate creed[13] indicate that for whatever else may happen with Alphabet products, Google Search has a normative imperative to be empirically valuable and accurate. However, these theoretical justifications for why one may expect Google to be beneficial have not yet been tested empirically, which impairs the degree to which we can have confidence in Google's value for complex areas of politics like direct democracy.

With this and Chapter 1, we outlined the current state of the literature on direct democracy, ballot measures, and Internet politics. In this chapter, we clearly explicated our theory about Google's capacity to benefit those who use Google Search for direct democracy, and outlined where this work fits in the overall Internet politics literature. We now move to begin the empirical portion of this book demonstrating the impact of Google Search access on returns for ballot measure topics, how users click, what users learn, and how other political attitudes and behaviors are affected by Google Search—including important interactions such as time spent searching, ideology, and prior political knowledge.

Notes

1 The main page is https://ballotpedia.org/Main_Page.
2 This chapter does not pretend to be a definitive history of the Internet. For that, please see Hafner and Lyon (1998) or Chadwick (2006) who do excellent reviews of both the technological development as well as the regulatory framework. Our purpose here is to highlight the relevant aspects of the Internet's history to appropriately place this study in the Internet politics literature.
3 Obviously, the news industry has evolved over time, and in some cases reporters have more leverage over their work than they had in the past. However, for most reputable news outlets, the editorial process remains robust and indicative of a prestigious organization.
4 This is where the discussion about the impact of social media becomes important. As we clarify below, at one point, gaming Google's first page was nearly impossible. With the advent of social media and fake news, it has become less impossible. Google is aware of the issue and has taken positive steps to contain nefarious behavior (McAlone 2016; Wingfield, Isaac, and Benner 2016).
5 Google tweaked the algorithm to end "Googlebombs," which enabled websites to achieve up-ranking by getting thousands of sites to link in a coordinated fashion (Moulton and Carattini 2007).
6 PageRank also includes a dampening factor that reduces the impact of one website's links on subsequent websites by about 15% for each subsequent link. This step is necessary to avoid feedback loops and other anomalies of the algorithm, such as what to do about websites with no links. As such, it is merely a mathematical necessity to get the algorithm to converge; it does not have much consequence politically, and it is omitted from the above equation for simplicity of exposition.
7 See the appendix for additional information.
8 The students in the T-SPLOST experiment matched the diversity of the university, with 68% female, with an average age of 19. Racially, it was 13% Asian, 50% Black, 28% White, and 8% other race. It contained students from 32 majors.
9 We captured search histories and search returns for each treatment group; see appendix for details.
10 MTurkers were prompted to upload their search history screenshots as part of the post-test.
11 We would like to point out that "fake news" is not new. Fake news—information styled as news from a source styled as a reputable news outlet—was quite common in the heyday of yellow journalism. In fact, the bombing of the *USS Maine* in Havana,

Cuba, harbor was the source of fake news contributing to commencement of hostilities in the Spanish-American War (Mander 1982). Our point is just that this current variant of fake news is generally an Internet phenomenon, but the genre of fake news is not new.

12 *The Onion* is predicated on shining a light on the absurdity of the news gathering and making process in the American system as well as the ludicrous nature of many American news tropes.

13 The Google Code of Conduct can be found here: https://abc.xyz/investor/other/google-code-of-conduct.html.

References

Adamic, Lada A. and Natalie Glance. 2005. "The Political Blogosphere and the 2004 U.S. Election: Divided They Blog." Proceedings of the 3rd International Workshop on Link Discovery 1: 36–43.

Arasu, Arvind, Jasmine Novak, Andrew Tomkins, and Andrew Tomlin. 2002. "PageRank Computation and the Structure of the Web: Experiments and Algorithms." Technical Report, IBM Almaden Research Center, Brisbane.

Benkler, Yochai. 2013. "WikiLeaks and the Networked Fourth Estate." In *Beyond WikiLeaks: Implications for the Future of Communications, Journalism and Society*, edited by B. Brevini, A. Hintz, and P. McCurdy, 11–34. New York, NY: Palgrave Macmillan.

Bennett, W. Lance. 2004. "Gatekeeping and Press-Government Relations: A Multi-Gated Model of News Construction." In *The Handbook of Political Communication*, edited by Lynda Kaid, 283–313. Mahwah: Lawrence Erlbaum.

Berinsky, Adam J., Gregory A. Huber, and Gabriel S. Lenz. 2012. "Evaluating Online Labor Markets for Experimental Research: Amazon.com's Mechanical Turk." *Political Analysis* 20 (July): 351–68. doi:10.1093/pan/mpr057.

Bond, Robert M., Christopher J. Fariss, Jason J. Jones, Adam D. I. Kramer, Cameron Marlow, Jaime E. Settle, and James H. Fowler. 2012. "A 61-Million-Person Experiment in Social Influence and Political Mobilization." *Nature* 489 (7415): 295–8. doi:10.1038/nature11421.

Bond, Robert M. and Solomon Messing. 2015. "Quantifying Social Media's Political Space: Estimating Ideology from Publicly Revealed Preferences on Facebook." *American Political Science Review* 109 (1): 62–78. doi:10.1017/S0003055414000525.

Brin, Sergey and Lawrence Page. 1998. "The Anatomy of a Large-Scale Hypertextual Web Search Engine." *Computer Networks and ISDN Systems* 30 (1): 107–17.

Buddenbrock, Frank. 2016. "Search Engine Optimization: Getting to Google's First Page." In *Google It: Total Information Awareness*, edited by Newton Lee, 195–205. New York, NY: Springer.

Carr, Nicholas. 2011. *The Shallows: What the Internet Is Doing to Our Brains*. New York: W. W. Norton & Company.

Chadwick, Andrew. 2006. *Internet Politics: States, Citizens, and New Communication Technologies*. New York: Oxford University Press.

———. 2008. "Web 2.0: New Challenges for the Study of E-Democracy in an Era of Informational Exuberance." *I/S: A Journal of Law and Policy for the Information Society* 5 (1): 9–42.

Chadwick, Andrew and Philip N. Howard. 2010. "Introduction: New Directions in Internet Politics Research." In *Routledge Handbook of Internet Politics*, edited by Andrew Chadwick and Philip N. Howard, 1–9. New York, NY: Taylor & Francis.

Coppock, Alexander, Andrew Guess, and John Ternovski. 2015. "When Treatments Are Tweets: A Network Mobilization Experiment over Twitter." *Political Behavior* 38 (1): 105–28. doi:10.1007/s11109-015-9308-6.

Curran, James, Natalie Fenton, and Des Freedman. 2016. *Misunderstanding the Internet.* New York, NY: Routledge.

Deuze, Mark. 2005. "Popular Journalism and Professional Ideology: Tabloid Reporters and Editors Speak Out." *Media, Culture & Society* 27 (6): 861–82. doi:10.1177/0163443705057674.

DiMaggio, Paul, Eszter Hargittai, Celeste Coral, and Steven Shafer. 2004. "Digital Inequality: From Unequal Access to Differential Use." In *Social Inequality*, edited by Kathryn M. Neckerman, 359–74, 390, 392–400. New York: Russell Sage Foundation.

DiMaggio, Paul, Eszter Hargittai, W. Russell Neuman, and John P. Robinson. 2001. "Social Implications of the Internet." *Annual Review of Sociology* 27 (January): 307–36.

Drezner, Daniel W. and Henry Farrell. 2007. "Introduction: Blogs, Politics and Power: A Special Issue of Public Choice." *Public Choice* 134 (1–2): 1–13. doi:10.1007/s11127-007-9206-5.

Druckman, James N. and Cindy D. Kam. 2011. "Students as Experimental Participants: A Defense of the 'Narrow Data Base.'" In *Cambridge Handbook of Experimental Political Science*, edited by James N. Druckman, Donald P. Green, James H. Kuklinski, and Arthur Lupia, 41–57. New York, NY: Cambridge University Press.

Duggan, Maeve and Aaron Smith. 2016. "The Political Environment on Social Media." *Pew Research Center: Internet, Science & Tech.* October 25. www.pewinternet.org/2016/10/25/the-political-environment-on-social-media/.

Entman, Robert M. 2004. *Projections of Power: Framing News, Public Opinion, and U.S. Foreign Policy.* Chicago, IL: University of Chicago Press.

Epstein, Robert. 2016. "Subtle New Forms of Internet Influence Are Putting Democracy at Risk Worldwide." In *Google It: Total Information Awareness*, edited by Newton Lee, 253–60. New York, NY: Springer.

Epstein, Robert and Ronald E. Robertson. 2015. "The Search Engine Manipulation Effect (SEME) and Its Possible Impact on the Outcomes of Elections." *Proceedings of the National Academy of Sciences* 112 (33): E4512–21. doi:10.1073/pnas.1419828112.

Farrell, Henry. 2012. "The Consequences of the Internet for Politics." *Annual Review of Political Science* 15 (1): 35–52. doi:10.1146/annurev-polisci-030810-110815.

Federal Communications Commission. 2010. "National Broadband Plan." Government. *FCC.gov.* www.fcc.gov/national-broadband-plan.

Gesenhues, Amy. 2013. "Google's Hummingbird Takes Flight: SEOs Give Insight on Google's New Algorithm." Blog. *Search Engine Land.* http://searchengineland.com/hummingbird-has-the-industry-flapping-its-wings-in-excitement-reactions-from-seo-experts-on-googles-new-algorithm-173030.

Ghonim, Wael. 2012. *Revolution 2.0: The Power of the People Is Greater Than the People in Power: A Memoir.* Boston, MA: Houghton Mifflin Harcourt.

Gillespie, Tarleton. 2014. "The Relevance of Algorithms." In *Media Technologies: Essays on Communication, Materiality, and Society*, edited by Tarleton Gillespie, Pablo J. Boczkowski, and Kirsten A. Foot, 167–94. Cambridge: MIT Press.

Google. 2014a. "Google Inside Search." Blog. *How Search Works Overview.* www.google.com/search/about/insidesearch/howsearchworks/index.html.

———. 2014b. "Google Inside Search." Blog. *Crawling & Indexing.* www.google.com/search/about/insidesearch/howsearchworks/crawling-indexing.html.

Hafner, Katie and Matthew Lyon. 1998. *Where Wizards Stay up Late: The Origins of the Internet*. New York, NY: Simon and Schuster.

Halpern, Daniel and Jennifer Gibbs. 2013. "Social Media as a Catalyst for Online Deliberation? Exploring the Affordances of Facebook and YouTube for Political Expression." *Computers in Human Behavior* 29 (3): 1159–68. doi:10.1016/j.chb.2012.10.008.

Hindman, Matthew. 2009. *The Myth of Digital Democracy*. Princeton: Princeton University Press.

Hunt, Elle. 2016. "What Is Fake News? How to Spot It and What You Can Do to Stop It." *The Guardian*. December 17, sec. Media. www.theguardian.com/media/2016/dec/18/what-is-fake-news-pizzagate.

Kahn, Richard and Douglas Kellner. 2004. "New Media and Internet Activism: From the 'Battle of Seattle' to Blogging." *New Media & Society* 6 (1): 87–95. doi:10.1177/1461444804039908.

Khondker, Habibul Haque. 2011. "Role of the New Media in the Arab Spring." *Globalizations* 8 (5): 675–9. doi:10.1080/14747731.2011.621287.

Lee, Jessica. 2013. "No. 1 Position in Google Gets 33% of Search Traffic [Study]." *Search Engine Watch*. June 20. http://searchenginewatch.com/article/2276184/No.-1-Position-in-Google-Gets-33-of-Search-Traffic-Study.

Lee, Newton. 2016. "To Google or Not to Google." In *Google It: Total Information Awareness*, edited by Newton Lee, 3–53. New York, NY: Springer.

McAlone, Nathan. 2016. "Google Does a Better Job with Fake News than Facebook, but There's a Big Loophole It Hasn't Fixed." *Business Insider*. November 19. www.businessinsider.com/google-has-a-fake-news-loophole-2016-11.

McCombs, Maxwell. 1997. "Building Consensus: The News Media's Agenda-Setting Roles." *Political Communication* 14 (4): 433–43. doi:10.1080/105846097199236.

McCombs, Maxwell E. and Donald L. Shaw. 1972. "The Agenda-Setting Function of Mass Media." *Public Opinion Quarterly* 36 (2): 176–87.

Maheshwari, Sapna. 2017. "10 Times Trump Spread Fake News." *The New York Times*. January 18. www.nytimes.com/interactive/2017/business/media/trump-fake-news.html.

Mander, Mary S. 1982. "Pen and Sword: Problems of Reporting the Spanish-American War." *Journalism History* 9 (1): 2–9.

Merton, Robert K. 1968. "The Matthew Effect in Science: The Reward and Communication Systems of Science Are Considered." *Science* 159 (3810): 56–63. doi:10.1126/science.159.3810.56.

Moulton, Ryan and Kendra Carattini. 2007. "Official Google Webmaster Central Blog: A Quick Word About Googlebombs." Blog. *Webmaster Central Blog*. January 25. http://googlewebmastercentral.blogspot.com/2007/01/quick-word-about-googlebombs.html.

MOZ.com. 2013. "2013 Search Engine Ranking Factors: Survey and Correlation Data." Industry Research. *MOZ.com*. September.

O'Reilly, Tim. 2010. "What Is Web 2.0? Design Patterns and Business Models for the Next Generation of Software." In *Online Communication and Collaboration: A Reader*, edited by Helen Margaret Donelan, Karen Kear, and Magnus Ramage, 225–35. New York, NY: Routledge.

Page, Benjamin I. 1996. "The Mass Media as Political Actors." *PS: Political Science & Politics* 29 (1): 20–4. doi:10.2307/420185.

Page, Lawrence, Sergey Brin, Rajeev Motwani, and Terry Winograd. 1999. "The PageRank Citation Ranking: Bringing Order to the Web." *Technical Report 422*. Stanford InfoLab: Stanford University. http://ilpubs.stanford.edu:8090/422/.

Pariser, Eli. 2011. *The Filter Bubble: How the New Personalized Web Is Changing What We Read and How We Think*. London, UK: Penguin.

Pole, Antoinette. 2010. *Blogging the Political: Politics and Participation in a Networked Society*. New York, NY: Routledge.

Richey, Sean and Junyan Zhu. 2015. "Internet Access Does Not Improve Political Interest, Efficacy, and Knowledge for Late Adopters." *Political Communication* 32 (3): 396–413. doi:10.1080/10584609.2014.944324.

Rieder, Bernhard. 2012. "What Is in PageRank? A Historical and Conceptual Investigation of a Recursive Status Index." *Computational Culture* 2: 1–17.

Rogers, Ian. 2002. "Google Page Rank—Whitepaper." *Ian Rogers*. www.sirgroane.net/google-page-rank/.

Rombough, Jourdan. 2013. "Learn About Google PageRank & How It Works." *Optimization Theory*. December 7. www.optimizationtheory.com/how-pagerank-works/.

Schudson, Michael. 2001. "The Objectivity Norm in American Journalism." *Journalism* 2 (2): 149–70.

Schwartz, Barry. 2009. "Google's Vince Update Produces Big Brand Rankings; Google Calls It a Trust 'Change.'" Blog. *Search Engine Land*. http://searchengineland.com/google-searchs-vince-change-google-says-not-brand-push-16803.

Shane, Scott. 2017. "From Headline to Photograph, a Fake News Masterpiece." *The New York Times*. January 18. www.nytimes.com/2017/01/18/us/fake-news-hillary-clinton-cameron-harris.html.

Shirky, Clay. 2008. *Here Comes Everybody: The Power of Organizing Without Organizations*. New York, NY: Penguin.

Singer, Jane B. 1997. "Still Guarding the Gate? The Newspaper Journalist's Role in an On-Line World." *Convergence: The International Journal of Research into New Media Technologies* 3 (1): 72–89. doi:10.1177/135485659700300106.

———. 2014. "User-Generated Visibility: Secondary Gatekeeping in a Shared Media Space." *New Media & Society* 16 (1): 55–73. doi:10.1177/1461444813477833.

Smith, Aaron. 2009. "The Internet's Role in Campaign 2008." *Pew Research Center: Internet, Science & Tech*. April 15. www.pewinternet.org/2009/04/15/the-internets-role-in-campaign-2008/.

Sullivan, Danny. 2012. "The Penguin Update: Google's Webspam Algorithm Gets Official Name." Blog. *Search Engine Land*. http://searchengineland.com/the-penguin-update-googles-webspam-algorithm-gets-official-name-119623.

Sunstein, Cass R. 2009. *Republic.com 2.0*. Princeton, NJ: Princeton University Press.

Teresi, Holly and Melissa R. Michelson. 2015. "Wired to Mobilize: The Effect of Social Networking Messages on Voter Turnout." *Social Science Journal* 52 (2): 195–204. doi:10.1016/j.soscij.2014.09.004.

Vargas, Jose Antonio. 2012. "How an Egyptian Revolution Began on Facebook." *The New York Times*. February 17. www.nytimes.com/2012/02/19/books/review/how-an-egyptian-revolution-began-on-facebook.html.

Wakabayashi, Daisuke and Mike Isaac. 2017. "In Race Against Fake News, Google and Facebook Stroll to the Starting Line." *The New York Times*. January 25. New York Edition, sec. B.

Wingfield, Nick, Mike Isaac, and Katie Benner. 2016. "Google and Facebook Take Aim at Fake News Sites." *The New York Times*. November 14. www.nytimes.com/2016/11/15/technology/google-will-ban-websites-that-host-fake-news-from-using-its-ad-service.html.

Zillien, Nicole and Eszter Hargittai. 2009. "Digital Distinction: Status-Specific Types of Internet Usage." *Social Science Quarterly* 90 (2): 274–91. doi:10.1111/j.1540-6237.2009.00617.x.

3

GOOGLE SEARCH RETURNS ON BALLOT MEASURES

Do Google searches for information related to ballot measures return valuable information for searchers? What types of websites are returned, and what is the quality of the information on those websites? These are the empirical questions motivating this chapter. Having established the practical importance of political knowledge in direct democracy and the theoretical justification for examining Internet search activity, this chapter puts our first hypothesis to the test. In Chapter 2, we laid out our theory that Google Search will result in empirically and normatively valuable information for searches on direct democracy because Google has an ethical and economic incentive to produce valuable search results. Moreover, direct democracy is a dense, complex area of politics that is likely to cover difficult-to-research topics. These are exactly the kinds of information environments where Google's PageRank algorithm should produce its most effective results. Thus, the hypotheses we test in this chapter are: 1) Google will present mainstream media (newspaper and television) websites higher in the rank order than other websites; 2) Information on the first page of Google results will be high-quality information relevant to the search being performed.

Testing these hypotheses is a crucial first empirical test for our theory about the value of Internet search for direct democracy. If the content related to direct democracy is so obscure or difficult to find that searchers do not have Google return usable information, then there is certainly no reason to think there is any educative value or down-the-line effects on attitudes or behaviors more broadly. Furthermore, this chapter deals with one of the main critiques of Internet search in the recent literature, which is the concern that search results can be gamed or intentionally biased to produce a specific result. This is a serious threat to external validity in this study, and is a serious concern for anyone who might use search engines for any reason at all. Direct democracy is the type of place where nefarious actors could—with little trouble—try to create false information environments to shift the vote one way or the other. However—while accepting these questions and possible issues as legitimate—these concerns are fundamentally empirical questions, and they have yet to be tested as such.

This chapter continues in the following manner: first, we highlight the research in social and computer science specific to understanding search results and behavior. Next, we discuss the data and how it was obtained, outline the hypotheses we test with our experiments, and describe the experimental procedures. We use a combination of observational quantitative and qualitative data to deeply explore the search results on our three ballot measures. Because the control group did not have access to Google, we have to rely on data from the treatment groups only. This makes our data purely observational. However, using a process tracing methodology (George and Bennett 2005) allows for multi-method analysis, which is extremely valuable in an area where there has not been much empirical, behavioral research before. We conclude with thoughts about how this chapter informs our theory, and a discussion about how other researchers might use the same methodology for other areas of interest.[1]

The Importance of Google Search Results

As Lee (2016) points out, Google is one of the most trusted companies in the world. Search engines, as a group, are more trusted than many traditional media companies (Reputation Institute 2017). The cornerstone of this level of trust are the normatively and empirically valid results search engines—specifically Google—bring back for their users. Based on PageRank, the sources that are the best possible matches for the search terms one enters should be on the first page. Coupled with the fact that many users do not ever go beyond the first page of results (Buddenbrock 2016), this makes Google's first page of results fundamentally important.

Despite the level of trust Google has among the public or its market share, critics point out that search results can be gamed. Epstein and Robertson (2015) demonstrate that small changes in the return some links get can change the effects of the search results for users. They create a mock search engine and game the results to create different results for different users who are performing the same searches. These changes result in differences in attitudes and prospective behaviors. Furthermore, Epstein (2016) and Moulton and Carattini (2007) detail the ways people and organizations have been "Googlebombed" in the past. By crowdsourcing links, individuals were able to troll unsuspecting victims by having their name or associations linked with less-than-flattering Google Search results. This is a serious critique, and explains why this chapter is necessary.

Concerns about Googlebombs or gaming search results to produce outcomes are problematic from both a normative and empirical perspective. Normatively, these biased outcomes would create conditions where people could no longer trust the results Google returned to them. Empirically, this bad information would result in errors in judgment or action for those who might rely on the information to make decisions. Regardless of either of these results, whether or not Google produces biased outcomes is an empirical question. Interestingly, despite relevant critiques about the power of Internet search engines, Epstein and Robertson do not test their theory with real-world data. More to the point, we cannot find any studies that actually examine the results of real-world search behavior against expected returns on a given research topic. Thus, this chapter presents an important first in the Internet politics literature. We test our hypothesis with actual, real-world search activity and data.

Results

The experimental procedures and environments for each of the ballot measures are detailed in Chapter 2. For this chapter, we simply focus on the search results returned in each of the environments. Basically, as subjects entered the lab, began their research "on the street," or participated through MTurk, they were asked to research their ballot measure, specifically. Many subjects used the name of measure and the state, but some changed their search terms in the middle of their search, or simply searched the name of the measure. The evidence presented here is about the quality of those returns, and we note where important changes in search behavior (i.e., changing search terms) begat differences in search results.

In all three experiments the main concern is the *type* of website returned to subjects. Websites are coded in one of nine categories. The categories are: Blogs, Information, Interest Groups, Irrelevant, Newspapers, Television, Government, YouTube, and Google. We also coded, when possible, for advertisements on search returns. The only experiment in which advertisements were clicked was the T-SPLOST experiment, and all of the ads clicked referred to groups supporting or opposing the ballot measure. Thus, those ad clicks led to interest group websites, which—when clicked—are coded as interest group clicks.[2]

The coding rules for each type are as follows:

1. **Blogs**: Individuals posting opinion or analysis without an editor.
2. **Information**: Information for education with no identifiable agenda; no advertising.
3. **Interest Group**: Group with a position on the issue and/or a professional organization.
4. **Irrelevant**: Website return or click with no ballot measure-specific information or relevance.
5. **Newspaper**: Information and/or opinion; advertising, editors.
6. **Television**: TV clips and/or links from local broadcast networks.
7. **Government**: Government information (i.e., ".gov" domain).
8. **YouTube**: Links to YouTube or other similar video hosting sites (i.e., Vimeo).
9. **Google**: Clicks back to Google or returns for other Google services.

T-SPLOST: Quantitative

We begin with the results from the T-SPLOST experiment. The details of this ballot measure are described in Chapter 1, and an explanation of the experimental procedures can be found in Chapter 2. The relevant facts, for review, are that this measure was placed on the ballot after months of planning, had widespread support by the business community and local governments in the Atlanta region, and deals with a notoriously difficult area of public policy in Georgia: roads and transportation options. This is not to say support was universal, but there was clearly an alignment of interest among key components of the elite levels of government and policymaking in Georgia.

To get an impression of the types of information returned for subjects, we created the graph in Figure 3.1. This figure shows the average search position for Google Search returns by type. The value for any given website in the search return can range from "1"—which represents the first return presented to searchers—to "100"—which would be the last return on the tenth page of search results. This means lower averages represent increased likelihood of a given type of webpage (i.e., newspaper, government, etc.) being returned earlier in the search result list. This is crucial because most users do not go past the first page, or even the first five results of the first page, of their search

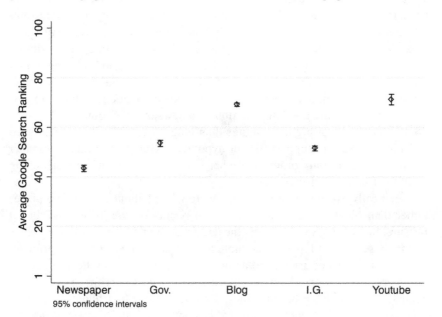

FIGURE 3.1   Average Google Search Results Ranking for T-SPLOST Experiment Subjects

Source: Student experiment, summer 2012.

Note: Search results captured on same day of experiments.

returns. Thus, if a website is going to be impactful, it needs to score low on this dependent variable. To get a sense of the distribution of website type—this is to say, if there are sites coming back near the first page of the returns as well as several pages away—we construct 95% confidence intervals around the means for each website type.

In Figure 3.1 we can see that newspapers have the lowest average Google Search return position for results on T-SPLOST. Two possible categories—information and television—do not show up in the figure. This is because there were no television or information pages returned on this measure during the time period we conducted our experiments. It is possible that as Election Day approached, returns from these sources may have increasingly populated search results. However, given the time period in which we conducted our study, we simply do not have anything to report from those sources. Overall, we see some support for our hypothesis from this simple visual examination. Newspapers have the lowest average followed by government and interest group sources.

Moving past a visual examination, we construct an ordinary least squares (OLS) regression to more precisely test our hypothesis that quality websites—such as newspapers or information sites—will be returned earlier than other types of websites for users' research on Georgia's 2012 T-SPLOST ballot measure. We use blogs as the omitted category because they are a question-able source of information, particularly when considering direct democracy. Blogs, as we define them for this study, present information or opinion without a professional editorial staff. Thus, while there may be good information on blogs at times, there is a sizable opportunity for blogs to advocate for a position without much quality control. We might expect, if Google returns norma-tively and empirically good information, that newspapers or other quality sites would be returned at higher rankings than blogs. These results are displayed in Table 3.1. We find support for our hypothesis: Google presents newspaper websites higher in rank order than other types of websites when researching T-SPLOST ballot measures.

Specifically, we find that newspapers are ranked about twenty-five places higher than blogs, on average, for search results on the T-SPLOST ballot measure. In fact, newspapers show the largest amount of difference from blogs among those website types we are able to code in the T-SPLOST experiment. Government websites are ranked about fifteen spots closer to the first results, and interest groups are about seventeen spots closer to the first page. These estimations are notable because they demonstrate our first hypothesis about Google Search results generating quality content is valid. However, as this simply gives us an estimate about where the results may be positions, it will be beneficial to see what the results on the first page of the T-SPLOST returns looks like for our subjects.

TABLE 3.1 Website Type as Determinant of Google Ranking, T-SPLOST

Variable	Transportation
Newspaper	−25.713***
	(0.000)
Government	−15.566***
	(0.000)
TV	Not returned
	—
Information	Not returned
	—
Interest Group	−17.600***
	(0.016)
YouTube	2.097***
	(0.000)
Ad	−15.136***
	(0.000)
Intercept	70.136***
	(0.000)
N	122
R^2	0.093

Note: Cells represent coefficients and robust standard errors of ordinary least squares regression models for the type of website determinants of Google rankings. "Blog" is the omitted category. "Not returned" means that Google did not return this type of website for any users in the sample. Robust standard errors in parentheses. Two-tailed significance test where $*p < 0.05$, $**p < 0.01$, $***p < 0.001$.

T-SPLOST: Qualitative

To investigate the quality of search results in a deeper way, we utilize George and Bennett's (2005) process tracing method. Process tracing is a valuable tool to hypotheses using qualitative data, and helps researchers demonstrate causality (Collier 2011). We are not concerned with causality, *per se*, but we do use the methods of process tracing to establish the validity of our main hypothesis for this chapter: Google Search returns bring back quality search results on the first page for those seeking information in direct democracy.

One of the first sites returned on the first page of results for all T-SPLOST subjects was "www.atlantaregionalroundtable.com."[3] This page contained a wealth of content on the transportation ballot measure Georgia voters would encounter. The organization responsible for this website was a coalition of businesses, local governments, and inter-governmental organizations. The Atlanta Regional Commission (ARC), an inter-governmental planning group, was the main catalyst bringing together a diverse set of interests to develop the Atlanta Regional Roundtable (ARR) (Atlanta Regional Commission 2017). For the purposes of this project, we coded the ARR as an interest group given the nature of its advocacy and composition. However, one could make the argument that this constitutes a government agency because of the heavy reliance on government partnerships within the organization. In any event, the main question is this: given the high proportion of returns containing this website, was quality information available?

Clicking through the ARR site gave any Internet user a wealth of information. The first thing to note is the three-step itemized list about the process for the ballot measure helping to inform anyone who clicked into the site. There was an interactive mapping tool where users could see the projects that might be in their area, a link for Google Earth "flyover tours" so prospective voters could see exactly what the current state of the transportation options were, and there were information sheets on every single region and the projects for the respective regions that would be funded by the ballot measure's new sales tax. On the website's right-sidebar, there were several helpful documents with facts, figures, and graphics to give researchers an in-depth view of any aspect of the project. Perhaps the crowning achievement of this webpage was the downloadable 157-page document containing the exact plans for every proposed project to be funded with the sales tax in or around Atlanta.

In Figure 3.2 there are examples of the kind of information available on the downloadable documents and other pages on the ARR website. The images in the figure are taken from pages one and four of the document, but they are representative of the information on all 157 pages. There are detailed maps, specific explanations, and exact calculations for the amount of money each project would cost. As noted in the figure and throughout the ARR website, much of the funding for these projects was expected to come from matching federal dollars. This information might have been very important to some prospective voters as they may have been wary of spending this amount of money from local and state sources alone. However, as is also made clear in these resources available on this website, there are almost no local dollars at stake in any of these prospective projects.

Moving to other returns very common on the first page of results, we find that transformatlanta.com,[4] beltline.org,[5] cobbchamber.org,[6] cleanaircampaign.org,[7] metroatlantatransportationvote.org,[8] and atlcbr.com[9] are all also on the first page for most T-SPLOST ballot search subjects. These websites are all coded as interest groups given their composition and because they take a position on the passage of the ballot measure. Looking at the content from these sites, it is clear that—despite their taking positions on the issue—their content was extraordinarily informative and exactly the kind of information we might hope, from a normative perspective, voters get before they make their choices on issues like taxes. For instance, the beltline.org[10] site returned on the first page of results for most users was an entire page with interactive maps and facts about the projects concerning the Beltline. At this time, the Beltline was in its initial development

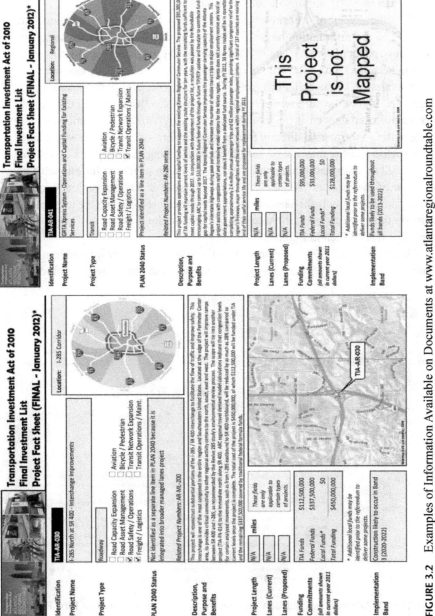

FIGURE 3.2 Examples of Information Available on Documents at www.atlantaregionalroundtable.com

Source: http://web.archive.org/web/20120710083658/www.atlantaregionalroundtable.com/documents/Fact_Sheets_Final_Investment_List_Higher_Resolution.pdf.

stages, so the T-SPLOST represented an opportunity for significant capital infusion. Even though the Beltline is an interest group advocating a specific position on the ballot measure, their website—which is returned on the first page for many searchers—is full of valuable information.

The other types of websites brought back on the first page of results for T-SPLOST are information (atlantaregional.com), government (atlantaga.gov), and a newspaper (ajc.com). The ARC site (atlantaregional.com) is coded as information because 1) the ARC did not take a stated position on their website for or against passage of the ballot measure, and 2) the ARC is an inter-governmental organization. For the purposes of coding the type of website, we felt that searchers who clicked on websites with the domain ".gov" would do so knowing they were getting information directly from a government source. Those who clicked on the ARC website may not be able to know anything about the site except that it was full of information. For the specific return on page one for our subjects, the title of the page is "Almost 25,000 Participate in Transportation Wireside Chats," and it presents the searcher with a press release detailing the mass phone canvass the ARR put on in the weeks leading up to the election. An image of the webpage can be seen in Figure 3.3.

Clearly, for T-SPLOST, subjects using Google to search for information were able to obtain high-quality, relevant information on the first page. We predicted

FIGURE 3.3 Atlanta Regional Commission Press Release Returned on First Page of T-SPLOST Search Results, Coded as "Information"

Source: Student experiment; summer 2012.

Note: Available at www.atlantaregional.com/about-us/news-press/press-releases/almost-25000-partici pate-in-transportation-referendum-wireside-chats-.

that newspapers would rank higher than other type of sites, and we find that this is the case. However, for T-SPLOST, we see that other types of sites (i.e., interest groups) that appear on the first page still generate high-quality information for searchers using Google to learn about direct democracy. While these results certainly help confirm our expectations, there are several limitations with which we must contend before we can truly confirm our hypothesis.

First, the T-SPLOST ballot measure experiment was performed in a lab with clean machines and no cookies in the browser. Furthermore, the experiment took only two weeks about a month before the election itself. This may affect the types of search results we have in this experiment. Thus, we need to see if there are differences when searchers are in a less sterile environment (i.e., non-lab), and if results change dramatically as searchers are looking for information closer to Election Day.

Charter School: Quantitative

To assess the quality of the search results for the charter school amendment, we use the same methods. An important difference in this experiment is that the participants were non-student adults who participated for a $2 payment at the end of their experiment. Those who were randomly selected to be in the treatment group are the subjects of concern in this section. As with the T-SPLOST, this analysis is observational, and only gives us the opportunity to examine the quality of the search results for the subjects who performed searches.

Turning to Figure 3.4, we can see there are both similarities and differences between the charter school ballot measure and the T-SPLOST ballot measures regarding the types of sites likely to be ranked closest to the first page. Recall that the lower the average Google Search ranking the closer to the first page a result is, and Figure 3.5 shows that information pages are the pages most likely to rank lowest. For the charter school amendment, newspaper webpages were numerically similar to their position in the T-SPLOST experiment, but here they are not as highly ranked as information pages or government webpages. Interest groups, which populated quite a few of the first page spots and were rather common overall for the T-SPLOST measure, do not rank as highly in the charter school experiment. Some of these differences can be attributed to the nature of the ballot measures, but some of this can also be attributed to the election type. The T-SPLOST measure took place during the summer primary election, while the charter school amendment took place during the fall general election cycle.

To get a more systematic look at the effect of site type on average search result ranking, we turn to Table 3.2. Using OLS again, we see that advertisements and YouTube returns are more likely to be ranked lower than blogs compared to all other website returns. This is the result of some adjustments with the way Google Search operated between the summer and fall of 2012. First of all, advertisements have been a part of Google Search returns for quite some time,

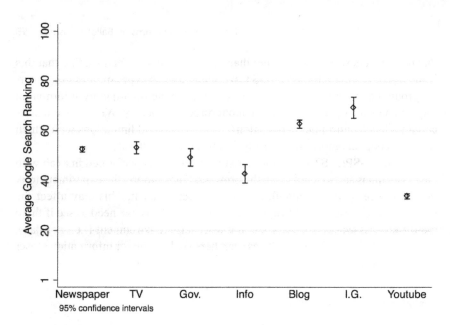

95% confidence intervals

FIGURE 3.4   Average Google Search Results Ranking for Charter Schools Experiment Subjects

Source: Field experiment, fall 2012.

Note: Search results captured on same day of experiments.

TABLE 3.2 Website Type as Determinant of Google Ranking, Charter School

Variable	Charter Schools
Newspaper	−10.240***
	(0.000)
Government	−13.351***
	(0.000)
TV	−9.518***
	(0.000)
Information	−19.918***
	(0.000)
Interest Group	6.657***
	(0.000)
YouTube	−28.985***
	(0.007)
Ad	−38.420***
	(0.002)
Intercept	63.718***
	(0.000)
N	51
R^2	0.084

Note: Cells represent coefficients and robust standard errors of ordinary least squares regression models for the type of website determinants of Google rankings. "Blog" is the omitted category. "Not returned" means that Google did not return this type of website for any users in the sample. Robust standard errors in parentheses. Two-tailed significance test where *$p < 0.05$, **$p < 0.01$, ***$p < 0.001$.

but what is different here is the extent to which ads were up-ranked. Most of the ads in all of these search results in our experiments had some connection to the ballot measure (i.e., in T-SPLOST, they were ads from interest groups, which is replicated here). However, the ads were a much bigger part of the search returns for the charter school amendment. For YouTube—which is the general code for any video content—we found that charter school search results brought back information from clips news organizations or citizens had done to discuss charter schools or the charter school amendment. In terms of quality information, government, and newspapers—in that order—are all ranked lower on average compared to blogs. These general results suggest that our basic hypothesis is not as well satisfied for the charter school ballot measure, but the real test is the in-depth explorations via process tracing.

Charter School: Qualitative

One of the interesting differences between the T-SPLOST and charter school experiments was the timing of the experiment relative to the election. The T-SPLOST experiments were a bit more than a month before Election Day, which may explain why there are subtle—but important—differences in the way the search returns presented themselves to searchers. For instance, for the charter school amendment, most returns contained a cluster of news stories at the top of the first page. In fact, subjects returns captured, on Election Day or a few days before Election Day, the prominent news stories from *The New York Times* (Rich 2012), CNN (Krache 2012), and Patch.com—which is a blog site dedicated to local issues. Below these search results, the overwhelming majority of charter school searchers had information from Ballotpedia.org or votesmart.org. Beyond these information sites, searchers had a wealth of television and newspaper sites that came up on the first page as well. An example of a common search result first page is displayed in Figure 3.5. This page was obtained on November 6, 2012, which is the day before Election Day. It shows that the quality of information regarding the charter school ballot measure was quite high on the first page, which lends evidence to our theory despite the overall quantitative evidence that other types of information was seeping toward the front page.

Consider Ballotpedia.org as an example of the kind of information anyone searching for information on the charter school amendment might find. An image of this site from October 2012 is on display in Figure 3.6. This website, which routinely came up on the first page of search results for subjects in this experiment and was one of the more utilized websites, has an immense amount of quality, verified information. Ballotpedia.org is associated with the Lucy Burns Institute, a 501(c)(3), and is designed to be accessible for anyone seeking high-quality information about down-ballot races and issues in the United States (Ballotpedia 2012). As displayed in Figure 3.7 for the 2012 charter school amendment, Ballotpedia.org had a short synopsis of the measure, the text of the measure itself,

Google

georgia charter school amendment

Web　Images　Maps　Shopping　News　More▼　Search tools

About 1,110,000 results (0.15 seconds)

News for georgia charter school amendment

Georgia's Voters Will Decide on Future of Charter Schools
New York Times - by Motoko Rich - 17 hours ago
At issue in **Georgia** is who should decide whether a **charter school** can open. Supporters of the **amendment** say a commission focused ...

All eyes on Georgia: Washington as voters consider charter school questions
CNN (blog) - 19 hours ago
Georgia Votes: The President Blurs and Charter School Amendment
Patch.com - 9 hours ago

Georgia Charter Schools Amendment 1 (2012) - Ballotpedia
ballotpedia.org/.../Georgia_Charter_Schools_Amendment_1_(2012)
A **Georgia Charter Schools Amendment** will appear on the November 6, 2012 ballot in Georgia as a legislatively referred constitutional amendment.
Background - Support - Opposition - Polls

A Look at Georgia Charter School Amendment on Tuesday's Ballot ...
www2.wsav.com/.../look-georgia-charter-school-amendment-tuesday...
3 days ago - (Savannah, GA) It's an issue that likely interests every parent out there. It's your child's education. Tuesday's election includes a ballot issue you ...

Georgia Charter Schools Amendment - Project Vote Smart
votesmart.org/elections/ballot.../georgia-charter-schools-amendment
Nov. 6, 2012 Georgia Amendment 1 **Georgia Charter Schools Amendment**

Home | Vote Smart Georgia
www.votesmartgeorgia.com/
FACT: Amendment 1 CHANGES the CONSTITUTION and permanently alters ... The **Georgia Charter School Amendment** will get a "No" vote from me despite ...

Georgia's charter school amendment drawing most interest and ...
jacksonville.com/.../georgia/.../georgias-charter-school-amendment-d...
Oct 20, 2012 - ATLANTA | Of the two constitutional **amendments** on this fall's ballot, the one dealing with **charter schools** has generated the most attention and ...

Charter school parents explain why we need Amendment One | Kyl...
blogs.ajc.com/.../charter-school-parents-explain-why-we-need-amend...
Oct 25, 2012 - **Charter** amendment foes twist conservative language to make their case ... **Georgia charter schools amendment** gets boost from RNC ...

Charter school amendment would set off gold rush | Jay Bookman
blogs.ajc.com/.../charter-school-amendment-would-set-off-gold-rush/
Oct 24, 2012 - ... to pass **Amendment 1**, the state **charter schools amendment**, you get the ... would begin in **Georgia** the moment the amendment is approved

Poll: 47% of GA. voters support charter school amendment | www...
www.wsbtv.com/news/news/.../ga...charter-school-amendment=SpE6
Oct 26, 2012 - A new exclusive Channel 2 Action News poll shows more **Georgia** voters are likely to vote in support of a controversial **charter school** ...

Tea party activists divided on Georgia charter school amendment ...
chronicle.augusta.com/.../georgia...tea-party-activists-divided-georgi
2 days ago - ATLANTA - The political movement that spread nationally in opposition to corporate bailouts and President Obama's health care overhaul ...

Searches related to georgia charter school amendment

georgia charter school association　　start charter school georgia
georgia charter school conference　　schools charter georgia
georgia charter school commission　　bascation charter school georgia

Gooooooooogle >
1 2 3 4 5 6 7 8 9 10　　Next

Advanced search　　Search Help　　Give us feedback

Google Home　　Advertising Programs　　Business Solutions　　Privacy & Terms
　　About Google

FIGURE 3.5　Sample Google Search Return for Charter Schools, 11/6/2012

Source: Google Search first-page return; field experiment, fall 2012.

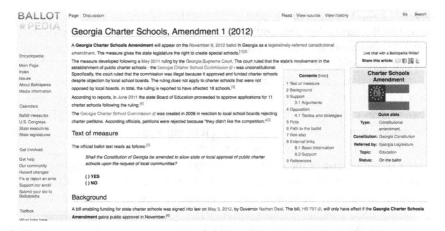

FIGURE 3.6 Partial Screenshot of Ballotpedia Page on GA Charter Schools Amendment, 10/1/2012

Source: Ballotpedia.org; Accessed at https://web.archive.org/web/20121001155333/http://ballotpedia.org/wiki/index.php/Georgia_Charter_Schools,_Amendment_1_(2012).

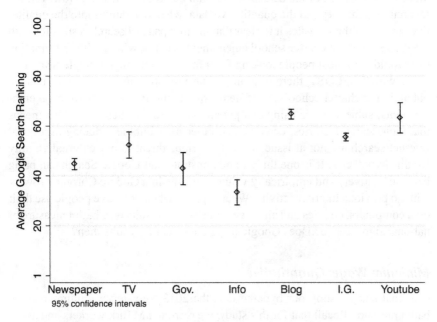

FIGURE 3.7 Average Google Search Results Ranking for Minimum Wage Experiment Subjects

Source: MTurk sample field experiment, fall 2013.

Note: Search results captured by subjects and submitted as part of their MTurk HIT.

and then a short background section explaining how the measure came to be. Not shown on the screenshot, but available at the source link, there are other sections detailing arguments for and against the measure, highlighting notable personalities and their positions on the measure, and a section showing the evolution of the measure through the legislative process in the Georgia General Assembly. This is a remarkable amount of information, all of which is sourced with links to those sources clearly labeled at the bottom of the page. Searchers who encounter this link on their first page—particularly if it is one of the returns at the top of the page—may not need to spend much time researching at all.

For the other pages that were commonly returned on the first page of the charter school subjects, we see a mix of newspaper and television. One of the explanations for why newspaper and television returns hover around the middle of the back compared to the information is due to types of sites brought back for the charter school amendment. Some results that are from the *Atlanta Journal-Constitution* are from their opinion writers, which we did not count as newspaper sources. These are coded as blogs, which is how the *Atlanta Journal-Constitution* references these writers on ajc.com. Thus, while it may seem like there are more newspapers represented than the quantitative data suggest, digging into the content reveals that not all is as it seems. A legitimate critique to be made of this section of the data analysis is on our coding scheme. However, the fact remains that beyond the quantitative data, when one delves into the qualitative aspects of the websites it is clear that the first page of search results for both T-SPLOST and the charter school amendment is dense with quality information that would help most people looking for information through Google Search.

As with T-SPLOST, there is an important limitation to the search results we obtain in the charter school amendment experiment. In both experimental environments, subjects were using computers that were not their own. This means that their search histories, cookies, and other filter bubble inducing aspects of Internet search are not at issue. This is a serious threat to our external validity for this hypothesis. It is one thing to demonstrate that Google Search can bring back normatively and empirically valuable results in a Google Chrome browser with no previous Internet activity. What happens when you have people use their own computers, cookies and all, to generate search results on a ballot measure of national significance? Does Google bring back quality results then?

Minimum Wage: Quantitative

Our final study testing our hypothesis is the 2013 New Jersey minimum wage ballot measure. Recall that for this study, we recruited MTurk workers and asked them to upload both their search history as well as ten pages of search results from the search they performed as part of the HIT. As with the previous two studies, we create a graph with the average search ranking for the types of websites with 95% confidence intervals displayed in Figure 3.7. The first thing to notice is that the confidence intervals are much wider in this study for all categories when compared to the previous two studies. This is because, unlike before, subjects were using their own browsers where they may be signed in, and the variation in search return is the result of cookies and other filter bubble qualities. Moreover, due to the difficulty of gathering an MTurk sample from a specific state, these MTurkers are from all over the United States. Geography and Internet service provider can have effects on search results, so these are factors to consider as well when assessing the differences between these search return measures and the previous studies.

For MTurk subjects searching for Minimum Wage ballot measure information, information pages were much more likely to be front loaded toward their first page of results. Government, newspaper, and television returns were the next types of sites to be ranked lowly—in other words, near the first page of results. These preliminary results comport with our main hypothesis, and—once again—give credence to our theory that Google is a secondary gatekeeper bringing quality information to Google Search users at higher levels than less helpful information. Even while subjects are located squarely within their own filter bubbles, using their own machines, we still find that quality websites are generally lower ranked as we expect. However, as with previous analyses, this figure is merely impressionistic, so it behooves us to move to more rigorous analysis.

As demonstrated in Table 3.3, information websites are, on average, about thirty spots lower than blogs on the search returns. The next lowest ranking type

TABLE 3.3 Website Type as Determinant of Google Ranking, Minimum Wage

Variable	Minimum Wage
Newspaper	−20.115***
	(1.137)
Government	−20.474***
	(5.415)
TV	−12.302***
	(1.796)
Information	−30.318***
	(1.613)
Interest Group	−8.660***
	(1.269)
YouTube	−1.628
	(2.545)
Ad	Not returned
	—
Intercept	64.351***
	(1.003)
N	27
R^2	0.102

Note: Cells represent coefficients and robust standard errors of ordinary least squares regression models for the type of website determinants of Google rankings. "Blog" is the omitted category. "Not returned" means that Google did not return this type of website for any users in the sample. Robust standard errors in parentheses. Two-tailed significance test where *$p < 0.05$, **$p < 0.01$, ***$p < 0.001$.

of website is newspaper, which is barely lower ranked than government web-sites. In terms of our hypothesis, these results confirm our basic theory. These are the types of sites we expect to be the most information-rich, and these are the types of sites that are ranked lowest. What makes these results so compelling is the filter bubble aspects at work. Those who are critical about the quality of search results because of the nature of filter bubbles and Internet enclaves are not wrong to voice their concerns, but they are generally talking about anecdo-tal accounts of Internet search return anomalies. Furthermore, those who are concerned about the outright gaming of search results are also talking about a particularly unlikely scenario. These search results, coupled with the previ-ous studies, demonstrate that—at least on direct democracy searches—Google returns generally quality information nearer the top of the search returns.

One note of caution is our N for this analysis. Unlike the other experiments, we had to rely on the subjects to screenshot and upload their search return results rather than having the absolute control to capture these results ourselves. Thus, it is possible there is some systemic skew or bias in these results. There is no clear reason to think there would be systemic bias, but our lack of control does introduce this possibility. However, one way we are able to mitigate these con-cerns is to note that these results—both the graph and the model—follow from the previous experiments where we had total control. This replication makes any concerns about bias less acute, but they do, nonetheless, exist.

Minimum Wage: Qualitative

Another way to minimize concerns about the self-reporting of ballot measure search results is to process trace the returns from the results we do have to see what the quality of returns was for these subjects. As has been demonstrated in the previous two experiments as well as by the computer science work on search results, Google Search returns are generally very similar from individual to individual even inside filter bubbles. Generally, a return or two will be differ-ent, but if we find some level of uniformity among the first page of results from those who submitted their returns, we can have some consolation that Google Search returns on the minimum wage measure were as quality-rich as the previ-ous studies.

As with the charter school amendment, a common return—often within the first page's top returns on all search histories—is Ballotpedia.org. Once again, as demonstrated in Figure 3.8, Ballotpedia gives searchers exceedingly valu-able information. The details of the ballot measure and its implications are laid out plainly in the first section of the page. Moreover, this page is much longer than the charter school ballot measure page. There is more information about the history of the measure, there are campaign ad videos from competing inter-est groups, and there is Rutgers-Eagleton poll and Monmouth poll data at the bottom of the page as well.[11] Two things are important to take away from the

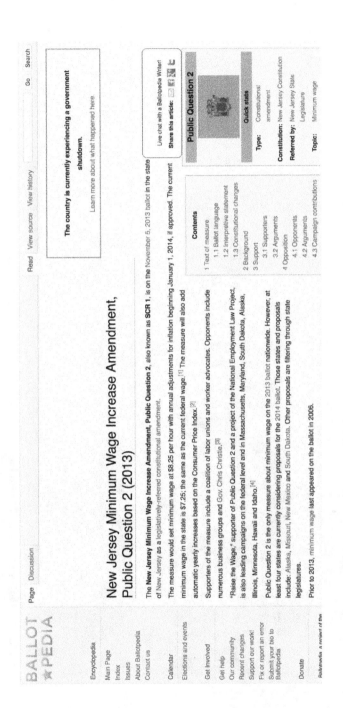

BALLOT ★PEDIA

Page   Discussion   Read   View source   View history   Go   Search

The country is currently experiencing a government shutdown.

Learn more about what happened here.

Encyclopedia
Main Page
Index
Issues
About Ballotpedia
Contact us
Calendar
Elections and events
Get involved
Get help
Our community
Recent changes
Support our work!
Fix or report an error
Submit your bio to Ballotpedia
Donate
Ballotpedia, a project of the

New Jersey Minimum Wage Increase Amendment, Public Question 2 (2013)

The **New Jersey Minimum Wage Increase Amendment, Public Question 2,** also known as **SCR 1,** is on the November 5, 2013 ballot in the state of New Jersey as a legislatively-referred constitutional amendment.

The measure would set minimum wage at $8.25 per hour with annual adjustments for inflation beginning January 1, 2014, if approved. The current minimum wage in the state is $7.25; the same as the current federal wage.[1] The measure will also add automatic yearly increases based on the Consumer Price Index.[2]

Supporters of the measure include a coalition of labor unions and worker advocates. Opponents include numerous business groups and Gov. Chris Christie.[3]

"Raise the Wage," supporter of Public Question 2 and a project of the National Employment Law Project, is also leading campaigns on the federal level and in Massachusetts, Maryland, South Dakota, Alaska, Illinois, Minnesota, Hawaii and Idaho.[4]

Public Question 2 is the only measure about minimum wage on the 2013 ballot nationwide. However, at least four states are currently considering proposals for the 2014 ballot. Those states and proposals include: Alaska, Missouri, New Mexico and South Dakota. Other proposals are filtering through state legislatures.

Prior to 2013, minimum wage last appeared on the ballot in 2006.

Contents

1 Text of measure
  1.1 Ballot language
  1.2 Interpretive statement
  1.3 Constitutional changes
2 Background
3 Support
  3.1 Supporters
  3.2 Arguments
4 Opposition
  4.1 Opponents
  4.2 Arguments
  4.3 Campaign contributions

Live chat with a Ballotpedia Writer!
Share this article:

Public Question 2

Quick stats

Type: Constitutional amendment

Constitution: New Jersey Constitution

Referred by: New Jersey State Legislature

Topic: Minimum wage

FIGURE 3.8   Partial Screenshot of Ballotpedia Page on NJ Minimum Wage Amendment, 10/5/2013

Source: Ballotpedia (2012).

ACC Association of Corporate Counsel

LEXOLOGY®

Search by keyword | Jurisdiction | Work area | Firm name

(any) | (any) | (any)

Search   Reset

E-mail address: | Password:

Log In   Request new password

View original | Forward | Print | Read Later

Tweet   G+1 0   in Share 0   Like 0

Register Now As you are not an existing subscriber please register for your *free* daily legal newsfeed service.

If you have any questions about the service please contact customerservices@lexology.com or call Lexology Customer Services on +44 20 7234 0606.

Register

New York raises minimum wage rate; New Jersey may not be far behind

Sills Cummis & Gross PC
David I. Rosen, Galit Kierkut and Damon W. Silver, Esq.

USA
April 3 2013

Sills Cummis & Gross P.C.

In his State of the Union Address on February 12, 2013, President Obama called on Congress to raise the federal minimum wage to $9.00 per hour, from its current hourly rate of $7.25. Although it remains unclear whether Congress will heed the President's call, various states, including New York and New Jersey, have already enacted or are actively considering new minimum wage rates that exceed the existing federal minimum wage rate "floor."

New York's newly passed budget provides for incremental minimum wage rate increases at the end of 2013, 2014 and 2015, culminating in a $9.00 per hour rate. This Fall, following Governor Christie's conditional veto of a wage rate increase bill, NJ voters will be asked to vote on a proposed Constitutional amendment, which would initially raise the minimum rate to $8.25 and thereafter would potentially raise it further every year based on the Consumer Price Index ("CPI"). Details on both of these developments follow.

Author page »

▼ Related USA articles

New Jersey minimum wage hike now up to voters

New Jersey Governor vetoes minimum wage increase, legislature puts issue on November ballot

New Jersey minimum wage referendum on November ballot

New Jersey minimum wage bill vetoed by Governor Christie

New Jersey voters approve minimum wage increase

More articles »

▶ Popular articles from this firm

"I use the newsfeeds to follow legislative changes and industry trends relevant to my division. I find the articles to be of a good quality and the topics are well researched and presented in a very user-friendly format."

Bernd Schlenther
Senior Manager, Central Risk Unit

FIGURE 3.9 Partial Screenshot of Lexology.com Blog Post on NJ Minimum Wage Ballot Measure, April 2013

Source: Lexology.com; Accessed at https://web.archive.org/web/20141026101922/www.lexology.com/library/detail.aspx?g=1d5d05e0-b07d-4f16-9e3f-083bf720c954.

Ballotpedia pages on charter school and minimum wage. First, in both cases, Ballotpedia has high-quality, well-sourced information. Second, the depth of information on Ballotpedia is clearly increasing over time. The charter school amendment and the minimum wage amendment are roughly one year apart, but the content on Ballotpedia is clearly getting better and more in-depth. As Ballotpedia continues to be returned at the top of the first page of results, this bodes well for prospective voters using Internet search as their method for research on ballot measures.

Moving past Ballotpedia, other first page results for minimum wage experiment subjects included roughly five newspaper or television/radio sources. These returns—from NJ.com,[12] njspotlight.com,[13] and nj1015.com[14]—all had mainstream, quality information about the ballot measure. The content on these sites contained traditional reporting about the issue, quotes from elected officials on both sides of the debate, and discussed the implications of the measure for New Jersey's economy. While there was some variability among the returns for MTurkers, these sites were almost uniformly found on the first page of results, and confirm our hypothesis that newspaper or other reputable news information should be ranked near the top of the first page.

An interesting change that occurred on minimum wage was the emergence of blogs on or near the first page. Per our theory, we suggest that blogs may not be helpful for citizens researching for information on direct democracy because these sites generally lack a true editor, and may be biased in some obvious—or more problematically—non-obvious way. Yet, on many MTurk subjects' first page of search results, jacksonlewis.com or lexology.com came back near the middle of bottom of the page. Looking at the pages—a partial image is available in Figure 3.9—one can see these are blogs, but clearly very professional blogs. In fact, they are blog posts by corporate and labor attorneys who are giving fairly impartial consideration of the implications for business and labor should the measure pass or fail. The Lexology.com post from attorneys at Sillis, Cummis & Gross, PC, as seen in Figure 3.9, links the New Jersey measure to the New York increase in minimum wage that occurred just prior to the debate beginning in New Jersey. On both blogs, there is valuable, even-handed coverage of the measures, which goes against our expectations for this type of website, but is exactly in line with our hypothesis regarding Google Search returns. Given the computer science basics and economic incentives of Google Search, we should expect Google to return valuable information. Over the course of three experiments, we show—empirically—this is the case, and even on types of sites where we might expect less valuable information (i.e., blogs), we still find normatively and empirically good information.

Conclusions

In this chapter, we test our first empirical hypothesis. We hypothesize that Google Search will return normatively and empirically valuable information for

Google Search users researching information on direct democracy. This is an important and open empirical question because few, if any, researchers have actually tested if Google Search actually brings back information users might find valuable given the purpose of their search. We test this across three ballot measures, in three election contexts, and with three different types of samples. In each case, we show that Google Search brings back high-quality, valuable information. We show with distributional plots and OLS estimations that our general hypothesis is confirmed, and we then use process tracing to go in-depth with the returns located on the first page to assess the value qualitatively. Regardless of the measure in question, the context of the election, or the nature of the subject Internet search environment, Google Search returns valuable information when used to research direct democracy.

There are, of course, important limitations to consider with this chapter. First, while we feel secure with the external validity provided using three different measures in three different election contexts, the fact is there are well over one hundred ballot measures on ballots in the United States in any given even-year general election. It is possible that, for some of these, there may be ideologues on either side of the debate who get their message or content pushed toward the lower rankings of Google Search returns. This situation is a constant threat to the validity of our position. However, as demonstrated here, the first page of Google Search results is generally heavy with news and information content about the ballot measure itself. It would take an inordinately powerful personality or group to get their partisan message pushed to the top of the Google Search results on a ballot measure, so this scenario seems unlikely.

Another limitation to consider is that the data we present here are purely observational. On some level, this makes sense because we are specifically interested in the returns brought back when subjects have a specific goal in mind. A possible control condition would be the returns brought back when subjects are not given a specific objective, but are rather allowed to do research on a topic of their choosing. Does Google Search bring back results relevant to the objectives subjects might have without prompting from study designers? We do not test this here, so our claims about the efficacy of Google Search pertain only to direct democracy. This is a limitation, but it is one with which we are comfortable. Our main goal in this chapter was to demonstrate the efficacy of Google Search on ballot measures, and we do so successfully.

Moving forward, researchers should replicate our results here with larger and more robust data sets: more ballot measures, more states, more areas of politics overall. Replication of these results will help outline the areas where Google Search is more and less helpful for bringing back quality information. Moreover, it may prove helpful to have researchers utilize Google's PageRank value as a dependent variable. We do not do that here, rather we rely on the specific placement of links within the first ten pages of search returns. One can imagine that using PageRank itself would be a valuable way to measure this concept now that we have this empirical evidence on how Google returns websites as a result of searches on direct democracy. The fundamental point is that this chapter is the first time this specific empirical question—Google Search returns resulting from politically motivated searches—has been systematically investigated. This represents an important leap forward in our understanding, but there is more work to do.

Having successfully demonstrated that Google returns quality information for searchers researching direct democracy, the next question revolves around the behavior of the searchers themselves. That is to say, what do subjects click on when they are in the process of learning about direct democracy measures? Answering this question helps us move beyond the simple stage where we are at this point. We can show Google returns valuable information, but do subjects click on this information? We turn to this question in the next chapter.

Notes

1 We have made all of our data available for other researchers at our personal websites. Anyone who would like to see the search returns or screenshots of websites may find those data there.
2 For more detail on the click behavior of subjects, see the next chapter.
3 We captured screenshots from our experimental subjects to code our data. However, one can also see the websites by searching "archive.web.org," which is a website devoted to cataloging the history of the Internet over time. Archive.org is a 501(c)(3), nonprofit organization.
4 Transform Atlanta: pro-passage.
5 Atlanta Beltline: nonprofit that oversees a multi-purpose park build on old railroad tracks around downtown Atlanta (i.e., Beltline); pro-passage.
6 Cobb Chamber of Commerce: pro-passage; part of the ARR.
7 Clean Air Campaign: pro-passage.
8 Metro Atlanta Transportation Vote: pro-passage.
9 Atlanta Commercial Board of Realtors: pro-passage.
10 The webpage described here is available at https://web.archive.org/web/20120924191110/http://beltline.org/progress/planning/transit-planning/regional-transportation-referendum-transportation-investment-act/.
11 Due to space limitations, we cannot place the whole page in the text. The whole page is viewable at the link provided in the source information in Figure 3.8. We encourage anyone who wants to see the depth of information to access that link.
12 Online home for *The Star-Ledger* and *The Times of Trenton.*
13 An online newspaper focusing on the New Jersey State House.
14 One of the largest and strongest radio stations in the state.

References

Atlanta Regional Commission. 2017. "Welcome to the Atlanta Regional Commission." *Intergovernmental Organization.* www.atlantaregional.com/.
Ballotpedia. 2012. "Ballotpedia: About—Ballotpedia." Information. October 1. https://web.archive.org/web/20121001152636/http://ballotpedia.org/wiki/index.php/Ballotpedia:About.

Buddenbrock, Frank. 2016. "Search Engine Optimization: Getting to Google's First Page." In *Google It: Total Information Awareness*, edited by Newton Lee, 195–205. New York, NY: Springer.

Collier, David. 2011. "The Teacher: Understanding Process Tracing." *PS: Political Science & Politics* 44 (4): 823–30.

Epstein, Robert. 2016. "Subtle New Forms of Internet Influence Are Putting Democracy at Risk Worldwide." In *Google It: Total Information Awareness*, edited by Newton Lee, 253–60. New York, NY: Springer.

Epstein, Robert and Ronald E. Robertson. 2015. "The Search Engine Manipulation Effect (SEME) and Its Possible Impact on the Outcomes of Elections." *Proceedings of the National Academy of Sciences* 112 (33): E4512–21. doi:10.1073/pnas.1419828112.

George, Alexander L. and Andrew Bennett. 2005. *Case Studies and Theory Development in the Social Sciences*. Cambridge, MA: MIT Press.

Krache, Donna. 2012. "All Eyes on Georgia, Washington as Voters Consider Charter School Initiatives." News Blog. *CNN.com: Schools of Thought*. November 6. http://schoolsofthought.blogs.cnn.com/2012/11/06/all-eyes-on-georgia-washington-as-voters-consider-charter-school-initiatives/.

Lee, Newton. 2016. "To Google or Not to Google." In *Google It: Total Information Awareness*, edited by Newton Lee, 3–53. New York, NY: Springer.

Moulton, Ryan and Kendra Carattini. 2007. "Official Google Webmaster Central Blog: A Quick Word About Googlebombs." Blog. *Webmaster Central Blog*. January 25. http://googlewebmastercentral.blogspot.com/2007/01/quick-word-about-google-bombs.html.

Reputation Institute. 2017. "Global RepTrak 100 | Top Companies by Reputation | Most Reputable Companies." Accessed February 26. www.reputationinstitute.com/research/RepTrak-in-Country/Global-RepTrak-100.

Rich, Motoko. 2012. "Future of Georgia's Charter Schools on Ballot." *The New York Times*. November 6, sec. A.

4

CLICK BEHAVIOR AND DIRECT DEMOCRACY

In this chapter, we investigate whether users follow Google's advice and click on websites listed at the top of Google Search returns. Further, we investigate whether or not users follow the logical implications of Chapter 3 and click on mainstream media websites more than other sources, such as blogs. Using data from the charter school experiment, we also examine motivated reasoning—which is a serious concern when citizens are responsible for seeking out information for politics—as a possible explanation for search behavior. Finally, for a broader view and external validity, we use nationally representative survey data from the 2012 American National Election Study to investigate factors that correlate with searching for information about ballot measures online.

There are several empirical questions this chapter seeks to answer. Despite Google returning mainstream sources at the top due to the PageRank System, it could be the case that users search *deeper* to investigate other sources that are available. Conversely, it could be that users are seeking out information from sources *other than* the mainstream ones that are listed at the top. For our theory to hold it requires more than Google presenting mainstream informative websites on page one; it requires users taking those recommendations seriously and clicking websites that are top ranked. Chapter 3 shows these top-ranked websites are in fact mainstream information sources, but we must now verify that users click on those sources and thereby take Google's recommendations.

There are many reasons to suspect the users may search out alternative information. The well-known theory of motivated reasoning posits that people seek information that matches their prior beliefs (Kunda 1990; Lodge and Taber 2000). If this is true for using Google Search for researching information on direct democracy, then we can expect users to pursue sources of information that confirm their biases. Internet searchers who are looking to have their prior attitudes confirmed or find information that does so should dig deeper than the first page of results. We should see users pursuing information much farther down the Google rankings because they will be taking clues from the names and other information presented in the Google list of results. Users can see the name of the website and a brief description of what a webpage contains—including what it is titled—from the Google Search results, so they may use these heuristics to select which websites to click on.

If, however, our theory is correct, rather than relying on motivated reasoning and searching deeply for similarly minded websites, the dominant predictor of clicking on a website will simply be the position in ranking on the Google Search results (Buddenbrock 2016). Users will click top-ranked sites due to a need to quickly and efficiently sort through information combined with an inherent and often unconscious trust of Google's ability to present valuable information near the top of the rankings. Because of information overload and cognitive difficulties, we know humans often take shortcuts to process information (Lupia 1994; Popkin 1991; Popkin and Dimock 1999). Furthermore, given the ubiquity of Google or search engines more generally, most users will have successfully used Google in the past to obtain information. These two factors suggest that they will click on top-ranked search results rather than go looking for ideologically congruent sites.

Across all three experiments, we kept track of what the users clicked. This allows us to make a very important analysis of user–Google interactions based on click behavior. The first of which is simply what type of websites they are clicking. It is important to know if users are choosing mainstream sites such as newspapers, or if they are choosing less reliable sources to click on such as blogs. To this point, data of this kind and questions of this nature have been very difficult for researchers to obtain or answer because one must actually see what users click in order to determine whether or not they are examining reliable sources. The novelty of our research design is that it allows us to actually observe real click behavior on a salient political topic. Note that each of these experiments takes place during an election that has these actual ballot measures on the ballot. Therefore, there are many stories and posts about these ballot measures to be clicked. Our results generally cannot speak to occasions when someone might research political topics or questions that are not salient and, therefore, there is not a large amount of mainstream press coverage available to be ranked by Google. More to the point, our results speak only to ballot measures and direct democracy.

Beyond simply the type of site and the number of clicks users make while researching ballot measures, it is also important to know what prior factors predict why they are searching for information on ballot measures. We supplement our experimental results with 2012 American National Election Study (ANES) Direct Democracy Supplement data, which asks questions about whether or not respondents are involved in politics, whether or not they commonly use political media, and socioeconomic demographics. We use these questions to ascertain whether or not these factors are predictive of searching for information on ballot measures more generally among the American public.

As a test of motivated reasoning in click behavior, we use the position variable—measuring what position the websites are listed in the Google rankings—as a dependent variable in a series of models to see what encourages someone to dig deeper into results. For example, if the motivated reasoning theory is correct, we should expect those who are more ideological to search deeper into the results. In this case, the more ideological an Internet searcher is, the larger the position variable will be as what they click on will have a higher position number in the Google rankings because the user is trying to dig into the results to find information confirming their prior attitudes. Similarly, we may expect those who are simply more involved in participatory politics to seek out information that matches their prior beliefs by going deeper into the search results.

Predictions

Before we began our analysis, it is preferable to make some explicit predictions on what we believe will happened when subjects research ballot measures on Google. Since the PageRank algorithm explicitly privileges sites which have the most inbound links from other websites, it is thereby providing information that has been vouched for by outside sources by the prior inbound links. By definition, these popular websites must be "mainstream" to the extent that they are heavily linked. As such, unless many websites link to *un*informative sites and pages, the algorithm produces recommendations which are informative at the top of its search results.

Based on the observations above, we can predict that subjects will click on mainstream media websites more often than other websites. As we show in Chapter 3, Google consistently presents within the first page newspapers, government sites, and information sites. Based on these consistent results across all three samples, and prior evidence which shows Google users click on top-ranked sites, our predictions are that Google users will click on those mainstream information sources. This is not a function of an individual's desire to get accurate information *per se*, but is more a function of the need to get information easily and trust that Google will allow them to do so.

For our second prediction, we use questions from the pre-test battery collected before assignment to treatment in our experiments to determine if there are factors that produce deviation from Google's recommendations. Thus, our second test is whether or not engagement in politics predicts users clicking on results which are ranked farther down by Google. This may be due to the well-known behavioral pattern of motivated reasoning whereby those more engaged and interested in politics are more attracted to finding sources of information which have less cognitive dissonance. These users deviate from the recommendations of Google by seeking something beyond the information that is provided by the mainstream sites. Thus, the motivated reasoning theory predicts that partisanship, being ideological, political knowledge, and partisan attachment will predict users going beyond the first page and clicking results further down.

Note that there are no possible results to examine for the control groups. As these are essentially observational data based on non-representative samples, we should be cautious in interpreting their broad generalizability. However, it would be nearly impossible to get a nationally representative sample of participants to enter a lab and allow us to monitor their Google click behavior. As such, it is worthwhile to examine the behavior of the diverse and multiple samples that we evaluate below.

Click Behavior by Website Type: Graphical Analysis

As with the previous chapter, we code the search results according to a specific set of coding criteria. To gather these data, we use the captured user browser history for every experimental subject in the treatment groups. Using the same criteria as before, we code all clicks in this histories by whether the clicks are on blogs, newspapers, television station websites, governmental websites, interest group websites, or any information sites such as Ballotpedia. Using this categorization system allows us to show the proportion of clicks for each user for each category in the graphs that follow. In other words, what these graphs show is the percentage of each user's clicks in a particular type. For example, if we see in Figure 4.1, 7% of users had 100% of their clicks to newspaper websites. This is an efficient way to present these complicated results. The displayed distribution of clicks shown in the graphs below contain most of the data available in this experiment on this topic. The key point from examining all three graphs, is that the vast majority of users' click patterns were dominated by mainstream sources of information.

Starting with Figure 4.1, we see that the vast majority of users had a high percentage of their clicks going to newspapers and information sites in the charter school amendment experiment. Thirty percent of users only click information sites. Through content analysis of the newspapers and information webpages that were actually clicked, we see these were highly informative, edited, and presented both sides in a relatively fair manner, as would be expected in a modern newspaper. Although the information sites such as Votesmart.com and Ballotopedia.com are relatively new, they also displayed high-quality information. Thus, for most users searching for Google for this topic leads them to click on edited, high-quality information that is not overtly biased.

Now turning to the New Jersey minimum wage experiment in Figure 4.2, we see that the results are replicated from Figure 4.1. In this experiment, most clicks are for newspaper and information sites. There are very few other sites that are clicked on by these participants. Once again content analysis of the

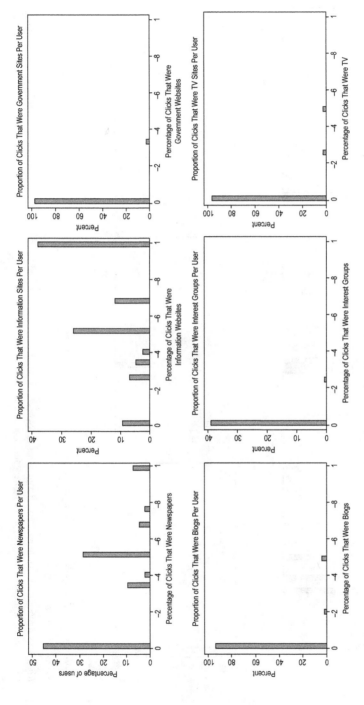

FIGURE 4.1 Click Behavior by Website Type, Charter School Amendment

Source: On-the-street, adult, non-student sample experiment, fall 2012.

Note: This figure shows that most users clicked either newspapers or information websites, and that for many users these were the only websites that they clicked in the charter school experiment. Very few users clicked other types of websites.

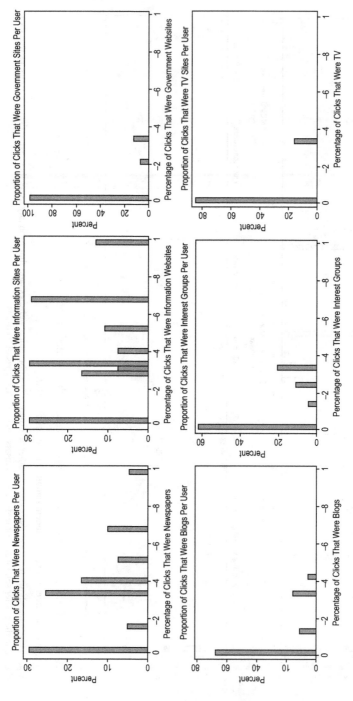

FIGURE 4.2 Click Behavior by Website Type, Minimum Wage Amendment

Source: MTurk sample experiment, fall 2013.

Note: This figure shows that most users clicked either newspapers or information websites, and that for many users these were the only websites that they clicked on in the minimum wage experiment. Very few users clicked other types of websites.

actual webpages that were clicked on shows that users would have been able to gain valuable information by reading these sites.

In Figure 4.3, we see a slightly different outcome. Newspapers and information sites are clicked often, as in the other two experiments, but additionally interest group sites are highly clicked as well. As we saw in Chapter 3, Google returned the highest number of interest group sites in this experiment. One thing that we can learn from this result is that users are clicking on what Google provides. In the page of results for the charter school and minimum wage experiments, almost no interest groups were returned in the search results, and so few were clicked. However, in the T-SPLOST experiment, interest groups commonly were included on the first page and they were clicked. While there has been a long literature that suggests that interest groups provide valuable heuristics for learning on ballot measures (e.g., see Lupia 1994; Lupia and McCubbins 1998), they do not provide unbiased information.

In sum, in all three experiments, we see that what Google returns on its front page is clicked with the most frequency, and—in terms of website types being clicked—we see that newspapers and information websites are clicked more than other types. These graphs give good evidence that our basic hypothesis about click behavior is correct. However, we cannot tell from these graphs why there is differentiation on why someone might, for example, click a newspaper or not. We now turn to multivariate analysis to examine the correlates of website click in our experiments.

Click Type Regression Analysis

For our click behavior models, we use the same coding system as in Chapter 3 for types of website as the independent variables. For the dependent variable, we create a dichotomous dependent variable for whether a website was clicked (1) or not (0) by the participant, from a list of the top 100 returned websites by Google.

In Table 4.1, we show that subjects click on mass media or informational websites most often. Using a logistic regression model, we estimate the likelihood of clicking on different types of websites. The data are clustered by participant, and we use robust standard errors. Compared to the omitted category of blog, we find across all three samples that newspapers are statistically significantly more likely to be clicked by subjects. Information websites (such as Votesmart. org) are statistically significantly more likely to be clicked in the charter school and minimum wage experiments, but were not returned at all by Google for the T-SPLOST experiment. Governmental and interest group websites were more likely to be clicked than blogs in only the T-SPLOST experiment. The other types of websites were not significantly different than blogs in any experiment.

Using the search histories of each participant, we find that around 89% of users never left the first page of search results, which matches independent

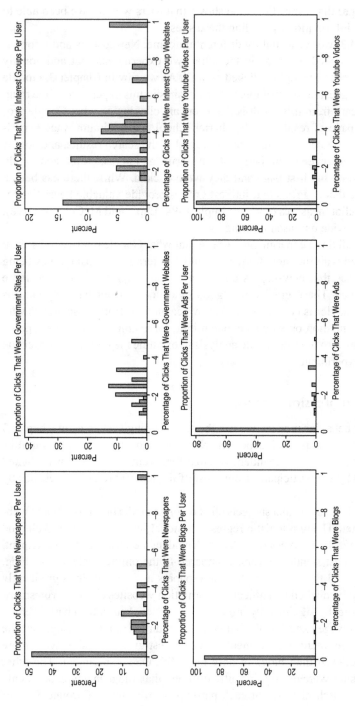

FIGURE 4.3 Click Behavior by Website Type, T-SPLOST Amendment

Source: Lab, student sample experiment, summer 2012.

Note: This figure shows that most users clicked either newspapers, government, or interest group websites, and that for many users these were the only websites that they clicked on in the T-SPLOST experiment. Very few users clicked other types of websites.

TABLE 4.1 Types of Websites Clicked

	Transportation	Charter Schools	Minimum Wage
Newspaper	1.733***	1.757**	1.394*
	(0.289)	(0.582)	(0.619)
Information	Not returned	4.393***	3.701**
	—	(0.580)	(0.626)
Government	1.660***	0.986	1.675
	(0.260)	(1.177)	(0.934)
Interest Group	1.761***	0.696	0.057
	(0.229)	(1.175)	(0.443)
TV	Not returned	0.134	1.073
	—	(0.927)	(0.653)
YouTube	0.475	Not clicked	Not clicked
	(0.478)	—	—
Intercept	−4.792	−5.815	−4.579
	(0.242)	(0.565)	(0.516)
N	76	42	19
Wald χ^2	73.26	249.89***	95.55***

Note: Cells represent coefficients and robust standard errors of logistics regression models for type of websites clicked by subjects. 'Blog' is the omitted category. 'Not clicked' means that no participant clicked this type of website. 'Not returned' means that Google did not return this type of website for any users in the sample. Robust standard errors in parentheses with two-tailed significance test where *$p < 0.05$, **$p < 0.01$, ***$p < 0.001$.

assessments of Google Search behavior; around 90% of searchers never go past the first page (Chitika 2013). Furthermore, in these three experiments, no subjects went past the third page. Thus, the dominance of newspaper articles in the top rankings by Google—shown in the previous chapter—probably promoted many searchers to click on that type of link. In sum, Google's PageRank algorithm highly ranks mass media sites for users to click, which they did, but pertinent questions still remain. One important empirical question is: can we discount the role of motivated reasoning in this observed click behavior?

Correlates of Click Behavior

There are two potential alternative explanations beyond website type to measure what gets clicked on by respondents, which we can test with the charter school amendment experiment[1] data. Unfortunately, the two determinants of what is clicked on cannot be measured in the same model. This is because one of the chief determinants, according to our hypothesis, is the position within the Google ranking. However, the other competing hypothesis, motivated reasoning, suggests that individual characteristics of the respondent will predict what they click on. Therefore, we estimate two separate regression models with separate predictors, but each shows what subject or search return characteristics correlate with clicking on a given website.

We use *position* first as an independent variable to see whether, along with the type of websites, position is a predictor of what is clicked. Beyond that, then we use *position* as a dependent variable by which we are measuring depth of search. Depth of search is important, for two reasons. First, we want to know who is motivated to search for results on the initial factors. Second, it could be that Google is presenting mainstream results that are not—in fact—accurate and is also interesting to see who searches for alternative viewpoints.

The first predictor we examine is *position*, which is measured from 1 to 100 based on the website's ranking in the first one hundred results returned by Google. Note that a more prominent ranking in Google is a lower number, and, therefore, we would expect a negative relationship between being clicked and the position variable. In other words, for this hypothesis, being ranked farther away from the first ranked site will lower the likelihood of a website being clicked. In this model, we estimate a logistic regression model, similar to Table 4.1, to see what increases the likelihood of a website being clicked.

In Table 4.2, we see that position is the dominant predictor in the model. Additionally, the same types of websites, newspaper and information, that were often clicked in Model 1 are again significant in this model. This shows that position is a highly motivating factor in a website being clicked. For example, if two newspapers have coverage of the same story, this model predicts that the website which is ranked higher by Google will be the one that is clicked. This is a powerful confirmation of the empirical claim that most people stay on the first page of Google returns.

TABLE 4.2 Page Characteristic Correlates for Website Clicks, Charter School Experiment

	Model 1		Model 2	
	Coeff.	*(Robust S.E.)*	*Coeff.*	*(Robust S.E.)*
Position	−0.008***	(0.001)	−0.006***	(0.001)
Newspaper	—	—	1.884**	(0.585)
Information	—	—	3.926***	(0.575)
Government	—	—	1.319	(1.195)
Interest group	—	—	1.506	(1.204)
Television	—	—	−0.058	(0.926)
Constant	−1.359***	(0.224)	−3.848***	(0.568)
Level 1 N	4368		4368	
Level 2 N	43		4	
χ^2	46.577***		229.715***	

Note: Cells represent coefficients and robust standard errors of logistics regression models for type of websites clicked by subjects. 'Blog' is the omitted category. Data from the charter school experiment. Robust standard errors in parentheses with two-tailed significance test where *$p < 0.05$, **$p < 0.01$, ***$p < 0.001$.

TABLE 4.3 User Characteristic Correlates for Website Clicks, Charter School Experiment

	Coeff.	(Robust S.E.)
Political knowledge	−0.378	(0.338)
Participation	0.126	(0.149)
Ideological	0.346	(0.344)
Independent	1.040	(1.009)
Age	0.019	(0.019)
Female	−0.655	(0.678)
Black	−0.752	(0.709)
Constant	543.019***	(1.167)
N	4888	
R²	0.000	

Note: Cells represent coefficients and robust standard errors of an OLS regression model for *position* of the websites clicked by subjects. Data from the charter school experiment. Robust standard errors in parentheses with two-tailed significance test where $*p < 0.05$, $**p < 0.01$, $***p < 0.001$.

Next, Table 4.3 uses data from a questionnaire-administered pre-treatment, to create standard predictors of motivated reasoning. The dependent variable in this model is the position of the website in Google rankings from 1 to 100, but only for those who actually clicked on a website. Thus, the dependent variable measures how far down in the Google rankings a searcher went to find information. If the motivated reasoning hypothesis is correct, participants who have more intense involvement in politics will click websites with a higher position score because they will be combing through search results looking for information confirming their prior attitudes. Otherwise, even those who are likely motivated reasoners are not immune from the ease and empirical validity of Google's first page of results.

The predictors we include are pre-test *political knowledge*, as measured by an open-ended quiz of political knowledge of the governmental topics. We include a measure of *participation* in politics which is a sum of those who previously commented on a website about politics, discussed politics, volunteered for a campaign, sent an email or letter to politician, donated money to a campaign, and attended a meeting (Cronbach's alpha = 0.81). We include a measure of being *ideological*, which is created by "folding" the 1–7 ideology into a new scale which runs from 0 for moderates to 3 from those extremely liberal or conservative. We include party identification by examining those respondents that chose *independent* compared to those that chose either Democratic or Republican. Additionally, we measure demographics on *age*, and whether they are *female*, or *Black*.

Education would have been an interesting predictor to include, but only thirteen respondents chose to fill this particular item out. Additionally, almost no respondents gave information for income. Remember that in this experimental environment, random people on the street were asked to fill out the survey. It is highly likely that being approached by someone they have never met before on the street and asked for personal information about education and income resulted in the survey respondents intentionally omitting these data for privacy reasons. Unfortunately, we cannot test these variables in this model due to missing data.

We see in Table 4.3 that none of these predictors is statistically significant. What this means is that, in this experiment, none of these factors actually predicts a participant digging deeper into the search results to find websites that match their predispositions. Combined with the prior model in Table 4.2, this shows that the dominant factor in a website being clicked is its ranking by Google. Of course, it could be that participants in our experiment are not searching in the same way that they would at home. External validity is an ever-present and legitimate concern. Therefore, we now turn to nationally representative survey data to adjudicate whether searching online is predicated by characteristics of the individual.

Why Use the Internet to Research Direct Democracy? A Model Using ANES Data

We have shown that searchers follow Google's suggestions by clicking top-ranked URLs. Our next question is a larger, meta question. What makes someone, in the real world, take the time to search online for information about ballot measures? We know what they click on after they have searched for information, but why do they search? We can use survey data to explore the underlying correlates of online information searching. Up to now, we have investigated click behavior results using our three experiments, but we do not have a good sense about what the profile of Internet researchers is more generally. However, to give greater generalizability of our results, we turn to a nationally representative sample.

In 2012, the ANES added a special one-time survey component about ballot measures. Importantly, the ANES asked about the actual, specific ballot measures that were up for a vote in thirteen states.[2] For example, respondents from Arizona were asked about Arizona Proposition 114 which was about preventing crime victims from having to pay damages to a person who was injured while that person committed or attempted to commit a felony against the victim. This process was replicated for each ballot measure in each of the thirteen states in this study. This approach is vastly superior to previous survey methods that asked about ballot measures generally, such as questions about roll-off, without tying those answers to a specific ballot measure. As there are potentially many ballot measures for each respondent, depending on their state, asking general questions is not specific enough to obtain precise information. This novel survey design gives us access to exactly the type of information we need to answer our research question about correlates of searching.

The ANES describes their study in the following manner:

> The ANES 2012 Direct Democracy Study was a companion project to the ANES 2012 Time Series Study. It collected public opinion data concerning ballot measures such as referenda, initiatives, and state constitutional amendments subject to popular vote. Representative samples of adult U.S. citizens in 13 states were scientifically selected and completed pre-election and post-election questionnaires. There were 5,415 respondents.
>
> *(American National Election Study 2014, 1)*

The states studied were Arizona, Arkansas, California, Colorado, Florida, Massachusetts, Michigan, Missouri, North Dakota, Ohio, Oregon, South Dakota, and Washington.

In terms of subject selection, they state,

> Some respondents to the Direct Democracy survey received the questionnaire as part of the internet version of the ANES 2012 Time Series questionnaire. Other respondents received the Direct Democracy questionnaire separately, without completing the ANES Time Series questionnaire. Respondents were part of the GfK Knowledge Panel, an online probability sample. Pre-election data collection occurred from October 12, 2012 through November 6, 2012. Post-election data collection occurred from November 21, 2012 through January 30, 2013.
>
> *(American National Election Study 2014, 2)*

The recruitment to be included in this sub-sample of the ANES was accomplished in the following manner:

> Respondents who completed the Direct Democracy survey came from three groups, all of which were part of, or were recruited using the methods of, the GfK Knowledge Panel. The GfK Knowledge Panel is a large online panel of survey respondents who are invited to complete surveys several times each month on a variety of topics for a variety of investigators. Panelists were recruited using two probability sampling methods: address-based sampling (ABS) and random-digit dialing (RDD). Prospective panelists who did not have Internet access at the time of recruitment were furnished with free Internet service and free hardware to connect to the Internet.
>
> *(American National Election Study 2014, 6)*

The dependent variable measures whether or not the respondent heard anything online about a specifically mentioned ballot measure. It is derived from a question that asks "From which of the following sources have you heard anything about the ballot measure campaigns?" It is a dichotomous variable coded (1) for the 11% of respondents who selected "Internet sites, chat rooms, or blogs." One limitation is whether this actually measures whether or not they searched online, or simply heard anything from online sources about the ballot measures. There may be some respondents who did not directly search for this topic, but came into contact with this information by, for example, reading an online newspaper, and simply clicked a story they saw about the ballot measure. Still, almost all of the exposure to these blog posts or online stories must have derived from a choice the respondent made to click on the story or post, and as such the dependent variable at—a minimum measure—click behavior on ballot measure information.

Another point of interest is that these nationally representative data show only one in nine respondents say they got information online about ballot measures. While non-trivial, this number is not as robust as we may have expected. The correlations in Table 4.2 offer plausible explanation to this low level of searching.

The independent variables are all measured with standard questions that are typically asked in the ANES. First, we want to know about standard demographics and their correlation to online exposure to information about ballot measures. In Model 1, we include information on respondents' *education, income, age,* and whether they are *female, Black,* or *Hispanic* (see Mossberger, Tolbert, and McNeal 2007; Mossberger, Tolbert, and Franko 2012). In Model 2, we add predictors about their political sophistication, as those more sophisticated may be more likely to be motivated to search online (Luskin 1990; Davis 2005). These predictors are *political knowledge*—derived from a scale of 10 open-ended questions about politics—and *interest* in politics—measured on a one-to-five scale from "not at all interested" to "extremely interested."

In Model 3, we add predictors of their engagement in politics as those engaged may be more likely to be mobilized to search online (Mossberger, Tolbert, and McNeal 2007). We include a measure of being *ideological*, which is created from "folding" the seven-point ideology scale into a new scale which runs from 0 for moderates to 3 from those extremely liberal or conservative. We include party identification, comparing *Democrats* and *Republicans* to the omitted category of independents. As previous media usage for political information may predict search behavior on ballot measures, we include the summary variable of political media usage for *television, radio,* and *newspapers.* We also include a measure of IQ, called "WordSum." For the first time, the 2012 ANES included an IQ test. This WordSum IQ[3] test is basically a very high-level vocabulary test, but it correlates strongly with the more traditional IQ tests. Without getting into the endless debates over the validity or immutability of IQ, *WordSum* is certainly

TABLE 4.4 Individual-Level Correlates for Using the Internet to Search for Information About Ballot Measures

	Model 1		Model 2		Model 3	
	Coeff.	*(S.E.)*	*Coeff.*	*(S.E.)*	*Coeff.*	*(S.E.)*
Education	0.223*	(0.088)	0.161	(0.092)	0.139	(0.095)
Age	−0.049†	(0.027)	−0.084**	(0.029)	−0.084**	(0.029)
Female	−0.196	(0.182)	−0.076	(0.191)	−0.082	(0.192)
Income	0.007	(0.012)	0.008	(0.012)	0.008	(0.012)
Black	−0.121	(0.312)	−0.202	(0.317)	−0.151	(0.333)
Hispanic	−0.224	(0.270)	−0.230	(0.274)	−0.177	(0.279)
Pol. Know.	—	—	−0.003	(0.043)	−0.014	(0.044)
Interest	—	—	0.503***	(0.108)	0.499***	(0.109)
Media Attn.	—	—	−0.012	(0.031)	−0.016	(0.032)
Ideological	—	—	—	—	0.117	(0.105)
Democrat	—	—	—	—	−0.214	(0.295)
Republican	—	—	—	—	−0.295	(0.309)
WordSum	—	—	—	—	0.037	(0.053)
Constant	−2.420*	(0.379)	−3.723*	(0.532)	−3.697*	(0.580)
N	1304		1304		1299	
χ^2	14.56*		41.67***		43.47***	

Note: Cells represent coefficients and standard errors of logistic regression models for whether or not the respondent searched online for information about ballot measures. Data from the 2012 ANES Direct Democracy Study. Two-tailed significance tests where $†p < 0.10$, $*p < 0.05$, $**p < 0.01$, $***p < 0.001$.

a good test of current cognitive skills which may correlate with search behavior for information.

Table 4.4 presents the result of these three model specifications. We see that the dominant predictor of searching online for information about ballot measures is political interest. The only other consistent correlation that we find is with older respondents' being less likely to search online. This matches prior literature on how younger Americans are online more than older Americans (Pew Research Center 2017). These results may suggest an answer to the question as to why only 11% searched online, because the vast majority of Americans are not that politically interested. Also of note is that none of the demographic variables showed significance, which suggests that there are no meaningful differences between the levels of online searching across these groups. For example, men and women search at about the same level, as the descriptive statistics show that 11.5% of women and 9.5% of men searched online.

Conclusion

As we predicted, we find that users take Google's advice clicking on search returns on the first page 89% of the time. Most users do not dig deep. If Google suggests a top-ranked site, many users click that site. Almost all of our users did not go past the first page. The primary predictor of clicking a suggested site is simply its position. If Google recommends a site higher, it is much more likely to be clicked. One main implication of these results is that the impact of motivated reasoning is mitigated because of subjects' desire to get information fast and trust in the Google Search algorithm.

It is important to remember that our users are not a *tabula rasa* when it comes to Internet usage. Since Google is extremely popular, many of our participants probably have used Google in the past. As Google is generally deemed to be informative, its prior success in providing beneficial recommendations to gain information leads to more trust from its users that the top suggested links will be informative. In other words, the very success of the algorithm makes it more impactful on the click behavior of users, which in turn generates more usage of informative sites which will further generate trust in Google. While this aspect of usage might be interesting and informative for understanding Google's wide impact, we do not think this harms our hypothesis testing because we are trying to investigate Google usage in the real world. Trusting behavior based on prior usage would be just as common in the real world as would be within our experiment.

In addition to these basic results that showed that users take seriously the Google Search algorithm recommendations, we also find that there is no explicit explanation of why a few users ignore these initial recommendations and go deeper into the search results, such as being more ideological. Based on predetermined survey answers, we do not find that those more interested in politics, more engaged in political participation, and more ideological and partisan are more likely to pursue additional information than is provided within the first page of results.

An interesting question we cannot answer with these data is from the ANES results, which show respondents are searching because of their interest in politics. What we do not know is whether they find learning about politics to be enjoyable, or if they are trying to eliminate cognitive dissonance that they might have found on the front pages. By definition, the balanced reporting of mass media tends to report both sides of an issue, and will then report conflictual views to believers of one side. Because mass media often shows both sides, if you belong to one side, you will be exposed to alternative viewpoints from mass media. So perhaps the desire to search deeper into results is to try to find partisan media sources such as blogs that will present only one side of the nation. Additionally, it could simply be that these users are just more interested in political topics and thereby want to go to special sites that will talk about the matter at a more in-depth level. At this time, we cannot conclusively answer these questions, so we leave these for future research.

In the last two chapters, we have shown that the PageRank algorithm produces results that matched our initial predictions. Google recommends mainstream information at the top of its results. We have also shown that users take these results and click on highly ranked websites, which tend to be mass media and government websites. Based on these two facts that we have empirically demonstrated, in the next chapter we test whether the third and most important part of our basic theory. In the next chapter, we examine whether or not the users who clicked on these websites actually learn beneficial information about the ballot measures that they were researching.

Notes

1 The T-SPLOST experiment has missing data for some participants' pre-treatment characteristics, and the NJ Minimum Wage experiment data only returned 14 complete responses for what was clicked by the participant and what Google suggested to them. More to the point, motivated reasoning is based on some level of ideological or political reasoning, and of these three experiments, the charter school amendment makes a plausible best test for this aspect. Based on these missing data problems, we only examine GA charter school amendment in Tables 4.2 and 4.3. Without question, future research should examine this topic more closely.

2 Details about the survey can be found at this URL: http://electionstudies.org/study pages/anesspecialstudy2012directdem/anesspecialstudy2012directdemuserguide.pdf.

3 The WordSum IQ test is a vocabulary test that correlates at a very high level with traditional IQ tests and is an accepted measure of cognitive ability (see Miner 1957). Here, it is measured by a sum of the respondent's correct answers, which could range from 0 to 10.

References

American National Election Study. 2014. "Data User's Guide for the ANES 2012 Direct Democracy Study." Michigan University and Stanford University. http://electionstudies.org/studypages/anes_specialstudy_2012_directdem/anes_specialstudy_2012_directdem_userguide.pdf.

Buddenbrock, Frank. 2016. "Search Engine Optimization: Getting to Google's First Page." In *Google It: Total Information Awareness*, edited by Newton Lee, 195–205. New York, NY: Springer.

Chitika. 2013. "The Value of Google Result Positioning." *Chitika | Online Advertising Network*. http://chitika.com/google-positioning-value.

Davis, Richard. 2005. *Politics Online: Blogs, Chatrooms, and Discussion Groups in American Democracy*. New York: Routledge.

Kunda, Ziva. 1990. "The Case for Motivated Reasoning." *Psychological Bulletin* 108 (3): 480–98. doi:10.1037/0033-2909.108.3.480.

Lodge, Milton and Charles Taber. 2000. "Three Steps Toward a Theory of Motivated Political Reasoning." In *Elements of Reason: Cognition, Choice, and the Bounds of Rationality*, edited by Arthur Lupia, Mathew D. McCubbins, and Samuel L. Popkin, 183–213. New York, NY: Cambridge University Press.

Lupia, Arthur. 1994. "Shortcuts Versus Encyclopedias: Information and Voting Behavior in California Insurance Reform Elections." *American Political Science Review* 88 (1): 63–76. doi:10.2307/2944882.

Lupia, Arthur and Mathew Daniel McCubbins. 1998. *The Democratic Dilemma: Can Citizens Learn What They Need to Know?* Cambridge, UK: Cambridge University Press.

Luskin, Robert C. 1990. "Explaining Political Sophistication." *Political Behavior* 12: 331–61.

Miner, John B. 1957. *Intelligence in the United States*. New York, NY: Springer.

Mossberger, Karen, Caroline J. Tolbert, and Ramona S. McNeal. 2007. *Digital Citizenship: The Internet, Society, and Participation*. Cambridge, MA: MIT Press.

Mossberger, Karen, Caroline J. Tolbert, and William W. Franko. 2012. *Digital Cities: The Internet and the Geography of Opportunity*. Oxford, UK: Oxford University Press.

Pew Research Center. 2017. "Internet/Broadband Fact Sheet." Information Blog. *Pew Research Center: Internet, Science & Tech*. January 12. www.pewinternet.org/fact-sheet/internet-broadband/.

Popkin, Samuel L. 1991. *The Reasoning Voter: Communication and Persuasion in Presidential Campaigns*. Chicago: University of Chicago Press.

Popkin, Samuel L. and Michael A. Dimock. 1999. "Political Knowledge and Citizen Competence." In *Citizen Competence and Democratic Institutions*, edited by Stephen L. Elkin and Karol Edward Soltan. University Park, PA: Pennsylvania State University Press.

5

LEARNING HAPPENS

Political Knowledge and Three Ballot Measures

In Chapter 2, we described the skepticism of scholars and commentators about the Internet's ability to generate normatively positive effects for politics. Contrary to this dominant paradigm on Internet politics, we posited that ample reason exists to believe that search returns produce legitimate, normatively valuable results based on the computer science behind Google's PageRank algorithm and an understanding of the market conditions under which search engines operate. We supported our position with an empirical exploration of search returns in Chapter 3, and we showed in Chapter 4 that users click on informative websites. The current chapter focuses on the crucial next step: learning.

Our research question for this chapter is the following: Are citizens able to use Google searches to generate knowledge about ballot measures? Discovering the implications of Internet search behavior on political knowledge is crucial because if scholars and commentators agree on one thing, it is that being able to use the Internet to obtain accurate, helpful information is paramount in an increasingly wired and connected world. To gauge whether citizens can use the Internet to successfully research a political issue, we intentionally selected a challenging research area: ballot measures. Citizens have consistently been found to lack knowledge about ballot measures despite voting on them. Voters often find direct democracy difficult because they have less information for decision making, yet their choices have more direct consequences than typical elections. Voters do not vote on a party or politician in the context of ballot measures, but rather on the expected outcome of an entire policy, which is typically couched in hard-to-read language (Reilly and Richey 2011). These policy areas often have both avid supporters and detractors offering biased opinions, and they involve technical claims that are hard to adjudicate.

We created three experiments with student, adult, and Amazon's Mechanical Turk (MTurk) samples to test how Google searches affect learning about ballot measures. We randomly assigned Google access to half of the participants in each experiment, while the other half were not able to use the Internet and served as the control group. We monitored subjects' screenshots and search histories to identify what Google shows them and what they click. After computer access was removed, all participants completed an open-ended knowledge test on the most important aspects of these ballot measures to determine whether Internet research educated them. We find a large increase in political knowledge among the Internet users group compared to the control group. Despite the difficult topics and expected manipulation of information by ideologues, our results consistently show that Google provides almost exclusively mainstream and informative sites to searchers, who then click on the sites that are highly ranked. This outcome holds true despite inclusion of the participants' cookies, which presumably place them in their own filter bubble. In one experiment, a re-test after one week shows that the treatment group still knew more. In summary, these results show that individuals can use the Internet to successfully research ballot measures, and they provide clear evidence that information technology can facilitate voter preparation.

Theoretical Expectations

Ballot measures are typically low salience (Kenski and Stroud 2006; Smith and Tolbert 2004; Smith 2001), and they use obscure language (Reilly and Richey 2011). As a result, the general public typically knows very little about the presence or content of ballot measures they may encounter during election season (Lupia 1994; Reilly 2010). These facts make direct democracy a hard test for our theory. Based on our theory of Google as a gatekeeper, we posit that subjects will click on mainstream media websites more often because they are ranked higher than other types of websites (confirmed in Chapter 3) and because mainstream media contains pertinent valid information (confirmed in Chapter 4). In addition, these subjects will learn more than subjects who do not use it. Formally, then, we make the following predictions for this chapter:

> *Hypothesis 1*: Subjects randomly assigned to have Google access will have significant increases in political knowledge.
> *Hypothesis 2*: Subjects who use Google will know more about ballot measures one week post-experiment.

Hypothesis 1 concerns the *ability* of participants to actually learn from usage. Importantly, the null hypothesis—that Google searches on ballot measures have no educational effect—is a real possibility, for the reasons previously listed and outlined by the prior pessimistic scholarship (see Carr 2011; DiMaggio et al.

2004; Zillien and Hargittai 2009). Additionally, subjects may not read the top-ranked sites in depth, or pertinent, valuable content may not exist online on a given area of dense political information. A likely scenario is that good information is obscured by poor information, or simply that learning is difficult. Regardless of the reason, the point has never been empirically tested with actual search behavior from Internet users. By having users search for information on ballot measures using Google in real time, capturing their search history, and having relevant demographic and attitudinal measures, we are able to make validated claims about the normative benefits of Internet searches in politics for the first time.

Aside from knowledge simply being acquired, we predict that knowledge generated from searching the Internet will be temporally resilient. Because subjects who are using Google are agents rather than passive recipients, we expect to see political knowledge that withstands the passage of time. Hypothesis 2 is important because subjects may be more likely to notice information about the issue in the news or their life after the experimental exposure to the ballot measure and politics generally. Thus, being in this experiment may conceivably prime subjects to be more cognizant of our subject matter. If experimental subjects in the treatment still show higher levels of knowledge one-week post-experiment, we can attribute these gains to the experimental Internet research process demonstrating this kind of behavior generates robust, long-lasting effects on political knowledge.

Despite the fact that ballot measures are usually low salience, the ballot measures we use were extremely salient during the time of our study, making it difficult to find evidence for our theory. The salient nature of our ballot measures may have created conditions in which the public generally had high levels of knowledge, which could obscure significant differences between the treatment and control groups. As evidence for this salience, the mean political knowledge score for both T-SPLOST and charter school control conditions was quite high, and the minimum wage measure—while not particularly high—had significant amounts of national press coverage.

Research Design and Three Ballot Questions

Experimental Procedures

To test our hypotheses, we used three samples to account for possible internal and external validity issues arising from studying the Internet. The aspects and research goals of the three experiments are shown in Table 5.1. Basically, we have three experiments to allow for a re-test, to get a non-"Internet-savvy" sample, to get participants from more than one state, and to get participants inside their filter bubble. Because access and the ability to use the Internet to extract information is strongly correlated with socioeconomic and demographic groups (e.g., higher incomes and Whites) (DiMaggio et al. 2001; DiMaggio et al. 2004;

TABLE 5.1 Research Goals of Three Studies

	Transportation	Charter Schools	Minimum Wage
Sample	Student	Adult	MTurk
Knowledge Decay	One-week re-test	No	No
Filter Bubble	No	No	Yes
State	Georgia	Georgia	New Jersey
Recruitment Site	On campus	On the street	Online
Time Frame	Summer 2012	Fall 2012	Fall 2013
N	241	102	219

Zillien and Hargittai 2009), conducting multiple experiments with different sample composition is important for testing our theory.

First, to account for knowledge decay, we used a student sample from a mandatory introductory course in American government class at a large public university in the southeastern United States. The ballot measure in question was a "transportation special purpose local option sales tax" (T-SPLOST) referendum.[1] Subjects were incentivized to participate, but they were *not* incentivized to answer correctly. Subjects were randomly assigned into the treatment (Google access) or the control (no Google access) condition in the laboratory. In both conditions, subjects answered a pre-test questionnaire on demographics, political beliefs, generalized political participation and interest, and Internet usage. Treatment subjects were then sent to a computer that defaulted to Google as the homepage and used a newly installed, clean version of Google Chrome as the default browser.

The subjects were instructed to research the T-SPLOST ballot measure, but they were not told they would be expected to answer a follow-up quiz. They were also not told to research any specific phrase or wording; they chose their own way to research the topic, but most simply inputted "T-SPLOST ballot measure" into Google. As we describe in previous chapters, we copied their search history to ensure compliance with the instructions and to monitor their searches. We also copied their Google Search return pages up to the tenth page, and we found that every participant used Google to research T-SPLOST. Subjects were told that they had up to twenty minutes to perform their search tasks. In most cases, subjects took between five and ten minutes[2] at which point they indicated to the proctor they were done and ready to move along. Once finished with their search task, they were instructed to leave the computer and were given a post-test questionnaire without computer access. They were also not allowed to use any web-enabled device, including mobile phones. The control condition only filled out the pre- and post-test questionnaires, with no Internet access or use of any web-enabled device.

For the charter school ballot measure, we used an "on-the-street, in-person" non-student sample to exclude Internet-savvy participants—an important consideration for research of this type (Zillien and Hargittai 2009). Interviewers walked around the streets of Atlanta asking adult non-students if they were willing to participate in research for two dollars, not mentioning it was Internet research. While both college students and MTurkers are valid pools of subjects for convenience samples, with results generally reflecting larger, more representative samples (Berinsky, Huber, and Lenz 2012; Druckman and Kam 2011), these individuals may be more likely to extract beneficial information from the Internet because they are more likely to be computer savvy. By getting a non-student sample, we could overcome the typical external validity complaint that is often invoked against experiments using college students. The first question asked of potential subjects was the screener question: "Are you a college student?" Only those that were currently not students were allowed to join. The distribution of education matches that of Georgia, with about 40% of subjects not having any college education. Once the adult non-students agreed to participate, they were randomly assigned into either the treatment group, which had access to a laptop computer with a clean version of Google's Chrome web browser available, but no external help of any kind, or the control group. The rest of the procedures were similar to those described above.

Finally, to get participants inside their filter bubble and to broaden participants' geographic diversity, in the fall of 2013 we posted an ad on Amazon's Mechanical Turk website for U.S.-based MTurkers with an incentive of one dollar. Once in the experiment, the subjects were randomly assigned to the treatment group and instructed to use Google to search for information on New Jersey's Minimum Wage ballot measure, or to the control group and instructed to simply answer questions to the best of their ability. Although this real-world sample had less laboratory control, we have two controlled studies with the other experiments, in which we monitored participants closely. Through each of these experiments, we obtained the search histories for all of the treatment subjects during the experiment,[3] and we find that all three samples performed similarly. If we find similar treatment effects across multiple samples in multiple elections in two states, we can safely conclude that Google is an effective educational tool for political knowledge in direct democracy.

Data

Each experiment is a 1×2 post-test design in which we code for treatment (1) and control (0). The summary statistics by treatment and control groups for the data used in this research are presented in the appendix to this chapter. The tables in the appendix also show that unit homogeneity was achieved by random assignment to treatment and control groups, and therefore the effect on the dependent variable from assignment to treatment can be considered causal. Our dependent variable is *political knowledge* measures for each of the three referendums that subjects were instructed to research. We followed past research on surveillance political knowledge (Delli Carpini and Keeter 1996; Jerit, Barabas, and Bolsen 2006) and created a scale of open-ended questions about the referendum. These questions were the following:

1. How much additional percent in sales taxes will you pay if Amendment No. 1 passes?
2. How long will the tax be paid if Amendment No. 1 passes?
3. Which areas will get a new MARTA train line if Amendment No. 1 passes?
4. Which highways will get a new intersection if Amendment No. 1 passes?
5. Will Atlanta get money for the Beltline line if Amendment No. 1 passes?
6. Will Peachtree City get money for the Ropeway line if Amendment No. 1 passes?

The Cronbach's alpha of these six items is 0.72, suggesting they are a good fit and successfully measure the latent concept of knowledge about the transportation referendum. For the charter school amendment, we followed a similar procedure for constructing a knowledge scale as the dependent variable, but with five questions rather than six. The Cronbach's alpha of these five items is 0.43. The questions for this measure were the following:

1. If the amendment passes, if a local school system does not want to establish a charter school within its system, can the state approve a charter school anyway?
2. As proposed in the amendment, are the charter schools established going to be public or private schools?
3. Under current law, who has the legal right to establish charter schools?
4. If the amendment passes, who will have the legal right to establish charter schools?
5. Under the amendment, will the state, local school systems or private citizens be responsible for funding the charter schools?

The questions for the New Jersey minimum wage ballot measure were similar to the previous experiments, and again we used five questions to create the scale. The Cronbach's alpha of these five items is 0.732. The questions were as follows:

1. What will the new minimum wage be in New Jersey if the ballot measure currently under consideration passes?
2. What is the current minimum wage in New Jersey?
3. Why will there be annual increases in the new minimum wage?
4. If the federal minimum wage increases, will New Jersey's minimum wage also increase?
5. Does New Jersey Governor Chris Christie support raising the minimum wage?

Each of these open-ended dependent variables and their corresponding scales represent a stringent test of our theory because we asked subjects to recall information they only recently researched. These types of tests are notoriously difficult and constitute a very specific type of knowledge (see Delli Carpini and Keeter (1996) and Chapter 1 for more details). However, considering the voluminous literature on what constitutes political knowledge in a vibrant, democratic society (see Habermas 2006; Landemore 2013; Ober 2008) and the fact that scholars and policy makers are constantly concerned about acquiring fact-based knowledge for the citizenry at-large (Galston 2001; Lippmann 1922; Dewey 1927), testing political knowledge in this way is legitimate.

Results

Hypothesis 1: Google Usage Increases Political Knowledge

Figure 5.1 displays treatment effects with 95% confidence intervals in all three experiments and shows statistically significant positive treatment effects on political knowledge of around one standard deviation in all three experiments.[4] In all experiments, a few minutes of searching on Google led to websites that imparted beneficial information. The results clearly show that Internet research using Google benefited voters' knowledge of ballot questions. Also note that the charter school experiment used a non-student sample recruited on the street.

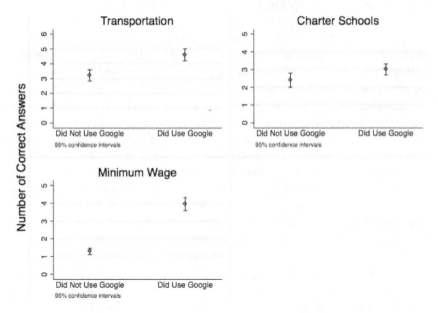

FIGURE 5.1 Treatment Effects for Political Knowledge on Three Ballot Measures

Source: Experiments (summer 2012, student; fall 2012, non-student; fall 2013, MTurk).

Even in this much older and less educated group, we found positive treatment effects for a ballot measure on the establishment and maintenance of charter schools in Georgia. The minimum wage experiment was done with MTurkers who researched the ballot question on their own personal computers, which had varied search histories and any number and type of cookies embedded in their browsers. The effects were large in this sample, which serves as deeper evidence of this effect in the world.

In any experiment, external validity is a constant concern. Our use of three different samples under various search and machine conditions obviates some of these concerns. For the minimum wage ballot measure, the screenshots subjects submitted make it clear that many subjects were logged into Google and thus were not only allowing cookies but also information from their various Google accounts such as Maps, Drive, and Plus. Yet, even with Google using all this information to create a possible filter bubble, which could confound our expected results, the treatment group knew significantly more than the control group. In sum, the large increase shows that voters can use information technology to boost their preparedness to answer ballot questions.

While the plots in Figure 5.1 provide evidence of the effectiveness of Google searches, looking inside the scale is also valuable to determine if Google assists with certain questions or types of knowledge more than others. To do this, we turn to Table 5.2, which displays logit models for each of the questions in all three scales. Questions for the T-SPLOST experiment are at the top of the table, charter school experiment questions are in the middle, and minimum wage questions are at the bottom. We also list the topics for each of the questions above the estimations to facilitate interpretation.

In the T-SPLOST set of models, we see that three of the six knowledge questions demonstrate statistically significant treatment effects. Subjects were able to correctly identify new MARTA lines (i.e., the only public transit in Atlanta), new intersections, and the benefit of the measure in helping to fund growth of the Beltline in metro Atlanta. Interestingly, subjects using Google did not differ significantly from the control in correctly answering questions about the tax percentage that the measure requested, the term of the tax, or the assistance that the measure would provide for the Ropeway line to Peachtree City. The last question—Ropeway—was a question distinct from those asked in the other two experiments. This question was intended to gauge whether Google access could help subjects discern false information from true facts about ballot measures. The Ropeway train line did not exist, and Peachtree City was not a part of the discussion about expanded MARTA access. While the treatment and control were not significantly different on this question, the coefficient being positive is instructive. This outcome suggests that subjects using Google were at least not getting this question wrong, which might be expected in an information overload situation.

For the charter school amendment, the results indicate the difficulty of learning about ballot measures. Recall for this experiment, we recruited subjects on

TABLE 5.2 Treatment Effects for Google Searches on Political Knowledge on Three Ballot Measures, by Question

T-SPLOST

	Tax Percent	Term of Tax	New MARTA Lines	New Intersections	Beltline	Ropeway
	Coefficient	Coefficient	Coefficient	Coefficient	Coefficient	Coefficient
Treatment	0.461	0.347	1.564***	0.622*	0.730**	0.386
	(0.302)	(0.288)	(0.280)	(0.264)	(0.275)	(0.259)
Constant	0.904***	0.783***	-0.519**	0.033	0.272	-0.272
	(0.203)	(0.198)	(0.190)	(0.184)	(0.185)	(0.185)
	$N = 241; \chi^2 = 2.35$	$N = 241; \chi^2 = 1.46$	$N = 241; \chi^2 = 33.71{***}$	$N = 241; \chi^2 = 5.61{*}$	$N = 241; \chi^2 = 7.17{**}$	$N = 241; \chi^2 = 2.24$

Charter Schools

	State Approval	Public Schools	Current Charters	Changes to Charters	Funding
Treatment	0.836*	0.197	1.396***	0.653	-0.664
	(0.415)	(0.444)	(0.422)	(0.408)	(0.478)
Constant	0.039	0.875**	-0.521	0.039	-0.875***
	(0.280)	(0.307)	(0.289)	(0.280)	(0.307)
	$N = 102; \chi^2 = 4.15{*}$	$N = 102; \chi^2 = 0.20$	$N = 102; \chi^2 = 11.63{***}$	$N = 102; \chi^2 = 2.60$	$N = 102; \chi^2 = 1.98$

Minimum Wage

	New Minimum Wage	Current Minimum Wage	COLA	Fed. Increases	Christie
Treatment	4.086***	3.954***	1.112***	1.874***	2.380***
	(0.459)	(0.552)	(0.316)	(0.394)	(0.354)
Constant	-2.721***	-1.333***	-0.620***	-0.159***	-1.304***
	(0.326)	(0.192)	(0.164)	(0.157)	(0.190)
	$N = 221; \chi^2 = 117.66{***}$	$N = 222; \chi^2 = 102.79{***}$	$N = 221; \chi^2 = 12.81{***}$	$N = 222; \chi^2 = 28.89{***}$	$N = 223; \chi^2 = 52.97{***}$

Source: Experiments (summer 2012, student; fall 2012, non-student; fall 2013, MTurk).
Note: * $p < 0.05$, ** $p < 0.01$, *** $p < 0.001$; Source: Ballot measure experiments.

the street who were not college students, and the sample group was therefore generally older and less educated. These subjects were also less likely to be computer savvy, and they spent much less time researching than the T-SPLOST subjects did on average. The two specific questions that the treatment subjects were more likely to get correct were those asking if there would be state approval of charter schools and who currently had the right to initiate charter schools in Georgia. This amendment was notoriously difficult, and it was written in a way that obscured the true intent of the measure's authors (Rich 2012). Treatment subjects only being able to generate statistically significant different results compared to controls on two of the five questions demonstrates the difficulty of learning objective facts about this measure. The questions with no differences between the control and treatment subjects were if charter schools are public schools, what changes are being made to charter schools, and how the schools are funded. Notably, the media coverage and popular knowledge about charter school funding is so dense and difficult to comprehend that our treatment subjects actually got this answer wrong more than the control subjects. The difference is not statistically significant, but it shows how even doing research on ballot measures may not ensure 100% accurate knowledge.

Finally, for the New Jersey minimum wage ballot measure in 2013, we see that Internet research is a significant predictor of correct answers across the board. The effects on these questions are notable because we cannot be sure that subjects in our control group did not do research on their own without our knowledge. This experiment represents an "intent to treat" environment in which we instruct the subjects on how to act, and we assume that the treatment subjects undertook research and the control subjects did not. Here, even under this high degree of external validity, we see the treatment had the hypothesized effect. This experiment may have had such uniformly positive effects compared with the other two because of the nature of the ballot measure question. The details of the New Jersey ballot measure were quite well known, and there was ample national media attention. Furthermore, the New Jersey question was—as a policy matter—exceedingly direct. The T-SPLOST and charter school measures were more complex and certainly more difficult to identify with any specific ideology or partisan group. Thus, it is possible that subjects could do a small amount of research and understand the broad implications by using heuristics. However, Google research clearly mattered because heuristics would not have helped subjects know that the law would pin minimum wage increases to inflation (i.e., COLA) or that as the federal minimum wage increased above the state minimum the state wage would follow.

On all three of these ballot measures we see that knowledge increases with Google access. A view inside the knowledge scales reveals that even though knowledge increased overall, difficult language and obscure concepts clearly made learning more difficult in some places. Nevertheless, we still show that Google access and research positively affect learning about ballot measures in

American politics. This important finding shows how search-engine results can be used for normatively valuable benefits in politics in the twenty-first century. However, there is more to knowledge than just its existence. How long are subjects able to retain knowledge once they get it?

Hypothesis 2: Internet Researching Using Google Is Robust to One-Week Decay

A serious threat to these findings is a recency effect whereby information gained through research using Google is quickly forgotten or is "shallow" (i.e., Carr 2011). To consider this problem, we re-contacted the treatment group in the T-SPLOST ballot measure experiment about a week after they researched the topic, and gave them the same test again. This re-testing was done in class, and the subjects were not told ahead of time that they would be re-tested. This second wave has some panel attrition, about 28%, and the reduced sample size works against finding a statistically significant effect. Furthermore, because this second wave is administered post-treatment, the control group may have done additional research on the topic because they were asked about it in the first wave. Yet, as we show in Figure 5.2, even after one week, those in the treatment group knew significantly more than the control group. This shows Internet research on topics pertaining to direct democracy leads to knowledge gains that

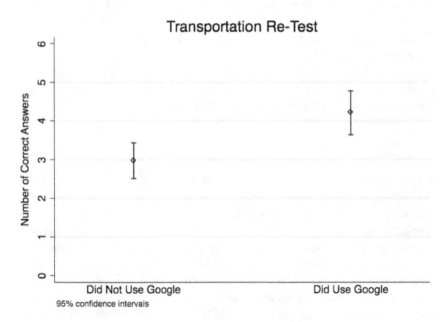

FIGURE 5.2 Treatment Effects on One-Week Knowledge Decay, Georgia T-SPLOST

Source: T-SPLOST Experiment, summer 2012.

TABLE 5.3 Treatment Effects on Political Knowledge, Imbalanced Covariates

Variable	T-SPLOST		Charter Schools		Minimum Wage	
	Coefficient	Robust S.E.	Coefficient	Robust S.E.	Coefficient	Robust S.E.
Treatment	1.168***	−0.244	0.814*	−0.395	3.833***	−0.405
Black	−0.285	−0.236	—	—	—	—
Age	—	—	0.006	−0.015	—	—
Female	—	—	0.109	−0.392	0.12	−0.249
Cut point 1	−2.736	−0.347	−3.949	−1.195	−0.746	−0.404
Cut point 2	−1.501	−0.245	−0.829	−0.704	0.686	−0.403
Cut point 3	0.073	−0.216	0.53	−0.699	2.007	−0.435
Cut point 4	1.217	−0.233	1.42	−0.709	2.83	−0.469
Cut point 5	3.078	−0.313	3.18	−0.778	4.201	−0.531
Cut point 6	5.014	−0.616	—	—	—	—
N		241	N	97	N	219
χ^2		4.36	χ^2	4.36	χ^2	122.40***

Source: Experiments (summer 2012, student; fall 2012, non-student; fall 2013, MTurk).

Note: Two-tailed significance tests where * $p < 0.05$, ** $p < 0.01$, *** $p < 0.001$.

last at least one week. Evidence of the Internet's ability to generate knowledge robust to time decay is an important contribution to this area of research, and it shows that knowledge from Internet searches may not be so shallow after all.

Thus, in two states considering three ballot measures, in the laboratory, on the street, or online, after a week's delay, and accounting for the filter bubble, Google usage increases political knowledge. As is common with random assignment, variables were occasionally imbalanced between the treatment and control groups. In Table 5.3, we include the variables that were imbalanced in regression models, and our findings remain positive and significant for Google usage for each experiment.

Conclusion

In this chapter, we find that Google research can effectively educate those willing to use it to learn about direct democracy. In prior chapters, we showed how the availability of search engines such as Google increases the "opportunity" to gain information, and here we showed that citizens have the "ability" to extract it effectively. This research shows that citizens can use the Internet to research ballot measures, and it helps to provide evidence to answer an important debate in political communication: Is the Internet beneficial for citizen competence? Our research clearly demonstrates that voters can use the Internet to research ballot measures to access useful information. This finding is important because voters have more access to information in a variety of locations, including through using their mobile phones. From a theoretical point of view, following Luskin's

(1990) framework, our work shows the only remaining issue for scholars of political knowledge is citizens' *motivation* to seek out information about politics. The Internet provides the *opportunity* because Google ensures they have the opportunity to find good information, and we find that citizens have the *ability* to extract valuable information through Internet usage.

The Internet has the potential to improve democracy, but we need to know that people are actually gaining from their usage of it. Consider that the sheer amount of information on the Internet facilitates exposure to broader perspectives than can be accessed through broadcast media. Crucially, the interactive nature of the Internet allows the receiver to ask questions through posts on blogs or message boards, which is impossible in unidirectional broadcast media. The interactivity should allow users of the Internet to clarify their misunderstandings and become more precise in their knowledge. Most importantly, users can access the Internet's information whenever they want, and they do not have to wait for the broadcast medium or printed page to be produced. Through 24-hours-a-day, 365-days-a-year access, the Internet provides nearly unlimited provision of almost the entirety of human knowledge. Important gaps in personal Internet access remain, but these are rapidly diminishing, and the current plan by the national government is to provide 100% access by 2020 or 2025 (Federal Communications Commission 2010).

As with most research, some aspects of our project leave questions open and provide avenues for future investigation. The first is that our project deals explicitly with direct democracy. Continuing this line of research is certainly important to discern if equally difficult, but more ideological and partisan areas of political behavior can benefit from directed research on the Internet. Much of the literature highlighting the potential negative impact of the Internet focuses on the areas of political behavior for which contention and conflict are salient aspects—unlike direct democracy, which is really just a black box of information for most voters. For instance, if individuals research conspiracy theories, would objectively good information be presented, and would the individuals use the links provided? Our research addresses these questions for direct democracy, but they are also vitally important to answer on political issues for which ideology and partisanship are more important intervening factors.

The second area for future research is to test how subjects use the Internet compared with other tools for research. We find the Internet helps establish political knowledge, but does it do so better than other, more traditional places for political information like print newspapers? That proposition is not tested here, but it is an extension of this work that will be informative. The third aspect for future research to address is an explicit test of PageRank for political websites. We did not obtain PageRank scores for all of the sites visited by our participants, so we are unable to explicitly test this proposition. This lack of testing is a drawback, but it does not diminish the fundamental empirical finding that mainstream sites are more likely to be pushed to the top of Google Search results. Despite these important areas of future research, the findings we present are still substantive and noteworthy. The Internet is a useful tool for direct democracy, and it can help generate better citizenship.

In the next chapter, we take a look down the line at attitudes that should be affected by increases in political knowledge. Specially, we look at confidence in vote choice in our experiments, and we use the 2012 ANES to assess how Internet use affects the ease of understanding ballot measures in a national sample. Confidence in vote choice and ease of understanding creates the mechanism for making citizens feel comfortable completing their ballots (i.e., decreases roll-off), which is a chronic problem in direct democracy elections. Then, in Chapter 7, we move to look at real-world data, which is the crucial missing link on Internet and politics research at this time—evidence and explorations about how Google Search behavior influences political behavior more broadly. Now that we have established that Google leads to political knowledge on ballot measures, we use innovative data and methods to assess what this knowledge looks like in practice.

Notes

1 The students in the T-SPLOST experiment matched the diversity of the university, with 68% female, with an average age of 19 years. The racial categories were 13% Asian, 50% Black, 28% White, and 8% other race. The participant group included students from 32 majors. This sample provides an excellent understanding of decision making among diverse groups of people, representing real-world situations. More details can be found in the appendix for this chapter.
2 The average search time for T-SPLOST was 10 minutes, 4 minutes for charter school, and 5 minutes for the minimum wage experiment.
3 MTurkers were prompted to upload their search history screenshots as part of the post-test.
4 We also find positive statistically significant treatment effects in ordered logit models shown in Web Appendix Table 5.

References

Berinsky, Adam J., Gregory A. Huber, and Gabriel S. Lenz. 2012. "Evaluating Online Labor Markets for Experimental Research: Amazon.com's Mechanical Turk." *Political Analysis* 20 (July): 351–68. doi:10.1093/pan/mpr057.
Carr, Nicholas. 2011. *The Shallows: What the Internet Is Doing to Our Brains*. New York: W. W. Norton & Company.
Delli Carpini, Michael X. and Scott Keeter. 1996. *What Americans Don't Know About Politics and Why It Matters*. New Haven: Yale University Press.
Dewey, John. 1927. *The Public and Its Problems*. New York, NY: Holt Press.
DiMaggio, Paul, Eszter Hargittai, Celeste Coral, and Steven Shafer. 2004. "Digital Inequality: From Unequal Access to Differential Use." In *Social Inequality*, edited by Kathryn M. Neckerman, 359–74, 390, 392–400. New York: Russell Sage Foundation.
DiMaggio, Paul, Eszter Hargittai, W. Russell Neuman, and John P. Robinson. 2001. "Social Implications of the Internet." *Annual Review of Sociology* 27 (January): 307–36.

Druckman, James N. and Cindy D. Kam. 2011. "Students as Experimental Participants: A Defense of the 'Narrow Data Base.'" In *Cambridge Handbook of Experimental Political Science*, edited by James N. Druckman, Donald P. Green, James H. Kuklinski, and Arthur Lupia, 41–57. New York, NY: Cambridge University Press.

Federal Communications Commission. 2010. "National Broadband Plan." Government. *FCC.gov*. www.fcc.gov/national-broadband-plan.

Galston, William A. 2001. "Political Knowledge, Political Engagement, and Civic Education." *Annual Review of Political Science* 4 (1): 217–34. doi:10.1146/annurev.polisci.4.1.217.

Habermas, Jurgen. 2006. "Political Communication in Media Society: Does Democracy Still Enjoy an Epistemic Dimension? The Impact of Normative Theory on Empirical Research." *Communication Theory* 16: 411–26.

Jerit, Jennifer, Jason Barabas, and Toby Bolsen. 2006. "Citizens, Knowledge, and the Information Environment." *American Journal of Political Science* 50: 266–82.

Kenski, Kate and Natalie Jomini Stroud. 2006. "Connections Between Internet Use and Political Efficacy, Knowledge, and Participation." *Journal of Broadcasting & Electronic Media* 50 (2): 173–92. doi:10.1207/s15506878jobem5002_1.

Landemore, Hélène. 2013. *Democratic Reason: Politics, Collective Intelligence, and the Rule of the Many*. Princeton, NJ: Princeton University Press.

Lippmann, Walter. 1922. *Public Opinion*. New York, NY: Free Press.

Lupia, Arthur. 1994. "Shortcuts Versus Encyclopedias: Information and Voting Behavior in California Insurance Reform Elections." *American Political Science Review* 88 (1): 63–76. doi:10.2307/2944882.

Luskin, Robert C. 1990. "Explaining Political Sophistication." *Political Behavior* 12: 331–61.

Ober, Josiah. 2008. *Democracy and Knowledge: Innovation and Learning in Classical Athens*. Princeton, NJ: Princeton University Press.

Reilly, Shauna. 2010. *Design, Meaning and Choice in Direct Democracy: The Influences of Petitioners and Voters*. Burlington, VT: Ashgate Publishing.

Reilly, Shauna and Sean Richey. 2011. "Ballot Question Readability and Roll-Off: The Impact of Language Complexity." *Political Research Quarterly* 64 (1): 59–67. doi:10.1177/1065912909349629.

Rich, Motoko. 2012. "Future of Georgia's Charter Schools on Ballot." *The New York Times*. November 6, sec. A.

Smith, Daniel A. and Caroline Tolbert. 2004. *Educated by Initiative: The Effects of Direct Democracy on Citizens and Political Organizations in the American States*. Ann Arbor: University of Michigan Press.

Smith, Mark A. 2001. "The Contingent Effects of Ballot Initiatives and Candidate Races on Turnout." *American Journal of Political Science* 45 (3): 700–6. doi:10.2307/2669246.

Zillien, Nicole and Eszter Hargittai. 2009. "Digital Distinction: Status-Specific Types of Internet Usage." *Social Science Quarterly* 90 (2): 274–91. doi:10.1111/j.1540-6237.2009.00617.x.

6

INTERNET RESEARCH AND INTELLECTUALLY SECURE DECISIONS IN DIRECT DEMOCRACY

To this point in the book, we demonstrate that Google returns quality search results for queries related to direct democracy (Chapter 3), users click on the most valuable returns (Chapter 4), and political knowledge is possible when using Google to learn information about direct democracy (Chapter 5). Much of this evidence comes from experiments, which are helpful for directing the causal arrow, but may lack a degree of external validity. Moreover, our concerns about the efficacy of Internet research—Google, specifically—do not stop at search results and political knowledge. Another important consideration, which is certainly important for direct democracy, is that citizens feel *confident* about their vote choice and research process, and—in a similar vein—do voters feel that the Internet makes ballot measures easier to understand and a more enjoyable experience?

If voters research ballot measures, but feel overwhelmed by the process, then we may have to question the utility of search as a positive force in direct democracy. Furthermore, a serious problem for direct democracy elections is "roll-off" (Magleby 1984; Reilly 2010; Wattenberg, McAllister, and Salvanto 2000). Roll-off happens when citizens vote for offices at the top of their ballots, but discontinue voting as they move down the ballot. One reason voters may do this is if they feel less confident about their vote choice, or—if they use Google or other search tools online—they do not feel their research efforts made their voting choices easier to understand. Thus, while this chapter may be focused on very specific attitudes (i.e., confidence in vote choice and ease of understanding), this is an important bridge between the previous chapters and Chapters 7 and 8 where we take a larger view on the impact of Internet search on direct democracy. This chapter begins to shift our focus into a broader category of concerns—such as attitudes—that lead directly into broader voter behaviors in the aggregate.

Vote Confidence and Ease of Understanding

We define "vote confidence" as a subject's certainty that their vote choice was the proper choice for themselves as far as they know. In some research, "voter confidence" often means confidence in the political system, or something like political efficacy (e.g., see Claassen et al. 2013). This is not the definition of voter confidence we are using. The measure we are using is, in some way, akin to Lau and Redlawsk's (1997) "voting correctly" or Baum and Jamison's (2006) "voting consistently." A key difference is that our focus is on the subjects' attitudes about their vote choice. Work on voting correctly empirically validates the choices of research subjects to verify if they actually vote "correctly" or "consistently." For our purposes, this is not necessary. There could be any number of reasons a conservative Republican might be in favor of the T-SPLOST or against the charter school amendment because there is no direct ideological or partisan corollary.[1] Similarly, it could be the case that liberals might vote against the T-SPLOST for ideological reasons that defy quick assumptions about supporting taxation for infrastructure purposes.[2] The main point is that we are not specifically concerned with whether or not the votes of subjects matched some specific choice, but rather if—after using Google for research—subjects express confidence in their vote choices.

Another way we can gauge the difficulty citizens have with direct democracy—and if Internet research makes these costs lower—is by assessing the ease with which they believe they understand the issues at hand or if they enjoy voting on their ballot measures. Ease of understanding and enjoyment from the voting process, like confidence in vote choice, are important characteristics when citizens make choices that have direct impacts on policy in the public sphere. If the issues citizens are being asked to vote on are so complex they cannot understand them or it becomes a cognitively painful process, then we have to reconsider the utility of direct democracy as a policymaking forum. As with vote confidence, we take subjects' expressed attitudes about their own ease of understanding and the degree to which they like voting on ballot measures. Unlike voting correctly, there is no accepted empirical validation measure for ease of understanding or measuring one's enjoyment gained from voting, so we link these concepts to the voter sophistication, political efficacy, ballot complexity, and roll-off literatures. We now turn to explore the main empirical findings to this point in political science on these and related concepts.

Vote Confidence

Vote confidence and discussions surrounding voters' confidence in their choices are implicit in much of the research on voter competence and sophistication. Political knowledge is generally considered a prerequisite for being confident in one's vote choice (Delli Carpini and Keeter 1996; Lau and Redlawsk 2006; Prior and Lupia 2008). As discussed in detail in Chapter 4—and demonstrated in our empirical findings—Google Search activity does produce political knowledge on ballot measures. So, if this is the case, does this also translate into confidence about one's vote choice in these elections? A concept related to vote confidence is "voter confusion" (Highly and McAllister 2002; Margolis 1977). As confusion increases we can expect confidence in one's vote choice to decrease. There are numerous studies that deal with these concepts, although—arguably—voter confusion has a larger and longer literature. Both of these concepts—confusion and confidence—help us understand what we might expect from subjects who are confronted with complex ballot measures.

Confidence in one's vote choice is driven by a myriad of factors. Some of these are theoretically relevant at the individual level such as political knowledge and interest in politics (Benoit, McKinney, and Holbert 2001; Lau and Redlawsk 1997; Lau, Andersen, and Redlawsk 2008). Using experiments, researchers have consistently shown subjects who were able to gain outside information for their vote choice are generally more confident with their choice. Lau and Redlawsk show this using a dynamic process tracing environment, while Benoit and colleagues (2001) use presidential debate viewing as outside information. Replicating Benoit et al. (2001) and Benoit and Hansen (2004) show general media exposure increases voters' confidence in their choices with cross-sectional data. This is an important replication because it shows that confidence is not an artifact of the lab. Importantly, we know time processing information increases one's confidence in vote choice (Lau and Redlawsk 2006). Time spent processing information is crucial because it allows a person the cognitive space to absorb the details of the information they find during their research. We add to this literature by highlighting the impact of Internet research on voters' confidence in their vote choice on ballot measures.

When it comes to voter confusion, few things in American politics are more confusing than direct democracy (Lupia 2001; Reilly 2010). Margolis (1977) claims that voter confusion is prevalent in American politics, and particularly so at the state and local level. Moreover, confusing ballots or other complex aspects of the voting process are demonstrated to decrease confidence in one's vote and the system overall (Atkeson and Saunders 2007). In a large-scale study of the voting system in the United States, Burden and Stewart (2014) show that voters' confidence in the electoral system and confidence in their own vote selections are directly related to the ease with which they are able to gain information. Elite messages also impact the level of confusion among the general public, which is particularly true for issues regarding referendums (Highly and McAllister 2002). This is an important and telling finding, which indicates that Google access should help make voters more confident in their selections on ballot measures.

Given that Google gives users access to high-quality information and users click on these resources, it is likely the case that Google access would result in higher levels of confidence in one's vote choice. In settings outside of politics, confidence in the choices being made propels decision-makers and those who are affected by their decisions to continue cooperating and finish their tasks (Sniezek 1992; Westbrook, Gosling, and Coiera 2005). We suspect this may be the same for direct democracy as well. Confidence in vote choice likely contributes to the willingness of voters to vote down their ballot. However, a legitimate counter hypothesis is that Google presents so much information that—even though the information is high quality—there is a crisis of choice for voters and their confidence actually decreases. Carr's (2011) "shallows" argument is predicated on Internet search biasing users toward short, almost trivial information retrieval. If there is not enough time or if users feel rushed, they may not feel very confident with their choice. Without confidence, voters may be less likely to continue filling out their ballot, and roll-off then becomes an issue. At this point, both of these suppositions are empirical questions.

Ease of Understanding and Efficacy

Beyond vote confidence, "ease of understanding" and getting enjoyment from the voting process may be a useful way to conceptualize voter utility from research using the Internet. Like vote confidence, ease of understanding is another dependent variable with a varied history in empirical research. Some research investigating ease of understanding is focused on voting systems, specifically. Herrnson et al. (2008) use a large-scale field study looking at which types of voting systems allow for the greatest ease of understanding among other dependent variables. While these studies are informative, they eschew other ways tools can help voters understand ballot measures. Much like vote confidence, several individual-level predictors are associated with ease of understanding. Voters' level of education, race, political knowledge, and political interest are all significant predictors of finding political information easy to understand (Prior and Lupia 2008). As with confidence, believing one can understand the questions being asked and understanding the implications of one's votes is likely an inducement to continue down the ballot. As ballots get difficult, we know that roll-off increases (Reilly and Richey 2011). Thus, anything that makes ballots easier to understand is a net positive for keeping people engaged in the voting process. Being able to make the empirical link between using the Internet for research and increases in attitudes about the ease with which voters understand ballot measures is an important empirical question.

Finally, a pivotal attitude for voter participation more generally is political efficacy. Efficacy has been studied for decades in American politics (Craig, Niemi, and Silver 1990; Finkel 1985; Morrell 2003; Morrell 2005; Niemi, Craig, and Mattei 1991). As a concept, efficacy is the result of both confidence in the choices one makes and a level of understanding that indicates one can connect the implications of the political choices and behaviors one faces.

Historically, media effects on efficacy have been mixed. Research on political talk radio shows it decreases political efficacy (Hollander 1995), as do some types of television (Baumgartner and Morris 2006; Mutz and Reeves 2005). Internet use, conversely, is associated with modest increases on general political efficacy in previous research (Kenski and Stroud 2006). Given this history, further research is in order on the impact of Internet use on political efficacy. For our purposes, we want to know, specifically, if Internet use makes the enjoyment of voting on ballot measures go up for citizens, which is a form of increased internal efficacy.

This chapter is crucial to extending the empirical evaluation of our theory out of the narrow focus on political knowledge or Google returns and into more practical aspects of direct democracy. When conceptualizing the utility of Google for ballot measures, we should remember that using Google to search for information is no different than reaching for a hammer when one is trying to nail two boards together. Google is the tool, like the hammer, and it is only as useful as the results it produces. There is certainly an aspect of user capacity involved— this is to say: Can people properly use Google and gain good information in doing so? The previous three chapters of this book demonstrate that, yes, Google does yield quality results and those results are used to gain political knowledge. This chapter's role is to make the link between capacity and knowledge acquisition and subtler, but substantively important, attitudes about one's utility from using Google. Before we can establish the mechanism between Google Search and political behavior in a real way, we need to establish that Google Search is associated with the appropriate attitudinal frame of mind to yield substantive political behaviors. If there is no evidence Google Search makes users more confident about their abilities or eases their understanding of ballot measures, then there is no reason to suspect there may be linkages to real-world behavior.

Our basic research questions are as follows: Are Google users more confident with their vote choice compared to those who do not use the Internet to research ballot measures, and does using the Internet for research make ballot measures easier to understand? To these questions, we develop the following hypotheses:

> *Hypothesis 1*: Subjects using Google will be more confident about their vote choice than subjects in the control group.

We test this hypothesis using data from the T-SPLOST and charter school amendment experiments.[3] Note that there is a reasonable counter expectation that Internet research may make subjects less confident. There is likely a time component to this because, as Carr (2011) points out, limited or shallow research may be more problematic than no research at all.

These measures make excellent tests for this hypothesis because of the difference in research environments.[4]

To generate external validity and to test an aspect of our theory with a nationally representative sample, we use two questions from the 2012 ANES that most appropriately tap into how Internet research decreases costs for voters. The questions are worded thusly: "How hard or easy was it to understand the effects of each of the following ballot measures from this election?" The possible answer choices are "Very easy" (7), "Easy" (6), "Somewhat easy" (5), "Neither hard nor easy" (4), "Somewhat hard" (3), "Hard" (2), and "Very hard" (1). The dependent variable is constructed by adding together the responses from all of the ballot measures. This includes up to eleven ballot measures answers per respondent. Then, this sum was divided by total number of responses (eleven), to make the resultant average directly comparable to the above scaling. The specific hypothesis for this question is as follows:

Hypothesis 2a: Respondents who use the Internet to do research on ballot measures will report that their ballot measures were easier to understand compared to respondents who do not do research online.

The second question we use connects to both ease of understanding, confidence, and political efficacy. Specifically, the ANES asked subjects if they "enjoyed" voting on ballot measures. For someone to enjoy voting, they must have the requisite levels of political efficacy and knowledge to express this attitude (Finkel 1985; Morrell 2005). This is another good test for the attitudinal utility of Internet research. Our hypothesis is as follows:

Hypothesis 2b: Respondents who use the Internet to do research on ballot measures will report they like to vote on ballot measures more than those who do not do research online.

The independent variable is worded as "From which of the following sources have you heard anything about the ballot measure campaigns?" This is a dichotomous variable for the 11% who selected "Internet sites, chat rooms, or blogs." This measure of Internet research is a hard case. The question simply asks if the subjects have minimally engaged with these sources. The survey does not ask how long respondents spent doing research, nor does it inquire about the types of sites subjects are using. Therefore, if there is a significant finding here, we have a robust, hard-test case for Internet research being useful for making ballot measures easier to understand.

Of course, there are also important control variables to consider. We know that believing politics is easy to understand is significantly correlated with important attitudes and qualities like increased political knowledge (Delli Carpini and Keeter 1996) and political interest (Prior 2010). Demographic factors like age, race, gender, and education are also key controls for political sophistication (Highton 2009; Lewis-Beck et al. 2009; Verba, Burns, and Schlozman 1997).

Results

As part of the post-treatment battery of questions, subjects in the T-SPLOST and charter school amendment experiments had a question asking them about their level of confidence in their vote choice. The dependent variable is worded as "Thinking about your vote choice [ballot measure name], did you have enough information so that you chose the correct answer for yourself? Not at all confident (0), somewhat confident, (1), confident (2), and very confident (3)." Because this is an important aspect to the hypotheses from the experiments, we should recall that the average T-SPLOST treatment subject spend nearly fifteen minutes researching the ballot measure before they completed the post-treatment portions of their survey. The average charter school amendment subject spent roughly three minutes on their research. These differences in search times, as we have described in other places, are likely the result differences in lab versus on-the-street style research environments.

T-SPLOST

First, we visually examine the effect of search on subjects' confidence in their vote choice for the T-SPLOST measure. The treatment effects can be seen in Figure 6.1. Clearly, there are significant positive effects on subjects' confidence when they used Google to do research on the T-SPLOST measure. Given the

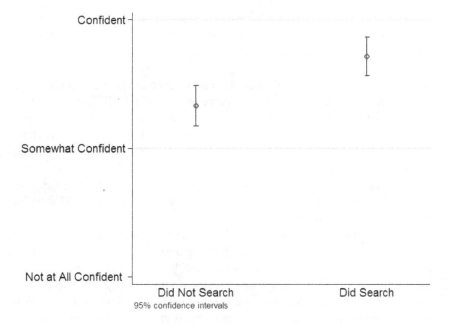

FIGURE 6.1 Treatment Effects for T-SPLOST on Vote Choice Confidence

Source: T-SPLOST experiment, summer 2012.

TABLE 6.1 The Impact of Google Search on Vote Confidence

Variable	Model 1: T-SPLOST	Model 2: Charter School
	Odds Ratios	Odds Ratios
	(S.E.)	(S.E.)
Searched	2.242***	0.604
	(1.392)	(0.220)
Cut point 1	−1.843	−2.264
	(0.238)	(0.369)
Cut point 2	0.534	−0.439
	(0.185)	(0.266)
Cut point 3	2.175	0.619
	(0.233)	(0.272)
N	241	100
χ^2	11.26***	1.91

Note: Ordered logistic regression displaying odds ratios for the T-SPLOST and charter school treatments. Two-tailed tests where *$p < 0.05$, **$p < 0.01$, ***$p < 0.001$.

number of subjects for this experiment ($N = 241$), the 95% confidence intervals are fairly narrow. Overall, subjects in the control condition were between "somewhat confident" and "confident" with a mean of 1.33. In the treatment condition, the 95% confidence interval nearly reaches "confident"; the mean for subjects in this condition is 1.71. The differences here seem to be subtle, to be sure, but substantive. This is an important finding because it suggests that Google Search activity creates the conditions where voters will be more secure in the choices they have made. Of course, knowing there is a significant treatment effect does not tell us much about the substantive impact. To do this, we turn to odds ratios using an ordered logit model for treatment effects (Long and Freese 2006).

In Table 6.1, we see the treatment effects as odds ratios for both the T-SPLOST and charter school amendment experiments. In Model 1, the odds ratio for the T-SPLOST Google treatment is 2.24 ($p = 0.001$), which means that the treatment represents a 124% increase in the odds of being more confident in one's vote choice. Despite the seeming subtlety of the treatment effects in Figure 6.1, the model demonstrates this is a very impactful effect from the treatment condition. Subjects who were in the Google treatment doing research on the transportation ballot measure are much more confident about their vote choices. To see how durable this is, we turn to the charter school amendment.

Charter School Amendment

For the charter school amendment, the effects are not realized. As we see in Figure 6.2, the effects in this experiment are negative, but not significant. This is a puzzling finding given the very clear effects from the T-SPLOST treatment.

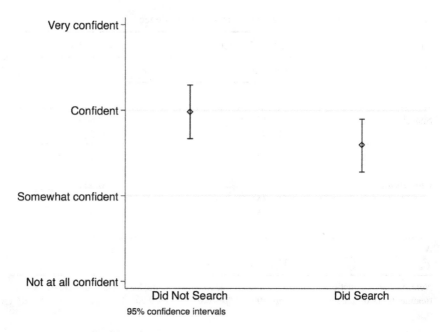

FIGURE 6.2   Treatment Effects for Google Search on Charter School Vote Choice
Confidence

Source: Charter school amendment experiment, fall 2012.

What is obvious from the figure is that the confidence intervals overlap to an extent that makes it difficult to explain much of what is happening beyond these simple impressions. To move to a more substantive explanation, we turn to ordered logits with odds ratios once again.

The odds ratio for the treatment effects in the charter school experiment is 0.75, which means that being in the treatment condition decreased the odds of moving to an increasing level of confidence in vote choice by 25%. This is a sizable decrease, but a non-significant one ($p = 0.433$), which matches the results from Figure 6.2. The main question here is this: why the differences between the experiments?

On some level, it is difficult to say why these differences exist given the lack of statistical significance in the charter school experiment. As we stated previously in this chapter, the T-SPLOST treatment subjects simply spent more time doing research on their ballot measure. We contend that the time these subjects spent is more like what citizens do in real life when citizens make the conscious choice to do research on something.[5] This is to say, when someone decides to do research online, they take their time, and spend a non-trivial amount of time doing research. We do not have a specific definition of "non-trivial," but ten minutes or more seems be uncontroversial for that definition.

Conversely, the subjects in the charter school amendment treatment did their research in a much more hurried way. They were approached on the street, agreed to participate, and likely wanted to continue doing whatever it was they were already doing. There is every reason to believe that some people might do online research in this manner. Consider, for instance, people who do quick research on their Internet-enabled smartphones or tablets while waiting in line at a checkout counter. These people are doing research—and may learn what they wanted to learn—but they may not be overly confident in what they learned.

Given the findings in the experiments, it is important to add some context and external validity to these findings. We do this by relying on the 2012 ANES just as we did in Chapter 4. The value here is that with mixed findings in the experiments, we need some way to demonstrate the effects—to the extent they exist—in the larger world. Furthermore, by nationally representative survey data we are able to account for some of the characteristics that make it likely citizens would be more or less politically sophisticated overall, which certainly affects citizens' attitudes on vote choice. Experiments are useful for causality, but these experiments call for more external validity.

External Validity

ANES 2012 Results: Confidence/Ease of Understanding

The details about the 2012 ANES are explicated in Chapter 4, so we will not go over them here. The relevant information, for this chapter, is that the 2012 ANES had a special set of questions for subjects in several states with numerous ballot measures. By adding the time-series study responses with their direct democracy-specific responses, we are able to get a very good sense of how attitudes and citizen demographics affect direct democracy behavior and attitudes in a nationally representative sample. This survey is a crucial and enormously valuable resource.

The dependent variable for these analyses is worded as "How hard or easy was it to understand the effects of each of the following ballot measures from this election?" While the word "confident" is not explicitly used in this question, this question does tap into a similar attitude construct as the question used in the experiments. Furthermore, one's confidence in vote choice and the ease of understanding political information both play an important role in political behavior in direct democracy. What makes these two dependent variables useful for this chapter is that in both questions respondents are being asked about their level of intellectual security in the effects of the ballot measures as far as they know. The experimental subjects were asked about the confidence in their choices, while respondents in the ANES were asked about the ease of understanding the effects. We cannot be sure these respondents voted on the ballot measures, but we can see if anything (i.e., Internet usage) contributed to their ease of understanding. The answers for the question range from one to seven where '1' means "very hard" and '7' means "very easy." The dependent variable is constructed by adding together the responses from all of the ballot measures for each respondent and dividing by seven.

The independent variable is worded as follows: "From which of the following sources have you heard anything about the ballot measure campaigns?" This is a dichotomous variable where '1' represents those who said "Internet sites, chat rooms, or blogs," and '0' for those who reported any other source for research. As noted in the discussion about the limited research dealing with voter confidence, there are several control variables that are important for modeling voter confidence.

First, we control for demographic factors. *Education* is measured zero through six, with zero meaning the respondent did not finish high school and six representing respondents with graduate degrees. Just as more educated voters are more likely to turn out (Wolfinger and Rosenstone 1980), we suspect more educated voters will be more confident in their vote choice. We measure economic status with *income*, which is measured as a categorical variable increasing in $5,000 increments. Next, *age* is a continuous control variable measuring respondents' reported age. *Black, Hispanic,* and *female* are dichotomous variables measuring these self-reported characteristics about the respondents. Finally, we control for *political knowledge* and *political interest*. These two control variables are fundamental to gaining some explanatory power in our model (Dalton 2013; Delli Carpini and Keeter 1996; Verba, Schlozman, and Brady 1995). Those with increased levels of political knowledge or political interest should be the respondents who are most likely to feel their ballot measures were easy to understand. This follows from previous research on voter confidence, and these variables also predict lower levels of roll-off on ballot measures (Magleby 1984; Reilly 2010; Reilly and Richey 2011). Thus, if we are able to see some significant effects from doing research online, it is good evidence for external validity for our experimental results.

Figure 6.3 displays the means and 95% confidence interval for the dependent variable from the 2012 ANES. As we can see from this figure, those who used the Internet to seek out information on their ballot measures report their measures being much easier to understand. The confidence intervals are very clearly not overlapping, which means this is a significant difference. This figure, as with the previous graphs, simply gives us an impressionistic understanding of the impact of Internet research on respondents' perceptions of ease of understanding. To truly understand the effect of Internet research compared to other predictors of political sophistication, we turn to an ordered logit model.

Moving on to Table 6.2, we have three sets of models. The first is a simple bivariate model, the second is the model with demographic controls only, and the third model is the full model including controls for interest and political knowledge. In the first model, it is clear the bivariate effect is positive and significant.

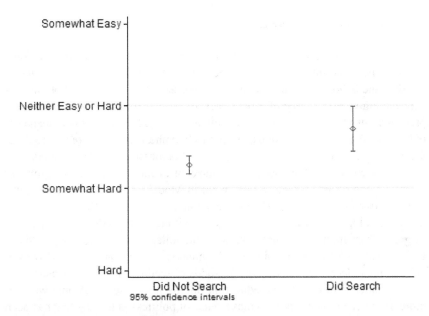

FIGURE 6.3 Effects of Internet Research on Ease of Understanding Ballot Measures, 2012 ANES

Source: 2012 American National Election Study, Direct Democracy Supplement.

TABLE 6.2 Ordered Logit Models for Ease of Understanding

	Model 1	*Model 2*	*Model 3*
Internet Search	0.665**	0.690**	0.495*
	(0.223)	(0.230)	(0.232)
Education	—	0.154*	0.068
	—	(0.072)	(0.074)
Age	—	0.027	−0.014
	—	(0.023)	(0.025)
Female	—	−0.319*	−0.183
	—	(0.152)	(0.157)
Income	—	0.018	0.016
	—	(0.010)	(0.010)
Black	—	0.287	0.299
	—	(0.255)	(0.259)
Hispanic	—	0.143	0.130
	—	(0.184)	(0.184)
Political Knowledge	—	—	0.103**
	—	—	(0.040)
Political Interest	—	—	0.246**
	—	—	(0.079)
Cut points suppressed for space.			
N	562	541	541
χ^2	8.86*	29.80***	51.53***

Note: 2012 ANES Direct Democracy supplement; Standard errors in parentheses. *$p < 0.05$, **$p < 0.01$, ***$p < 0.001$.

The coefficient is 0.665 and is significant ($p < 0.01$). This means that doing research using the Internet increases the ordered log-odds of feeling that understanding the ballot measures in one's state was easy by 0.665. Based on the evidence in Figure 6.3, this significant effect should not surprise us. Furthermore, we predicted this would be the case. The limitation here is the simple bivariate nature of this test. We need a more robust test of this hypothesis to feel more secure about the general effect of the Internet on making ballot measures easier to understand.

In the second model, we see some of the control variables exerting significant effects on the dependent variable as well. In Model 2, *education* has a significant positive effect, while *female* has a significant negative effect. Interpreting the ordered log-odds, we see that for a one-unit increase in education (i.e., such as going from high school graduate to some college), the ordered log-odds of feeling that ballot measures are easy to understand increase 0.154. However, being female decreases the ordered log-odds of feeling that ballot measures are easy to understand 0.319. The education finding makes sense. People who are more educated are better able to make sense of politics—a finding that has been replicated with some consistency. The finding for being female is less clear, but it is possible that women are just more likely to be honest about their lack of understanding ballot measures. We know that ballot measures are extremely difficult to understand in many cases (i.e., see Reilly and Richey 2011), but there is no reason to think there is a gender bias outside of women being biased toward honesty in survey responses. Focusing on the independent variable of interest—Internet search—we see it is still positive and significant, and is actually more substantively impactful in this second model. Thus, while controlling for demographics, Internet search is still a significant positive predictor of viewing ballot measures as easier to understand.

Finally, in Model 3, we turn to the fully specified model. Importantly, we see here, again, that the independent variable—Internet search—is positive and significant. The extent to which it increases the log-odds of easing the understanding of ballot measures is smaller compared to the other models, but given the range of control variables here its statistical significance is important. The effects of the demographic control variables are gone in this model because of the introduction of two powerful control variables: *political knowledge* and *political interest*. Political knowledge significantly increases the odds that someone feels understanding their ballot measures is easy. Similarly, political interest also significantly increases the odds that someone feels understanding ballot measures is easy. These findings conform to previous research, and are initiative to some degree. Political knowledge and political interest are two of the most enduring attitudes and concepts predicting political sophistication and engagement. If these variables were not significant there would be something seriously wrong. However, despite their effects, we still see significant positive effects from using the Internet for researching ballot measures. Thus, we see the Internet can not only increase one's confidence in one's vote choice (when given time), but it can also increase the chances someone feels their understanding of ballot measures is easier. With these two sets of findings, we now turn to the final attitude of interest—enjoyment from voting.

ANES 2012 Results: Enjoyment From Voting on Ballot Measures

Another interesting question asked by the ANES in 2012 was whether the responded enjoyed voting on each one of these ballot measures. Enjoyment from voting is a version of internal political efficacy. From this theoretical position, we can hypothesize that the increased information that would be derived from Internet searching reduces cognitive costs and thereby makes the experience of voting on ballot measures more enjoyable. We expect these reduced cognitive costs will correlate eventually was less roll-off. To test this hypothesis, we create an ordinal logistic regression model that predicts whether the enjoyment of voting on ballot measures is correlated with Internet searches. The dependent variable is derived from a question that asks, "Do you like, dislike, or neither like nor dislike voting on ballot measures?" The possible responses are, "Like a great deal (7)," "Like a moderate amount (6)," "Like a little (5)," "Neither like nor dislike (4)," "Dislike a little (3)," "Dislike a moderate amount (2)," and "Dislike a great deal (1)." The control variables in the model are the same as in Table 6.2.

Table 6.3 shows across three models that Internet searches on ballot measures increase the likelihood that the respondents "like" voting on ballot measures.

TABLE 6.3 Ordered Logit Models for "Enjoying" Voting on Ballot Measures

	Model 1	Model 2	Model 3
Internet Search	0.530**	0.442**	0.305†
	(3.19)	(2.60)	(1.78)
Education		0.090	0.040
		(1.73)	(0.75)
Age		−0.025	−0.053**
		(−1.54)	(−3.18)
Female		0.006	0.006
		(0.92)	(0.88)
Income		−0.286**	−0.200
		(−2.73)	(−1.85)
Black		−0.004	−0.0451
		(−0.02)	(−0.27)
Hispanic		−0.243	−0.227
		(−1.61)	(−1.50)
Political Knowledge			0.002
			(0.07)

(Continued)

TABLE 6.3 (Continued)

	Model 1	Model 2	Model 3
Political Interest			0.344***
			(6.22)
Cut points suppressed for space.			
N	1248	1198	1198
χ^2	10.11**	28.70***	72.39***

Note: 2012 ANES Direct Democracy supplement; standard errors in parentheses. †p < 0.10, *p < 0.05, **p < 0.01, ***p < 0.001.

This is consistent for the bivariate model, the model that includes demographics, and the model that includes political knowledge and political interest. The *p*-value for Internet search in the model that includes political knowledge and political interest is 0.075. While this is marginally above the traditional levels of statistical significance, it is instructive to consider the other variables in the model. The results in Table 6.3 also show that political interest correlates with enjoying the process of voting on ballot measures. Interestingly, these results show a statistically significant negative relationship in the third model, but is not significant in the second model. The other control variables do not have a statistically significant impact on enjoying voting on ballot measures. In sum, across three models these results show that searching for information on ballot measures on the Internet makes it a more enjoyable experience for the respondent, and this implies that they will be more likely to vote on it and not roll-off.

Conclusions

This chapter shows that Google Search can have deeper level impacts—by increasing voter confidence—when Google users take the time to use the engine. When they spend shorter amounts of time—as in the charter school amendment experiment—the effects are null. Both of these findings match expectations we have from the previous literature on Google and Internet search. Basically, if citizens are given the time, using Google for research creates externalities beyond simply knowing more about politics. They can feel more confident in their choices they make as a result of their information.

From the ANES data we find that Internet search is also related to being able to understand ballot measures and to increased levels of enjoyment for voting on them. Those who reported using the Internet to find information on ballot measures are significantly more likely to report they find ballot measures easy to understand even, and they are more likely to like voting on ballot measures even when controlling for important variables. This means that the Internet decreases the costs associated with direct democracy in real ways. These findings are extremely important for making the link between Google, knowledge gained from search, and actual behavior on direct democracy—which we theorize will make voters less likely to roll-off.

The main reason decreasing costs is so important is because direct democracy is one of the costlier forms of political activity in the United States. Citizens are constantly flustered and befuddled by questions being asked on ballot measures, and they have a difficult time trying to get engaged at all. This goes not just for average citizens but for more active members of society as well, such as petitioners (Reilly 2010; Yonk and Reilly 2012). Thus, the crucial test is if Google Search or Internet activity can decrease the costs of participating on ballot measures, and the best way to measure this is through roll-off. As we detailed in this chapter, there is ample reason to believe that the findings here on vote confidence, ease of understanding, and enjoyment would translate to lower levels of roll-off. However, this specific empirical question is not answered here. We do so in the next chapter.

Notes

1 Recall these are "hard issues" (see Chapters 1 and 2).
2 As we outlined in previous chapters, there was a great deal of cross-pressure activity on all three ballot measures. This was particularly the case for the T-SPLOST and charter school amendments. The Sierra Club came out strongly against T-SPLOST, while African American political leaders were very much in favor of the charter school measure. Both of these facts reflect the "hard" nature of these issues.
3 Due to time limitations with the MTurk study, we did not ask this question in that experiment. This is a limitation, but one with which we are comfortable because of the NES data and capacity to generalize from a national sample.
4 Recall that T-SPLOST respondents spent an average of 10 minutes doing research, while charter school subjects spent around 4 minutes on average.
5 This could be anything, by the way, so we are not limiting our expectations about how citizens research to politics. If you decide you want to choose between two movies playing at the theatre—and this is a purposeful, direct choice—then it makes sense that you would spend quality time—something up to or greater than fifteen minutes—to do research on your film options. Someone who does this would likely be very confident in their choice in the end. Similarly, if you decide to see a movie, but do not do research until you are confronted with your choice—in the ticket line, perhaps—then you may know more about the film than someone who does not do research, but you may not be as confident in your choice. In this case, ignorance creates bliss, so to speak.

References

Atkeson, Lonna Rae and Kyle L. Saunders. 2007. "The Effect of Election Administration on Voter Confidence: A Local Matter?" *PS: Political Science & Politics* 40 (2): 655–60.

Baum, Matthew A. and Angela S. Jamison. 2006. "The Oprah Effect: How Soft News Helps Inattentive Citizens Vote Consistently." *The Journal of Politics* 68: 946–59.

Baumgartner, Jody and Jonathan S. Morris. 2006. "The Daily Show Effect: Candidate Evaluations, Efficacy, and American Youth." *American Politics Research* 34 (3): 341–67.

Benoit, William L. and Glenn J. Hansen. 2004. "Presidential Debate Watching, Issue Knowledge, Character Evaluation, and Vote Choice." *Human Communication Research* 30 (1): 121–44. doi:10.1111/j.1468–2958.2004.tb00727.x.

Benoit, William L., Mitchell S. McKinney, and Lance R. Holbert. 2001. "Beyond Learning and Persona: Extending the Scope of Presidential Debate Effects." *Communication Monographs* 68 (3): 259–73. doi:10.1080/03637750128060.

Burden, Barry C. and Charles Stewart III. 2014. *The Measure of American Elections.* Cambridge, UK: Cambridge University Press.

Carr, Nicholas. 2011. *The Shallows: What the Internet Is Doing to Our Brains.* New York: W. W. Norton & Company.

Claassen, Ryan L., David B. Magleby, J. Quin Monson, and Kelly D. Patterson. 2013. "Voter Confidence and the Election-Day Voting Experience." *Political Behavior* 35 (2): 215–35.

Craig, Stephen C., Richard G. Niemi, and Glenn E. Silver. 1990. "Political Efficacy and Trust: A Report on the NES Pilot Study Items." *Political Behavior* 12 (3): 289–314.

Dalton, Russell J. 2013. *Citizen Politics: Public Opinion and Political Parties in Advanced Industrial Democracies.* 6th Edition. Washington, D.C.: CQ Press.

Delli Carpini, Michael X. and Scott Keeter. 1996. *What Americans Know About Politics and Why It Matters.* New Haven, CT: Yale University Press.

Finkel, Steven E. 1985. "Reciprocal Effects of Participation and Political Efficacy: A Panel Analysis." *American Journal of Political Science* 29 (4): 891–913.

Herrnson, Paul S., Richard G. Niemi, Michael J. Hanmer, Peter L. Francia, Benjamin B. Bederson, Frederick G. Conrad, and Michael W. Traugott. 2008. "Voters' Evaluations of Electronic Voting Systems: Results From a Usability Field Study." *American Politics Research* 36 (4): 580–611. doi:10.1177/1532673X08316667.

Highly, John and Ian McAllister. 2002. "Elite Division and Voter Confusion: Australia's Republic Referendum in 1999." *European Journal of Political Research* 41 (6): 845–61.

Highton, Benjamin. 2009. "Revisiting the Relationship Between Educational Attainment and Political Sophistication." *The Journal of Politics* 71 (4): 1564–76. doi:10.1017/S0022381609990077.

Hollander, Barry A. 1995. "The Influence of Talk Radio on Political Efficacy and Participation." *Journal of Radio Studies* 3 (1): 23–31.

Kenski, Kate and Natalie Jomini Stroud. 2006. "Connections Between Internet Use and Political Efficacy, Knowledge, and Participation." *Journal of Broadcasting & Electronic Media* 50 (2): 173–92. doi:10.1207/s15506878jobem5002_1.

Lau, Richard R., David J. Andersen, and David P. Redlawsk. 2008. "An Exploration of Correct Voting in Recent U.S. Presidential Elections." *American Journal of Political Science* 52 (2): 395–411. doi:10.1111/j.1540–5907.2008.00319.x.

Lau, Richard R. and David P. Redlawsk. 1997. "Voting Correctly." *American Political Science Review* 91 (3): 585–98. doi:10.2307/2952076.

———. 2006. *How Voters Decide: Information Processing During Election Campaigns.* Cambridge, UK: Cambridge University Press.

Lewis-Beck, Michael S., William G. Jacoby, Helmut Norpoth, and Herbert F. Weisberg. 2009. *The American Voter Revisited.* Ann Arbor, MI: University of Michigan Press.

Long, J. Scott and Jeremy Freese. 2006. *Regression Models for Categorical Dependent Variables Using Stata, Second Edition.* College Station, TX: Stata Press.

Lupia, Arthur. 2001. "Dumber than Chimps? An Assessment of Direct Democracy Voters." In *Dangerous Democracy? The Battle over Ballot Initiatives in America*, edited by Larry Sabato, Bruce A. Larson, and Howard R. Ernst, 66–70. Lanham: Rowman & Littlefield.

Magleby, David B. 1984. *Direct Legislation: Voting on Ballot Propositions in the United States*. Baltimore, MD: Johns Hopkins University Press.

Margolis, Michael. 1977. "From Confusion to Confusion: Issues and the American Voter (1956–1972)." *American Political Science Review* 71 (1): 31–43. doi:10.1017/S0003055400259285.

Morrell, Michael E. 2003. "Survey and Experimental Evidence for a Reliable and Valid Measure of Internal Political Efficacy." *Public Opinion Quarterly* 67 (4): 589–602.

———. 2005. "Deliberation, Democratic Decision-Making and Internal Political Efficacy." *Political Behavior* 27 (1): 49–69.

Mutz, Diana C. and Byron Reeves. 2005. "The New Videomalaise: Effects of Televised Incivility on Political Trust." *The American Political Science Review* 99 (February): 1–15.

Niemi, Richard G., Stephen C. Craig, and Franco Mattei. 1991. "Measuring Internal Political Efficacy in the 1988 National Election Study." *The American Political Science Review* 85 (4): 1407–13.

Prior, Markus. 2010. "You've Either Got It or You Don't? The Stability of Political Interest over the Life Cycle." *The Journal of Politics* 72 (3): 747–66. doi:10.1017/S0022381610000149.

Prior, Markus and Arthur Lupia. 2008. "Money, Time, and Political Knowledge: Distinguishing Quick Recall and Political Learning Skills." *American Journal of Political Science* 52 (1): 169–83. doi:10.1111/j.1540–5907.2007.00306.x.

Reilly, Shauna. 2010. *Design, Meaning and Choice in Direct Democracy: The Influences of Petitioners and Voters*. Burlington, VT: Ashgate Publishing.

Reilly, Shauna and Sean Richey. 2011. "Ballot Question Readability and Roll-Off: The Impact of Language Complexity." *Political Research Quarterly* 64 (1): 59–67. doi:10.1177/1065912909349629.

Sniezek, Janet A. 1992. "Groups Under Uncertainty: An Examination of Confidence in Group Decision Making." *Organizational Behavior and Human Decision Processes, Group Decision Making* 52 (1): 124–55. doi:10.1016/0749–5978(92)90048-C.

Verba, Sidney, Kay Lehman Schlozman, and Henry E. Brady. 1995. *Voice and Equality: Civic Voluntarism in American Politics*. Cambridge, MA: Harvard University Press.

Verba, Sidney, Nancy Burns, and Kay Lehman Schlozman. 1997. "Knowing and Caring about Politics: Gender and Political Engagement." *The Journal of Politics* 59 (4): 1051–72. doi:10.2307/2998592.

Wattenberg, Martin P., Ian McAllister, and Anthony Salvanto. 2000. "How Voting Is Like Taking an SAT Test: An Analysis of American Voter Rolloff." *American Politics Quarterly* 28 (2): 234–50.

Westbrook, Johanna I., A. Sophie Gosling, and Enrico W. Coiera. 2005. "The Impact of an Online Evidence System on Confidence in Decision Making in a Controlled Setting." *Medical Decision Making* 25 (2): 178–85. doi:10.1177/0272989X05275155.

Wolfinger, Raymond E. and Steven J. Rosenstone. 1980. *Who Votes?* New Haven, CT: Yale University Press.

Yonk, Ryan M. and Shauna Reilly. 2012. "Citizen Involvement & Quality of Life: Exit, Voice and Loyalty in a Time of Direct Democracy." *Applied Research in Quality of Life* 7 (1): 1–16. doi:10.1007/s11482–011–9142-x.

7

REAL-WORLD APPLICATIONS

Does Google Use Correlate With Real-World Political Behavior?[1,2]

Our experimental results in the previous chapters clearly show that Google searches produce political knowledge, and they show that using the Internet to learn about measures can increase the confidence citizens have in their vote choice. However, it is also important to consider how often citizens engage in online research about ballot measures before elections and whether it actually motivates any real-world behavior. To examine whether voters engage in Internet research for ballot questions we again use 2012 ANES data, and we use aggregate data on real-life Google searches. Google Insights for Search (I4S)[3] allows researchers to collect such data on Internet searches over time and by state. This process allows us to avoid two common problems that have affected past research relaying only on survey data to assess the effects of information technology on voter preparation. The first problem is social desirability bias in responses to survey questions, which arises from voters exaggerating their level of preparedness to answer ballot questions. The second problem is inherent in experimental studies; specifically, known difficulties exist with external validity and generalizability of results because participants may engage in unrealistic behavior in the laboratory (i.e., they use Google to do research in the context of a study, but they may not use it in their everyday lives). Google Search data mitigate these concerns because they accurately reflect the true patterns of Internet searches in individual states.

Because of the 2012 ANES Direct Democracy supplement, we are able to start by testing the correlation between using the Internet for research on ballot measures and the extent to which survey respondents report rolling off on ballot measures. Then, using cross-sectional time-series (XSTS) models of 2008 Google Search data measured weekly from November 1, 2007, to December 1, 2008, we find a large increase in searches for the *exact name* of a ballot measure, starting six weeks before the election. These results are robust even after controlling for differences in state demographics, state-level economy, and state election characteristics. We also find increases in search behavior in a particular state based on the *topics* being voted on in that state's ballot measures. For example, only California has a large increase in Google searches for the phrase "gay marriage," the topic of California's ballot question Proposition 8, around election time. This multi-method, multi-source research provides clear evidence that citizens take advantage of the Internet to research ballot measures, and it shows that information technology can facilitate voter preparation.

Beyond simply demonstrating search-engine usage as Election Day nears, we also use Google I4S query share data to correlate roll-off on ballot measures with Google Search volume. Our test shows that Google searches in a state for ballot measure names and topics one week before the 2008 presidential election correlate with actual roll-off on those ballot measures. This finding demonstrates that the more Internet searches there are for a ballot measure, the less likely voters are to not answer the question. These results provide external validity for our experimental results in the previous chapters, and taken together they suggest that the Internet can help direct democracy by exposing voters to websites that provide information about ballot measures.

We know that an increase in searches for health-related issues occurs during flu outbreaks and flu season (Eysenbach 2009; Polgreen et al. 2008; Ginsberg et al. 2009). The increase of these types of searches by individuals during health crises demonstrates that when people are concerned about their health, they turn to the Internet for additional information. Therefore, when ballot issues are presented to voters, it is plausible that they will turn to Internet searches for additional information. Mellon (2014) shows that Google Trends data is a reliable measure of issue salience for a range of general political issues as well. To investigate this potentiality on ballot measures, we have three hypotheses. Hypothesis 1 is that the proportion of Internet searches on a state ballot measure will increase within the state as the election becomes closer. Hypothesis 2 is that the proportion of Internet searches for the topic of the ballot measure will increase at a greater rate as the election approaches in the state where the ballot measure is relevant.[4] Hypothesis 3 is that that the more Internet searches there were for a ballot measure in the week before the election, the less likely voters were to roll-off (not vote down the ballot, by not answering the ballot questions).

While these hypotheses are intuitive, a real possibility exists that we could find a null result because voters may not search the Internet for these measures in these states. They may simply rely on information from other sources to inform their vote—such as newspapers or broadcast media—and not search for the information online. Prior research on civic competence suggests that voters will in fact not devote time to doing due diligence for voting. Conversely, national trends could make citizens research these topics throughout the United States. If these searches are not a direct desire for information on these ballot measures and are merely due to people searching for daily issues and activities, continual searches across states should be apparent rather than specific searches within the state voting on the measure. These searches should be consistent through Election Day, not increase in the days leading up to the election, and not correlate with roll-off. This pattern would be particularly true for well-known ballot measures such as Proposition 8 in California. Searches on gay marriage or Proposition 8 could be done from all over the country; however, according to our hypotheses we should see a specific increase in attention in California, demonstrating that voters are becoming more familiar with the ballot measure and the arguments for each side and showing a negative correlation with roll-off. Thus, in order to test our hypothesis, we need a null hypothesis that compares the states that have the ballot measure to states that do not have the ballot measure over time.

While our tests with Google Insights for Search are novel and original, we first need to establish the baseline expectation that Internet search is related to roll-off. To do this, we use the 2012 ANES. As described in previous chapters, this data set has a bounty of useful questions that help us contextualize and generalize our experimental findings. Here, we use the 2012 data to make the connection between Internet research and roll-off. Roll-off is a serious problem in direct democracy (Magleby 1984; Reilly 2010; Reilly and Richey 2011; Wattenberg, McAllister, and Salvanto 2000), so anything that can be isolated as a mitigating factor is worthy of study and exploration.

2012 ANES Data

The 2012 ANES contains a question that specifically asks whether respondents rolled off on a ballot measure—that is choosing an answer and not skipping the ballot measure. As a first step to measure whether Internet searches correlate with roll-off, we use this nationally representative survey data to test if the respondents expressing that they chose to *not* vote on the ballot measure correlates negatively with performing Internet searches on the ballot measure. To measure roll-off, we used the following question asked in the 2012 ANES, "Did you vote 'Yes,' 'No,' or abstain (did not vote) on the following ballot measures?" We code responses for abstains as (1), and sum them up across all eleven ballot measures. This creates a measure that goes from zero (0) to eleven (11) depending on how many ballot measures the respondents expressed rolling-off.

Because this is a count of the number of ballot measures of the respondent rolled-off, we use a negative binomial regression model (Hilbe 2007). We can empirically test whether this is a good choice by analyzing the p-value of the alpha statistic of the likelihood-ratio test. If this test has a statistically significant p-value, then the dependent variable has a Poisson distribution and a negative binomial, and therefore a negative binomial regression model is necessary. The likelihood-ratio test shows an alpha statistic with the p-value of 0.000, which clearly shows this dependent variable requires a negative binomial regression model.

Table 7.1 shows respondents who reported doing research on ballot measures using the Internet negative for increasing counts of rolled-off ballot measures across all three models. This means respondents who said they researched on the Internet were less likely to say that they abstained from voting on the ballot measure. Note that in Model 3, Internet searches has a p-value of 0.073, which is just barely outside the traditional $p \leq 0.05$ level of significance. However, given that this result is in line with our expectations, we are comfortable with this estimate as being significant. There are several legitimate critiques that one could make of using survey responses as metrics for behaviors like roll-off. It is very likely that asking survey respondents whether or not they voted is rife with social desirability bias. However, the advantage of this approach is that it allows us to examine a nationally representative sample and determine whether respondents at least *say* they chose to vote on these ballot measures. In our next section, we go further and use Google Search data from Google Trends to assess if states with higher search volumes see less roll-off.

TABLE 7.1 Negative Binomial Regression Models for Roll-Off

	Model 1	Model 2	Model 3
Internet Search	−0.649**	−0.570*	−0.451+
	(−2.58)	(−2.26)	(−1.79)
Education	—	−0.257***	−0.156*
	—	(−3.59)	(−2.14)
Age	—	−0.095***	−0.054*
	—	(−4.14)	(−2.27)
Female	—	−0.023*	−0.026**
	—	(−2.39)	(−2.66)
Income	—	0.294	0.169
	—	(1.95)	(1.12)
Black	—	0.303	0.386
	—	(1.23)	(1.58)
Hispanic	—	0.198	0.295
	—	(0.93)	(1.40)
Political Knowledge	—	—	−0.099**
	—	—	(−2.75)
Political Interest	—	—	−0.267***
	—	—	(−3.68)
Constant	0.267***	1.831***	2.696***
	(3.39)	(5.89)	(7.71)
N	1362	1304	1304
χ^2	5.873*	56.33***	83.16***

Note: 2012 ANES Direct Democracy supplement; standard errors in parentheses. $+p < 0.10$, $*p < 0.05$, $**p < 0.01$, $***p < 0.001$.

Google Trends Search Data

Google provides data generated by I4S or Google Trends.[5] To use I4S or Trends, a researcher inputs a search term, news item, or image of interest. One may modify the search terms by location of searches—such as by states—or by time ranges to address a specific research question. Researchers can filter their search volume results by type of search, country/location, year, and category. The "type of search" function classifies searches as web searches, image searches, news searches, or product searches. The "country" specification permits choosing nearly any country in the world, or one can specify their search as "worldwide." When one chooses a country for the specification—for state politics research this would most likely be the United States—I4S has a "sub-region" specification allowing for state specific search volume returns.

We collected time-series data within a particular state and also obtained cross-sectional data. To make cross-state comparisons, researchers need measures that assess the same phenomenon in the same way for all states in question, which I4S accommodates. With the location filter set to "United States," Google allows searching by sub-region (i.e., states). As a result, we were able to search for the exact same terms, images, news stories, or products for every state within the same period. This filter provides two choices for comparison, and one allows researchers to include all 50 states plus Washington, D.C., together for a specific search and time range. We combined these data sets to get XSTS data by searching by each state individually and then combining the 50 states together.

What Are the Data?

Google normalizes and scales the data generated by I4S. The normalization process is done by Google by using the search term being investigated by the researcher (i.e., "Michigan Medical Marijuana") and another baseline search term (i.e., "baseball") that can be compared with the researcher's search term in all geographic regions (Carneiro and Mylonakis 2009).[6] The comparison search term is used because it has a stable and predictable search volume over time (Carneiro and Mylonakis 2009). It is important to note that Google does not use comparison search terms that are constant or present a flat line if graphed, but rather it uses terms that are highly predictable for any given time of year. For example, the baseline term "baseball" has a very predictable pattern that increases during the baseball season every year, and Google uses that predictability as a reference to normalize a search term. Google has a repository of these baseline terms, all of which have been shown to produce predictable and stable results for normalization (Carneiro and Mylonakis 2009; Ginsberg et al. 2009).

As a search term increases or decreases in volume over the period set in the filters, it is compared to the baseline term in all geographic locations in the location filters. For instance, if one searches the United States as a unit for

"California Gay Marriage" over the months October 2008 to November 2008, the results in Figure 7.1 appear. The figure demonstrates the search term volume for California Gay Marriage in all 50 states and is normalized to reflect relative "query shares" (Shimshoni, Efron, and Matias 2009).[7] The figure shows two graphs; one is the trend line for query shares over the time period specified, and the second is a density chart by state for relative query share score. The search

FIGURE 7.1   Google I4S Results Page for "California Gay Marriage" October 2008 to November 2008

Source: Google Trends.

activity clearly peaks just before Election Day, and California has the highest amount of search activity.[8] Google obtains these normalized query shares by taking the total number of searches for a term in a defined geographic area, dividing that number by the total number of Internet searches in that area for the specified amount of time in question, and then normalizing the resulting value with a constant search term across all geographic sub-regions in the filter (Google, Inc. 2009; Shimshoni, Efron, and Matias 2009).

Google scales the data after this normalization process (Google, Inc. 2009). Data range from 0 to 100. As noted earlier, 100 reflects the highest amount of search volume within specified date and geographic constraints. Once Google establishes where the highest search volume occurs, it uses that reference point to scale the rest of the data points.

Thus, if the highest search volume for Michigan's medical marijuana ballot measure is in Week A and Week B shows half that search volume, the scaled value for Week B is 50. The scaled and normalized query shares only reflect the activity during the time specified, and they reflect the activity of the search terms or images being investigated (Google 2009). The limitations of this part of the data will be examined further later.

Past Usages of I4S Data

I4S is a new application that has only existed since 2004, and researchers are still discovering how it can be used to advance social science research. At present, several published political science journal articles and books have used I4S as a dependent or independent variable. Public health researchers often want to anticipate the next big pandemic. Various studies have shown that using Internet search term surveillance can correlate with outbreaks, in some cases well before the official declaration of the outbreaks. Since tools of this nature have only been available since 2004, researchers had to wait until some history of search terms had accumulated in order to utilize the data in any meaningful way. Polgreen et al. (2008) produce one of the earliest tests of search term data by using Yahoo search terms to correlate the onset of seasonal flu incidents as measured by public health offices and agencies. The researchers use a XSTS model to predict the likelihood of influenza-related activities being correlated with flu-specific search activity over a ten-week period. They find that their data are robust and validate their hypothesis. Ginsberg et al. (2009) replicate the study of Polgreen et al. with Google data.[9]

Ginsberg et al. take the 50 million most common search terms for influenza-like illnesses and create a normalized and scaled search volume score. They find, consistent with Polgreen et al. (2008), that this new search volume score or "trend" is also highly predictive of influenza-like illness reports by public health agencies. Their work is the basis for Google Flu Trends,[10] and the resulting I4S is useful for diseases other than the very common flu. Wilson and Brownstein

(2009) use I4S to predict the onset of *Listeria*, which is an uncommon disease. They successfully replicate the flu onset models by showing that *Listeria*-related public health reports are correlated with search term volume provided by Google Trends.[11] Their results demonstrate that even for a relatively uncommon disease like *Listeria*, I4S/Trends is a robust predictive tool. Furthermore, the robustness of this database has been replicated in Europe by French public health agencies (Pelat et al. 2009). Pelat and colleagues use I4S search volume data to replicate the findings of Ginsberg et al. (2009), and they do so for diseases other than the flu and in French. Thus, as Pelat et al. (2009) suggest, I4S has broad applicability and should be tested in areas other than public health.

Economists are also having success in using I4S to monitor economic conditions and activity. Choi and Varian (2012) demonstrate that I4S can successfully measure three economic activities: retail sales, home sales, and automotive sales. Research by Kholodilin, Podstawski, and Siliverstovs (2010) suggests that I4S volume is significantly correlated with consumption in the United States as well. Vosen and Schmidt (2011) add to this research by testing I4S capacity relative to survey-based indicators for consumption activity, and they find that I4S search term volume is a more accurate and robust predictor of various types of private consumption. Other research finds that I4S data correlate with unemployment rates accurately and more robustly than traditional measures such as initial claims (D'Amuri and Marcucci 2010). D'Amuri and Marcucci use the search term "jobs" in I4S. They perform a number of analyses using the best unemployment estimates in economics, and they demonstrate that the models perform better when the I4S term is included. I4S's ability to predict unemployment is replicated in numerous countries, such as Germany (Askitas and Zimmermann 2009), Italy (D'Amuri 2009), and Israel (Suhoy 2010). Finally, Mellon (2014) conclusively shows that Google Trends data is a robust marker for issue salience in American politics. However, these strong results in public health, economics, and public opinion do not mean that the data are without limitations.

Limits of the Data

These data possess strong potential usefulness to test the external validity of our experiments, but at least four significant limitations exist. The first limitation is the most evident: the raw search volume numbers are not available. Google does not provide these numbers publicly. They claim that their normalization and scaling process is the most efficient way to avoid the large discrepancies in search volume that one might expect between places like Rhode Island and California (Google, Inc. 2009). At this time, there is no way to know what the query share returns mean in terms of the actual number of people searching on the Internet. Crucially—and we stress this point—a threshold exists that searches must meet in order to register in Google I4S. If ten people search something, the search will not pass the threshold. Google will not release the exact threshold number but insists it must be a non-trivial amount of the search population. The fundamental point is that I4S query shares are a measure of *relative* search volume given the stated parameters by a researcher. Because Google uses a stable and predictable comparison term, the query share estimate should be an accurate reflection of the real numbers of people using those search terms relative to the other geographic areas involved. While this assumption is a serious limitation, it does not necessarily mean that these data cannot serve as a useful explanatory variable if construct validity can be established as has been done in public health and economics.

The second limitation is that the search terms used to generate the query shares have real consequences for the search volume returns. Thus, coding decisions when using these data are momentous. Searching for "Gay Marriage" rather than "California Gay Marriage" may change the results returned by I4S. Consequently, the theoretical basis for the search term used is of paramount importance. Furthermore, I4S allows the option to compare search volume across multiple search terms at once. While this function is important, it may not be useful when generating search volume data sets for political science. For instance, searching simultaneously for "California Gay Marriage" and "Gay Marriage" within the same temporal parameters (October 2008 to November 2008) demonstrates that—not surprisingly—"Gay Marriage" has a higher relative search volume than "California Gay Marriage." The trends of the lines produced by I4S are nearly identical with their peaks just before Election Day, but the values produced by I4S for the comparison are not interesting in themselves because they are calculated relative to each other. Thus, although this function is interesting as a descriptive tool for comparing search term validity, it does not add anything substantive to the point that query share values can be used as a predictive variable. The query shares produced in this instance are produced as a function of the other and therefore may hide the actual implication of the more specific search term—"California Gay Marriage."

The third limitation is that, like the search term coding decisions, temporal coding decisions are important. The normalization and scaling Google applies to the data are significantly affected by the time period in question. Thus, adding one month more or less than necessary can result in the effect being missed or over-represented. The fourth limitation is that these data are not drawn from a random sample of the population. Although the Internet is becoming ubiquitous and citizens are becoming much more adept at using it, any research using these data must take into consideration that they only relate to people who are using the Internet, and more specifically Google.

An additional consideration, which is not necessarily a limitation, is that these data are presented in the aggregate. As Ginsberg et al. (2009) state, it is impossible to connect any single individual with any particular search. Thus, researchers should be on guard against committing ecological fallacies with these data by making claims about individuals' behavior. Discerning individual behavior is not possible with these data. Furthermore, we cannot make claims about the quality of the billions of searches being performed. We cannot know, for instance, if a person searches for "California Proposition 8," that they will find information from a reputable source, which of the possibly thousands of websites returned that they visit, or if that specific search term is the only one they used to search for information. However, because we have demonstrated the validity of Google Search returns and their implications for political knowledge, we can confidently assume that information related to direct democracy generated by searching Google is reputable. Concerns about the quality of search behavior in the broader public with Google I4S data does not mean that we cannot draw conclusions from the data, but rather that we need to be careful in how we approach this data source and to what extent we broaden the explanatory power of these data.

Finally, researchers should be aware that the search parameters will greatly affect the type of data generated by I4S. As noted, the original data come either as a cross-section for the entire United States, or they can be generated by state as a time-series within the state specified in the filters. To get XSTS data, researchers can generate their time-series search inquiries individually for all 50 states and then combine the resultant data sets into one larger XSTS.

Hypothesis Testing

We believe that just as public health researchers are able to use Google I4S to accurately predict flu activity and economists can use it to gauge economic indicators, political science can use I4S to investigate important aspects of democratic citizenship. Through analyzing Google searches, we can determine if voters use the Internet to learn about direct democracy—a notoriously opaque aspect of the American electoral system.

As used by prior research (e.g., D'Amuri and Marcucci 2010; Shimshoni, Efron, and Matias 2009; Choi and Varian 2012; Choi and Varian 2009), our dependent variables to test Hypotheses 1 and 2 are normalized search term values—"query shares"—from Google I4S (Google, Inc. 2009; Shimshoni, Efron, and Matias 2009). Google obtains query shares by taking the total number of searches for a term in a defined geographic area, and dividing that value by the total number of searches in that area for the specified amount of time in question (Shimshoni, Efron, and Matias 2009). For example, we may have found that on California's Proposition 8—Same-Sex Marriage—has a "100" for Week X. Similarly, New York also might have a "100" query share for the same week. This situation does not mean that the absolute search volumes for those two states are the same. It simply means that, in California's case, Week X has the highest search volume for the weeks in which we set our search parameters. New York's searches could be more or less in absolute number, but Week X in New York is the week with the highest search volume for New York. The key, however, is that we do not expect any search volume in states where the search term is not a ballot question. Only the most highly salient ballot measures are searched in states where they are not on the ballot, and there are typically very few of those (e.g., California Proposition 8 in 2008). Thus, the data reflect the search activity within any one state for that term. This procedure allows for a very clear cross-sectional time-series analysis.

Google scales the data after this normalization process (Google, Inc. 2009). Data range from 0 to 100. As noted earlier, 100 reflects the highest search volume within the specified date and geographic constraints. Once Google establishes where the highest search volume occurs, it scales the remaining data points from there. Thus, if the highest search volume for Michigan's medical marijuana ballot measure is in Week A and Week B has half that search volume, then Week B's scaled value is 50. The limitation with these data—for both normalization and scaling—is that we cannot say specifically how many searches were performed on any one ballot measure. This situation is not problematic, however, because our hypothesis does not depend on absolute volume of searches, but relative search volume. Fortunately, the normalization and scaling do not preclude our ability to make claims about relative search volume *between* states. As a result, this new data source is a good first test for our hypothesis.

For our dependent variable, we gather Google I4S data for each ballot measure used in the 2008 election. Each ballot measure in the data set was also coded for topic. For instance, Michigan's Proposal 1 concerned the adoption of marijuana for medical use. So, to detect the "topic" search volume for this measure we searched "Michigan medical marijuana" in all 50 states separately for the weeks in the data set. And, as described above, to search for this ballot measure for the "name" data we searched "Michigan Proposal 1." This same process was repeated for each of the ballot measures in all 50 states.[12]

The limitation of this data, as previously stated, is that we do not have absolute search volume. However, given the evidence about the effectiveness and robustness of Google's search data, we can test how search volume increases as Election Day approaches. Shimshoni et al. (2009) note that the smaller temporal units introduce more variation in the data (I4S has the capacity to search by the day, week, month, and year—week is used in this chapter). As a result, the data we use bias our findings toward Type II findings.

Our key independent variable, *ballot measures by week*, measures the presence of a ballot measure in that state, weighted by the number of weeks before the election. Since these data are over time, we suspect that the number of searches will also grow over time as the election nears. Based on our hypotheses, we weight this variable by the distance in weeks before the election, up to 57 weeks. Thus, the 49 states without the ballot question are coded zero for all weeks, and the state with the ballot question is coded from 1 to 57, increasing by week. Creating an XSTS data set from Google I4S data for all 50 states, over 57 weeks, and using the 153 ballot measures available to voters across the country yields a data set of 436,050 possible observations. Some of these observations are lost because of non-returns by Google I4S, so we have an official data set of 435,694 observations for the XSTS. The results are also robust to a simple dichotomous indicator of the presence of the ballot question in the state.

The literature provides a number of variables that affect Internet usage, and we include those variables as controls. We include demographic controls for a state being in the West (California, Oregon, and Washington), per capita income, education level measured in percentage of the state's population with a college degree, age measured as the percentages that are over 65 (variable named *elderly*) and under 25 (variable named *youth*), and the percentages that are Black and Hispanic in the state. These data are from the 2000 Census. Electoral conditions may create a more stimulating election environment, which may lead to greater searching. Thus, we include a variable for the total number of ballot questions in the state in that election and the closeness of the presidential election in 2008. This competitiveness variable measures the closeness of the presidential election in each state by taking the final difference in electoral percentage of Obama and McCain as a proxy for overall closeness.

The data are over 57 weeks for each state and thus may be described as longitudinal, which is also known as XSTS (Wooldridge 2010, 6). Because the dependent variable is nested within states over time, we create an XSTS regression model to account for the within-state *and* between-state variability. This model accounts for changes in the same state over time. Traditionally, it is written as,

$$y_{it} = \alpha + X_{it}B + \mu_i + \varepsilon_{it} \tag{1}$$

for $i \in 1, \ldots, N$ and $t \in 1, \ldots, T_i$ and where **B** is a matrix of parameters to be estimated.[13] Most important for this research is that this data structure allows us to model how changes in the presence of state-level election factors influence searches aggregated from people living in that state. The results below are robust to other model specifications, including multilevel models and ordinary least squares regression with robust standard errors.

One central question to all longitudinal-data models is the issue of autocorrelation, which arises from prior lags of the dependent variable influencing later iterations of it (Baltagi 2001). This issue is important because as Drukker (2003, 168) states, "serial correlation in linear longitudinal-data models biases the standard errors and causes the results to be less efficient, [thus] researchers need to identify serial correlation in the idiosyncratic error term in a longitudinal-data model." If there is serial correlation, researchers need to correct for it. Wooldridge (2010, 282) developed a test for the presence of autocorrelation in longitudinal data. This test uses a first-differences model to test for autocorrelation, which is written as,

$$\Delta y_{it} = \Delta X_{it}B + \varepsilon_{it} \tag{2}$$

What the Woodbridge method does is estimate the matrix of parameters **B** by regressing Δy_{it} on ΔX_{it} and obtaining the residuals ε_{it} (Drukker 2003, 169). Wooldridge (2010, 282) shows that no serial correlation is present if the residuals from the full model and a lagged model correlate at -0.5, or formally written that $Corr(\Delta \varepsilon_{it}, \Delta \varepsilon_{it-1}) = -0.5$. With this knowledge, it is simple to test for the presence of autocorrelation in longitudinal data by checking if $Corr(\Delta \varepsilon_{it}, \Delta \varepsilon_{it-1}) = -0.5$. The Stata command *xtserial* preforms this test (see Drukker (2003) for more on this procedure). The results with these data show there is autocorrelation because it rejects the null hypotheses at $p \leq 0.000$. Thus, we need a model to estimate these results that accounts for the autocorrelation; the standard XSTS regression model written in Eq. 1 is inefficient and biased. Based on these results, we use a XSTS regression model with a disturbance term included that is first-order autoregressive.

Importantly, we must stress that we are not committing an ecological fallacy because we are making no claims about sub-groups within states. We are only testing whether the aggregate state-level density of searches is greater around elections for those states with ballot measures. The independent and dependent variables are both measured at the aggregate state level. That modeling specification does not make any inferential claims about individuals, which is the necessary element for it to be an ecological fallacy.

Figure 7.2 shows the level of searches for ballot question names in states that had a direct democracy election in 2008. The figure clearly shows that the

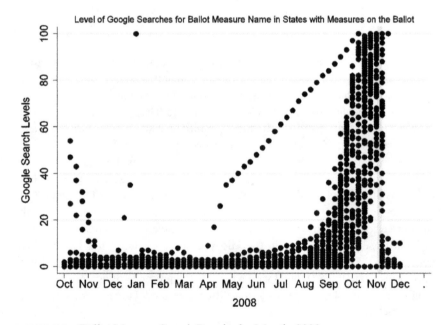

FIGURE 7.2 Ballot Measure Search Density by Month, 2008

Note: Data are Google I4S query values; the gray line in November indicates Election Day in Nov. 2008.

level of searches for the question name rises as the election approaches in the state, which suggests the upcoming election motivates citizens to research the ballot question. In addition, the search level remains high for a week or so after the election, showing that citizens were still researching the question after the election—probably to see what passed and what effect passage will have. This analysis is an interesting first-cut at investigating this relationship, but we test a more sophisticated XSTS model below.

Table 7.1 tests our first hypothesis and shows that we are correct with our theoretical assumptions about Google usage in states with ballot measures. The presence of a ballot question has a statistically significant positive effect on searches for that question's exact name in the states where the ballot question was present in the weeks leading up to the election. This finding shows that citizens use the Internet to research ballot questions in their state, and broader national trends are not driving both the presence of the ballot measure and the Internet searches. These results are also robust to a dichotomous measure of the presence of the ballot measure that is not weighted by week. In Model 2, we also see that the percentage of the area in a state that is urban lowers Internet searches for ballot names, while income greatly increases it. Interestingly, the average education level in the states does not have an effect. In models not shown, we removed income from the model, and education became positive and significant. Thus, the effect of education is moderated by income. Also, age has an impact because both *elderly* and *youth* are significant.

Table 7.2 shows that our second hypothesis is also supported for search volume for ballot topic. The presence of a ballot question has a statistically significant effect on searches for that question's topic in the states where the ballot

TABLE 7.2 Determinants of Internet Searches for Ballot Question Name, 2008

Variable	1	(S.E.)	2	(S.E.)
Ballot measure by week	0.318***	(0.004)	0.317***	(0.004)
Number of questions			0.012	(0.013)
Competition			0.000	(0.001)
West			0.061	(0.167)
Percent urban			0.000†	(0.000)
Unemployment			0.036	(0.031)
Income			0.047***	(0.001)
Education			−0.008	(0.010)
Male			−0.002	(0.015)
Elderly			0.042†	(0.023)
Youth			0.045*	(0.023)
Hispanic			0.004	(0.003)
Black			0.003	(0.004)
Intercept	0.059**	(0.022)	−2.616	(1.815)

(Continued)

TABLE 7.2 (Continued)

Variable	1	(S.E.)	2	(S.E.)
Observations	435,694		435,694	
Wald χ^2	5182.38***		5227.33***	
Modified D-W	0.282		0.282	
Baltagi-Wu LBI	0.431		0.431	

Source: Google I4S/Trends; U.S. Census Bureau.

Note: Cells represent unstandardized coefficients and robust standard errors of a XSTS regression model for determinants of change in the amount of Google searches about ballot measures names in 2008. Two-tailed tests for significance where † $p \leq 0.10$, * $p \leq 0.05$, ** $p \leq 0.01$, *** $p \leq 0.001$.

question was present. This finding shows that citizens use the Internet to research the topics of ballot questions. These results are also robust to a dichotomous measure of the presence of the ballot measure that is not weighted by week. In Model 2, we see that a state being in the West increases Internet searches for ballot question topics. In the model, we also find that income greatly increases it. Interestingly, age has no effect in that model, but having a greater percentage of the state that is Hispanic increases searches for ballot question topics.

As a further test, our third hypothesis is that search volume should serve as a proxy for voter interest in the aggregate. If voters are more interested, enthused, and mobilized with regard to a ballot measure, there should more Internet searches and less roll-off. "Roll-off" is the process whereby voters make top-of-the-ballot choices, but do not vote on the ballot questions on the same ballot. Thus, we hypothesize higher levels of Google Search volume in the week before Election Day should be correlated with lower percentages of roll-off. Using I4S, we can test this hypothesis for the first time with search data. Roll-off is a well-known problem, and causes for it have been extensively researched in political science literature (e.g., Reilly and Richey 2011).

Our independent variable is I4S query share output for two different terms for all 153 ballot measures on state ballots in the 2008 presidential election. We gather these data based on two types of search terms, with one search term being the specific *name* of the ballot measure itself (e.g., "California Proposition 8") for all 153 ballot measures. The second term we search is the *Topic* of the ballot measure for all 153 ballot measures on state ballots in the 2008 presidential election. Thus, instead of California Proposition 8 we search for "California Gay Marriage." This specification may seem broad, but those who would be searching this term in the date range in the states we specify are likely to be looking for information on the ballot measure about this topic.

The dependent variable for this analysis is *roll-off*. Its value is calculated by using the percentage point difference in turnout from the top office on the ballot (i.e., president in 2008) to the individual ballot measures. Ballot roll-off indicates that citizens vote for a top office but do not finish the entire ballot.

TABLE 7.3 Determinants of Internet Searches for Ballot Question Topic, 2008

Variable	1	(S.E.)	2	(S.E.)
Ballot measure by week	0.158***	(0.002)	0.157***	(0.002)
Number of questions	—	—	−0.013	(0.011)
Competition	—	—	0.001	(0.001)
West	—	—	0.528***	(0.148)
Percent urban	—	—	0.000	(0.000)
Unemployment	—	—	−0.023	(0.027)
Income	—	—	0.031**	(0.001)
Education	—	—	−0.017†	(0.009)
Male	—	—	−0.008	(0.013)
Elderly	—	—	0.012	(0.020)
Youth	—	—	0.026	(0.020)
Hispanic	—	—	0.006*	(0.003)
Black	—	—	0.001	(0.003)
Intercept	0.012	(0.020)	−0.383	(1.613)
Observations	435,694	—	435,694	—
Wald χ^2	4746.19***	—	4795.45***	—
Modified D-W	0.166	—	0.166	—
Baltagi-Wu LBI	0.388	—	0.388	—

Source: Google I4S/Trends; U.S. Census Bureau.

Note: Cells represent unstandardized coefficients and robust standard errors of a XSTS regression model for determinants of change in the amount of Google searches about ballot measures topics in 2008. Two-tailed tests for significance where † $p \leq 0.10$, * $p \leq 0.05$, ** $p \leq 0.01$, *** $p \leq 0.001$.

If we were trying to uncover a causal relationship between search level and roll-off, we would need to include control variables. But here, we only want to establish that I4S data taken a week before the election significantly correlate with actual electoral participation on ballot measures. Thus, we follow past research (e.g., Kholodilin, Podstawski, and Siliverstovs 2010) and do not present a kitchen-sink model packed full of control variables.

The results reveal a significant negative relationship, which supports our hypotheses. The search data on ballot question names has a negative correlation of −0.191 ($p = 0.02$) and topic searches are correlated at −0.150 ($p = 0.06$). Some may worry that our results are driven by the few ballot measures that have very high roll-off, but are coded zero for searches by Google. We use the Hadi (1992) method for detecting outliers and found eight significant outliers.[14] When we re-estimate the correlations omitting these outliers, we find that search data for question names have a negative correlation of −0.200 ($p = 0.02$) and topic searches are correlated at −0.151 ($p = 0.07$). These findings show that the results are robust to the omission of the outliers.

TABLE 7.4 Roll-Off and Internet Searches for Ballot Question Topic and Name, 2008

Variable	1	(S.E.)	2	(S.E.)	3	(S.E.)
I4S Topic Searches	−0.061†	(0.032)			−0.053†	(0.032)
I4S Name Searches			−0.049*	(0.021)	−0.046*	(0.021)
Intercept	12.871***	(0.884)	14.163***	(1.137)	14.561 ***	(1.156)
N	153		153		153	
F-test	3.49†		5.72*		4.27*	
R²	0.0226		0.0365		0.0539	

Source: Google I4S/Trends.

Note: Cells represent unstandardized coefficients and standard errors of an Ordinary Least Squares regression model for determinants of roll-off based on the amount of Google searches about ballot measures topics names in 2008. For significance with two-tailed test, † $p \leq 0.10$, * $p \leq 0.05$, ** $p \leq 0.01$, *** $p \leq 0.001$.

Our analysis also includes OLS estimations using I4S data as the independent variables in Table 7.4. We employ three modeling specifications to test the hypothesis that greater search volume significantly correlates with lower roll-off on ballot measures. Two independent variables represent the two methods of searches voters might perform when looking for information about their ballot measures. The first two models take these variables alone to test their effects, while the third specification estimates their effects on roll-off simultaneously. We also ran these models without the outliers mentioned above, and we find substantively similar significant correlations between both types of search volume and roll-off. We also ran these models using Rogers's (1993) robust standard errors on clustered on states, and we find substantively similar significant correlations between both types of search volume and roll-off. For simplicity, we present only one set of results in Table 7.4, the OLS results without robust standard errors and using all the data.

In Model 1, we test the effect of ballot topic search volume on roll-off. The effect of higher levels of search volume is negative and significant at the $p < 0.10$ level using a two-tailed test. In Model 2, we find that higher ballot name search volume is also significantly correlated ($p \leq 0.05$, two-tailed test) with lower levels of roll-off. The differences in levels of significance are not surprising because the *topic* variable has much more variance than the *name* variable. Nonetheless, these results suggest that ballot measures with high search volume scores are more likely to have voters participate on them. Furthermore, both measures of search volume are negative and significant, showing that Internet search volume correlates with roll-off.

The final model tests both variables' effects on roll-off, with negative and significant results for both *topic* and *name*.[15] However, this model stands apart because it demonstrates the robustness of the variables' predictive power.

Conclusion

To discover whether citizens are using the Internet to research ballot measures, we used subjective survey data and objective data on searches from Google. The ANES data showed a clear significant negative relationship between Internet searches and rolling off. Using Google Trends data, we also find a large increase in searches on both the exact name of the ballot measure and the general topic of the ballot questions starting about six weeks before Election Day in the state where the question is on the ballot. These results show that citizens do use the Internet to research ballot measures before Election Day. This finding is true for both the name of the ballot measure as well as the topic. This effect was found across states and demonstrates that American citizens do research prior to Election Day on these measures. This research shows that citizens use Google to research ballot measures, and it helps to provide evidence of the external validity of our experimental results. Our empirical test of external validity also shows that Google searches for ballot measures' names and topics in states one week before the 2008 presidential election correlate with actual participation on those ballot measures. This finding illustrates the desire of citizens to increase their ability to vote competently on these measures. It also contributes to earlier literature (Bowler and Donovan 2000; Lupia 1994; Lupia 2001) showing that voters have done research prior to arriving at the ballot booth. This research shows that voters actively search for information on ballot propositions, and our experiments show that if they do, they will become informed on the ballot measure.

With increased searches for both the topic and the ballot title closer to Election Day, voters are educating themselves to prepare to vote on these measures. By testing these two ways of searching, the research accounts for voters who may be unfamiliar with the exact title of a ballot measure because they are still seeking more information to assist them with their voting decisions. The findings strengthen support for use of direct democracy because they demonstrate that voters actively seek out information about these measures and prepare in the days leading up to the election. This interpretation supports the research that voters are able to vote their preferences (Bowler, Donovan, and Tolbert 1998; Bowler and Donovan 2000; Lupia 2001) and fulfill their expectations about direct democracy.

By using the Internet to research ballot measures, voters have more access to information in a variety of locations and frequently even from their mobile phones. Additionally, our research shows the promise of using the new Google Search data for political science research, which is beneficial in that they are non-obtrusive and an objective reflection of real-life behavior. We now turn to our final chapter to make some final remarks about our findings, and to set a course for future research in this area.

Notes

1 Shauna Reilly is a contributor to this chapter.
2 Portions of this chapter, used with permission, have been published in *State Politics & Policy Quarterly* under the title, "Using Google Search Data for State Politics Research: An Empirical Validity Test," in vol. 12, no. 2, pp. 146–59.
3 Google Trends was originally called Google Insights for Search (I4S). We use the names interchangeably.
4 We also find that fixed effects models, which only use dichotomous measures of the presence of the ballot measure in a state (and are not over time), have similar results (see Appendix Tables 1 and 2).
5 I4S is the easiest but not the only form of Google account. To access this data source one must first visit the following website: www.google.com/insights/search/#. Google Trends was, at one time, the less sophisticated version of I4S. Today, Google Trends and I4S use the same protocol. We use the terms "I4S" and "Trends" interchangeably. Trends/I4S allow users to set parameters for their search. After the search specifications and filters are selected, Google provides the search volume results in a downloadable spreadsheet.
6 According to Carneiro and Mylonakis (2009); Ginsberg et al. (2009); and Shimshoni et al. (2009), numerous comparison search terms are used by Google to generate the normalized data. Google claims that their rigorous tests generate reliable results regardless of the comparison search term because the comparison terms generally have stable and predictable volume over time and in comparison to one another. "Baseball" is used here as an example, but we have no way of knowing what term Google uses to generate the data normalization. Again, this is a limitation, but one that we are comfortable with given the robust results in this paper and other works we cite.
7 "Query shares" is the term Google uses to describe search volume.
8 It is important to note that searching for "Gay Marriage" with the same temporal filters generates essentially the same results, but because the search term is so much broader, the data are noisier and may not actually represent searches for the ballot measure. This situation highlights the importance of coding decision when using these data.
9 We have attempted to get the raw search term data from Google on numerous occasions. Polgreen, based on the footnotes in the 2008 article, is an employee or is at least professionally associated with Yahoo, while Ginsberg and a few coauthors, as noted by a footnote in the 2009 article, are employees of Google. Thus, to get the actual search term data it appears that one needs to be employed by the search-engine company.
10 www.google.org/flutrends/
11 It is important to note that the data returned by Google Trends and Google I4S are not generated any differently. Google I4S simply has the capacity for much more specific returns, which means it tends to have more validity.
12 Specifically, for both dependent variables we set the filters in I4S to create the longitudinal-data set. The filters can be set by a number of parameters. We chose to filter for web searches by state on every ballot measure from November 1, 2007, to December 1, 2008. This amount of time is good for two reasons. First, it allows us to get a large number of weeks in which voters could plausibly be looking for information on the upcoming election. Second, searching past the election allows us to test how much activity is going on after Election Day. Once the filters were set, we searched state by state for each ballot measure's query share. I4S provides Excel CSV files for the data obtained by the query search. The numbers returned by this process are the dependent variable. For further information about Google and the processes by which we garner the data visit this website: www.google.com/support/insights/bin/topic.py?hl=en topic=13975.

13 See Baltagi (2001) for more on XSTS models and this notation.
14 The Stata command *hadimvohi* tests outlier status. It rejects the eight ballot questions at the $p < 0.05$ level. For more details on this test, see Hadi (1994).
15 The *Topic* and *Name* variables are correlated at 0.1004 ($p = 0.2167$).

References

Askitas, Nikolaos and Klaus F. Zimmermann. 2009. "Google Econometrics and Unemployment Forecasting." *Applied Economics Quarterly* 55 (2): 107–20. doi:10.3790/aeq.55.2.107.

Baltagi, Badi H. 2001. *Econometric Analysis of Panel Data*. London, UK: J. Wiley & Sons.

Bowler, Shaun and Todd Donovan. 2000. *Demanding Choices: Opinion, Voting, and Direct Democracy*. Ann Arbor: University of Michigan Press.

Bowler, Shaun, Todd Donovan, and Caroline J. Tolbert. 1998. *Citizens as Legislators: Direct Democracy in the United States*. Columbus: Ohio State University Press.

Carneiro, Herman Anthony and Eleftherios Mylonakis. 2009. "Google Trends: A Web-Based Tool for Real-Time Surveillance of Disease Outbreaks." *Clinical Infectious Diseases* 49 (10): 1557–64. doi:10.1086/630200.

Choi, Hyunyoung and Hal Varian. 2009. "Predicting Initial Claims for Unemployment Benefits." http://static.googleusercontent.com/external_content/untrusted_dlcp/research.google.com/en/us/archive/papers/initialclaimsUS.pdf.

———. 2012. "Predicting the Present with Google Trends." *Economic Record* 88 (June): 2–9. doi:10.1111/j.1475–4932.2012.00809.x.

D'Amuri, Francesco. 2009. "Predicting Unemployment in Short Samples with Internet Job Search Query Data." *MPRA Paper 18403*. University Library of Munich, Germany. https://ideas.repec.org/p/pra/mprapa/18403.html.

D'Amuri, Francesco and Juri Marcucci. 2010. "'Google It!' Forecasting the US Unemployment Rate with a Google Job Search Index." *SSRN Scholarly Paper ID 1594132*. Rochester, NY: Social Science Research Network. http://papers.ssrn.com/abstract=1594132.

Drukker, David M. 2003. "Testing for Serial Correlation in Linear Panel-Data Models." *Stata Journal* 3 (2): 168–77.

Eysenbach, Gunther. 2009. "Infodemiology and Infoveillance: Framework for an Emerging Set of Public Health Informatics Methods to Analyze Search, Communication and Publication Behavior on the Internet." *Journal of Medical Internet Research* 11 (1): 1–10.

Ginsberg, Jeremy, Matthew H. Mohebbi, Rajan S. Patel, Lynnette Brammer, Mark S. Smolinski, and Larry Brilliant. 2009. "Detecting Influenza Epidemics Using Search Engine Query Data." *Nature* 457 (7232): 1012–14. doi:10.1038/nature07634.

Google, Inc. 2009. "Google Insights for Search: Analyzing Data." *Google Insights for Search*. www.google.com/support/insights/bin/topic.py?hl=en topic=13975.

Hadi, Ali S. 1994. "A Modification of a Method for the Detection of Outliers in Multivariate Samples." *Journal of the Royal Statistical Society: Series B (Methodological)* 56 (2): 393–6.

Hilbe, Joseph M. 2007. *Negative Binomial Regression*. 2nd Edition. Cambridge, UK: Cambridge University Press.

Kholodilin, Konstantin A., Maximilian Podstawski, and Boriss Siliverstovs. 2010. "Do Google Searches Help in Nowcasting Private Consumption? A Real-Time Evidence for the US." *SSRN Scholarly Paper ID 1615453*. Rochester, NY: Social Science Research Network. http://papers.ssrn.com/abstract=1615453.

Lupia, Arthur. 1994. "Shortcuts Versus Encyclopedias: Information and Voting Behavior in California Insurance Reform Elections." *American Political Science Review* 88 (1): 63–76. doi:10.2307/2944882.

———. 2001. "Dumber than Chimps? An Assessment of Direct Democracy Voters." In *Dangerous Democracy? The Battle over Ballot Initiatives in America*, edited by Larry Sabato, Bruce A. Larson, and Howard R. Ernst, 66–70. Lanham: Rowman & Littlefield.

Magleby, David B. 1984. *Direct Legislation: Voting on Ballot Propositions in the United States*. Baltimore, MD: Johns Hopkins University Press.

Mellon, Jonathan. 2014. "Internet Search Data and Issue Salience: The Properties of Google Trends as a Measure of Issue Salience." *Journal of Elections, Public Opinion and Parties* 24 (1): 45–72. doi:10.1080/17457289.2013.846346.

Pelat, Camille, Clement Turbelin, Avner Bar-Hen, Antoine Flahault, and Alain-Jacques Valeron. 2009. "More Diseases Tracked by Using Google Trends." *Emerging Infectious Diseases* 15: 1327–8.

Polgreen, Philip M., Yiling Chen, David M. Pennock, Forrest D. Nelson, and Robert A. Weinstein. 2008. "Using Internet Searches for Influenza Surveillance." *Clinical Infectious Diseases* 47 (11): 1443–8. doi:10.1086/593098.

Reilly, Shauna. 2010. *Design, Meaning and Choice in Direct Democracy: The Influences of Petitioners and Voters*. Burlington, VT: Ashgate Publishing.

Reilly, Shauna and Sean Richey. 2011. "Ballot Question Readability and Roll-Off: The Impact of Language Complexity." *Political Research Quarterly* 64 (1): 59–67. doi:10.1177/1065912909349629.

Shimshoni, Yair, Niv Efron, and Yossi Matias. 2009. "On the Predictability of Search Trends." *Google Research*. www.research.google.com/archive/google_trends_predictability.pdf.

Suhoy, Tanya. 2010. "Monthly Assessments of Private Consumption." White Paper 2010.09. *Bank of Israel*. www.bankofisrael.gov.il/deptdata/mehkar/papers/dp1009e.pdf.

Vosen, Simeon and Torsten Schmidt. 2011. "Forecasting Private Consumption: Survey-Based Indicators vs. Google Trends." *Journal of Forecasting* 30 (6): 565–78. doi:10.1002/for.1213.

Wattenberg, Martin P., Ian McAllister, and Anthony Salvanto. 2000. "How Voting Is Like Taking an SAT Test: An Analysis of American Voter Rolloff." *American Politics Quarterly* 28 (2): 234–50.

Wilson, Kumanan and John S. Brownstein. 2009. "Early Detection of Disease Outbreaks Using the Internet." *Canadian Medical Association Journal* 180 (8): 829–31. doi:10.1503/cmaj.1090215.

Wooldridge, Jeffrey M. 2010. *Econometric Analysis of Cross Section and Panel Data*. 2nd Edition. Cambridge, MA: The MIT Press.

8
CONCLUSIONS AND DIRECTIONS FOR FUTURE RESEARCH

Over the course of the preceding seven chapters we have shown that Google Search can be an incredibly powerful tool for citizens trying to make choices in direct democracy. Chapters 1 and 2 lay out the relevant literature, motivate our research questions, and lay out our general theory for Google as gatekeeper. In Chapter 3, we show that Google returns information relevant to ballot measures being searched in three different election contexts. Chapter 3 is an important first step in showing the utility of Google Search given concerns about gaming or biased results. In Chapter 4, we show subjects click on the best pages brought back on the first page of results, and we examine the correlates of Internet use for direct democracy in the United States using the 2012 ANES. It would be problematic if—even when given good results—users did not click on the most relevant sites Google returned. Based on the results in Chapter 4, this concern is trivial as subjects using Google acted rationally for information seeking. In Chapter 5, our results show that across three ballot measures, in the lab or on the street, with cookies or without cookies, and even when conducting a week-one re-test, Google Search produces political knowledge on ballot measures in American politics. The results from these chapters conclusively show that Google Search is a normatively and empirically beneficial tool for direct democracy.

To deepen our understanding of how Google Search impacts direct democracy, we expand our scope to attitudes and behaviors as a result of using Google. In Chapter 6, we demonstrate that using Google increases the confidence in vote choice and preparedness in the T-SPLOST experiment. Using ANES data, we show this quality has external validity as well. Users in the 2012 ANES direct democracy supplemental survey who used the Internet to research their ballot measure show increased levels of confidence compared to those who did not use the Internet to research ballot measures. Finally, in our last empirical chapter, we show that respondents in the 2012 ANES who did research on ballot measures using the Internet reported rolling-off less, and we show increases on Google I4S or Trends is correlated with both the state where the measure is on the ballot and it is negatively correlated with roll-off. These tests mean that people are using Google Search in the states where we would expect them to use it, and that in states where people use Google Search they are less likely to stop voting as they move toward ballot measures at the end of their ballot. These results mean that Google Search has instrumental value beyond the individual level. In other words, Google is good for direct democracy.

With this chapter, we aim to recap the importance of our research and direct future researchers with examples about how our methodology can be used. Our research is the first of its kind. Scholarship is replete with advocates and detractors of the Internet or Google, specifically. What is often missing from their praise or critique is a robust empirical investigation of their area of concern. Often, scholars have to rely on survey data, which is suboptimal when studying Internet behavior. Still other times, scholars may be able to examine Internet behavior, but there is often a lack of control or experimental design. Both of these problems are to be expected. Doing successful research on the Internet is hard, costly, and time-consuming. However, in this book we have taken a multi-method approach, and we are happy to share some best practices tips and advice for the future.

Why Study Search Algorithms

One of the things we show in this book is the importance of studying—through experimentation and behavior—the Google Search algorithm. The Google Search algorithm is the main tool citizens in modern democratic societies use for information. Because the search algorithm is explicated much more clearly than the processes that delineate traditional mass media, we can more easily understand how the provision of information will be assigned. In traditional mass media, it is unclear how the exact provision of information is provided even after decades of research on agenda setting and the editorial process. This is because the interview methodology of asking editors how they provide information, statistical analyses of quantitative textual data, or more subjective content analyses are still open to debate and interpretation. In fact, many scholars still have detailed and long running debates over how mass media provides information after many decades of intensive research (see Graber 2004; Iyengar 2015; McCombs 2014; Mutz 1998, for examples). Further, each micro-environment provides different stimuli that provoke editors, reporters, and other information sources to exhibit differential responses based on the local characteristics of media market. Thus, creating a grand and overarching theory of how information is provided is next to impossible with traditional mass media because each media market will have thousands of differential stimuli which will interact in an endless array of combinations.

The Google Search algorithm, however, is one solitary algorithm that provides over 50% of all news consumption (Lee 2016). Over a billion users use this one single algorithm that has a precise and clearly explicated logic that allows straightforward theory making. Because we can easily know how information is provided by understanding the necessary outcomes of the algorithm, we can derive from this knowledge a clear set of predictions that would not be possible in the near endless variations that exist in traditional mass media information provision. For example, an understudied and fascinating topic is how the psychology of editors affects their reasoning on the selection of news topics. As editors are human beings, they must have personality traits and other psychological factors that impact their decision making. But as all editors have a different psychological makeup, this necessarily implies that it is near impossible to create an overarching theory that would explain all news provision. And the psychology of editors is one of thousands of potential variables that affect agenda setting across the many media markets.

The Google Search algorithm is not influenced by psychology or other individualistic or local traits, and therefore studying its selection of news topics to up-rank to the front page is simply a matter of studying the underlying computer science of how the algorithm selects and processes the importance of individual pieces of coverage of news topics. This provides scholars with a chance to easily understand the provision of news in the modern information environment. By understanding the computer science of how a search engine provides and selects information (which will almost always will be an algorithmic process), it allows scholars to derive from the algorithm detailed hypotheses and predictions over how information will be provided. These theories can also be expanded to analyze how news provision will be affected across multiple platforms, software systems or applications.

For example, many scholars are interested in how social media is affecting political news viewership. Based on our successful analysis of the Google Search algorithm, the best and most logical way to proceed in understanding the effects of social media will be to understand the computer science of how the social media platforms such as Facebook or Twitter provide information. Since these algorithms are centralized and solitary, and also are determinative in the selection of the various news topics that users will see, by simply understanding how the algorithm selects information, scholars can easily understand how users will be provided with that information. After creating hypotheses based on the algorithm, we found that using experimental methods to empirically test the hypotheses derived from computer science theory was greatly beneficial for a full understanding of the impact of Google on users' political knowledge.

Survey Research Versus Experiments

The advantages of experiments over survey research should be clearer after reading this book. Survey research provides the benefit of generalizability, which is a clear and important advantage. Survey research can accurately be used in many settings to understand the political world, such as voting behavior, political participation and other more amorphous topics such as political trust and efficacy. Moreover, there are motivational, emotional, and psychological factors that can best be ascertained by asking the respondents how they feel. There would be no way to analyze these internal feelings and expectations, which are crucially important to understand the political world, without survey research. Indeed, we use survey questionnaires in our experiments to measure the political knowledge that was gained through Google usage. Also, many of our citations—such as how often users search the Internet—derive from survey research and are crucial to the study of Internet politics.

However, to truly understand how users engage with computers and with the Internet, nothing can beat the additional control that is gained through lab experiments. By controlling the information environment and having a record over what is provided by Google, which includes the vitally important ranking of the sites, we were able to test our theory. It would be next to impossible if users were not in an observational environment for us to verify the algorithm was acting in the way that we suggested. If we ask on a survey what Google showed the respondent, we would be relying on their memory, which would be faulty for this type of information. There would be no way to trust and verify that the websites that they say Google showed them after a certain search were listed in the correct order and if the information that they provided was accurate. It would be near impossible to expect the average person in a survey to remember how Google provided them information. The only way this can be done with scientific veracity is to conduct an experiment with observation of control. This aspect of our book is novel and we think it is a methodology that scholars can and should pursue in the future.

Additionally, our results on what users chose to click revealed fascinating information on the public processes information provided by Google. Remembering that 70% of all information searches on the Internet are gathered through Google (Lee 2016)—including information related to politics—it is crucial for scholars of Internet politics to understand how individuals select webpages to gain information. The dominant theory that has years of psychological research behind it is that of selection bias, or the related concept of motivated reasoning. We find that likely indicators of motivated reasoning are not nearly as important in the selection of information as PageRank. This shows the importance of observational control in a laboratory, as scholars may not immediately understand the importance of PageRank on what citizens choose to click on. The selection bias theory is highly intuitive and has years of prior research supporting it. Thus, it would be likely for scholars to assume that this would take place in the selection of which news source to click on. But by having participants in a laboratory in a controlled setting, we can view what they click on. In doing so, we find that the search algorithm provision is a much more important factor in deciding what they click on than selection bias. And since we further show that what they click on is what they learn, it was crucial to have environmental controls where we could observe directly what was provided, what they chose to click on, and what they learned. With this said, there are still several topics which we could not answer which are important to understanding Google's relationship to modern politics, which we now go over.

We Cannot Always Trust Google Results

First and foremost, having one company controlling a large percentage of the information dissemination in a modern politics suggests that we had better become highly concerned about Google's self-interest in promoting some results (see Epstein 2016; Epstein and Robertson 2015, for more on this concern). The results from our book shows that control of this algorithm is extremely important in determining the public sphere. If we define the public sphere as Habermas (2006) might—as the total sum of the conversation that we are having about politics and society in our national life—then we can be sure that the Internet is going to have a profound influence on that conversation. Currently, Google has a self-interest to promote and disseminate accurate information as that is their basic business model and "do-not-be-evil" principle: if you use Google, you will get the correct information. This business model has been transformative because once users understood that using Google gets them accurate information, they returned to it often. Which in turn made them view more advertising. Accuracy is the key to their business model. Thus, currently Google has a self-interest to promote accurate information about all topics and our research shows that the PageRank search algorithm supplies relevant mainstream sources that generally do provide accurate information. But, accuracy is only currently its business model, and that can change at any time.

Due to the nature of our book, only studying the algorithm in its current formation—which stresses accuracy—we can say nothing about Google manipulating the algorithm. For example, if there is ever a particular issue where Google is sufficiently threatened, or placed under financial pressure because of changes in the way advertising is processed, then it would be potentially advantageous for Google to change the algorithm to show results that benefit Google. That should alarm us. This publicly traded company still has most of its stock remaining in the hands of a relatively small group of people. Those people have specific and defined interests. Control over the algorithm gives them an inordinate amount of power over our public sphere.

One of the chief results of our book is that if you use Google you will gain accurate information about ballot measures, which leads to down-the-line attitudes making participation in direct democracy more likely. However, the implication of the results only exists under the current algorithm in its current specifications which are designed to produce accurate information. If and when Google decides to change those algorithmic assumptions in a way that may not be in parallel with democratic process, then we can be sure it will have profound negative consequences for our democracy. For instance, although they were initially reticent (Peyser 2016), Google recently took action to down-rank sites that engage in Holocaust denial based explicitly on the content of those sites. Even if Holocaust-deniers were to game the algorithm to promote their sites, engineers at Google have made it so those sites remain buried deep in the search results (Chokkattu 2016). However, since we cannot assume that the interest of Google will never be orthogonal to the interests of the country, this requires scholars to constantly monitor what the algorithm does to make sure that it is producing beneficial information.

A clear and specific role for scholars of Internet politics is to continue to monitor the output of Google to ensure that the algorithm is still designed to provide accurate information. This method should be extended to other massively influential Internet corporations such as Facebook and Twitter. Because these algorithms are proprietary, these corporations do not have to notify us when they change the underlying assumptions and goals of these algorithms. Yet due to their importance to our public sphere and having a successful informed democracy, it is crucial to have a third party verify that these corporations are acting in the public's interest. The research environment of modern universities provides a clear pathway to have uninterested unfunded third parties do rigorous scientific analysis of the veracity of the results that are provided by these corporations. As stated above, our methodological innovations in this book involving observational controlled lab studies are potentially highly beneficial for the further study of how these private corporations are potentially manipulating results, as well as the potential benefit of using these alternatives to Google for information gathering. Beyond this topic there are still many of the things that need to be learned, and let's investigate that now.

What Still Needs to Be Learned

In addition to the above topic of manipulated algorithm results not being able to be studied, we still need to know several important things that future research should consider. For example, we currently do not understand the extent to which differences by mode of access, such as mobile versus personal computers (PC) versus tablet, affect citizens' research experiences (see Pearce and Rice 2013 for some preliminary findings). One of the most basic assumptions of political behavior research is that users engage in cost-benefit analyses. The assumption simply is that political participants will choose the path that provides the most benefit with the least effort. With Internet searches, this calculation could easily be determined by the type of modal access if searching is less convenient on some types of systems.

For example, what is easy to access on a PC can be very different from what is easy for a mobile phone. Plausibly, there are important differences in what is easy to read and access on the much smaller screen and more difficult typing structure. If true, then mobile phone users will have important differences in the patterns of clicks on selecting information. Our results might not be instructive for tablets or mobile phone users, because all of the users in our experiments use either laptops or PCs, and with a dramatic rise of mobile phone usage a key question is whether these results are present across platforms.

Further, as the search algorithm becomes more specific to users' traits, it could be that the search results are in some way delineated differently across platforms. It was recently announced that Google will penalize websites for not being mobile friendly (Kennedy 2015). If Google is pushing websites that are not mobile friendly down in the ranking in its algorithm, we can expect those websites to be clicked on less and the information contained within them to be learned less often. This could perhaps have powerful political implications if marginalized voices are not able to create sophisticated websites that are mobile friendly, and then therefore these marginalized voices are further marginalized by their subsequent lower ranking on Google Search results.

Another profoundly important topic is how searchers will perceive candidate or policy information from Google searches, which could be more complicated than the "yes" or "no" questions provided by ballot measures. Due to the artificial nature of our experiment, we are giving the specific topic for voters to research. Ballot measures are not simple, and, in fact, one of our underlying assumptions is that this is a hard case for Google to educate users. But, we cannot discern what will happen if users search for non-factual morality-based policies that are often the most powerful in voters' decision making. We cannot address whether Google Search results that are biased toward mainstream information are going to be as educative for moral decision making. For example, it may be in a voter's interest to research topics which are more scientific, but due to the emotional pull that these moral issues have, they may be more likely to search for moral issues. By providing the ballot question either through referenda or initiative processes, the topic has been chosen for direct democracy voters. In an election with candidates, it is up to the user to select the topic to research on Google because there are many potential topics that are spoken about in an election period, and we cannot demonstrate with our book the effect of Google searches for candidates or policy.

An extreme example of this potential problem is conspiracy theories. In almost all cases, ballot measures are not about conspiracy theories or non-mainstream topics. However, in a general election context, it is possible that users might choose to research some conspiratorial theory about one of the candidates since the user chooses the topic to search. Our research, again, cannot speak to the validity of the Google Search algorithm in providing conspiracy theory search results. Yet, since we can assume that Google will provide mainstream information, it is likely that mainstream information will not contain conspiracy endorsement. The one fear, however, is the situation where no mainstream organization has yet written on the conspiracy theory, there will simply not be anything mainstream in the total web environment about the conspiracy to be up-ranked to the top of the search results. In this special case, the Google Search algorithm will suggest at the top of the search results conspiracy theory-endorsing websites with the most inbound links, because there is nothing else on the topic to suggest to users.[1]

This brings up the potential for intentional manipulation, where new conspiracy theories are quickly disseminated. The 2016 presidential election actually prominently featured this problem, which was widely termed "fake news." Next, we examine how to think about our positive results in the light of the fake news problem.

What to Do About Fake News?

When we started writing this book, it was still largely a hypothetical question as to whether there could be a successful large-scale effort to manipulate public opinion by manipulating information on the Internet. Well before the 2016 presidential election, we had actually written about this topic as a potential problem that could affect learning on the Internet, and other scholars discussed the potential for social media as a tool for information warfare (Manduric 2016). It is clear now that a large-scale coordinated effort to manipulate public opinion through the Internet was conducted on behalf of the winning candidate in 2016 (Davis and Haberman 2017; Sanger and Shane 2016). In Chapter 2, we listed these concerns as part of numbers four and five in our list of problems with lacking an editor to process information. At that time, we anticipated that this would be potentially done by alternative political campaigns and not an outside actor to the election.

We did not anticipate this would be a state-sponsored attack, with all the resources that states have, including vastly superior computing power and human capital than is typical of most hackers and other computer malcontents. Of course, the manipulation effort that was launched in 2016 featured much more than simply fake news. A major part of this effort was the hacking of websites and email accounts, and the generation of false stories that are disseminated through traditional state-sponsored media (Sanger and Shane 2016). However, one of the most effective sources of manipulation of public opinion in this effort was the generation of fake news about Hillary Clinton online. While it is impossible to precisely identify the cause for Hillary Clinton's loss, the 2016 election was so close that it is highly possible that this effort to distribute fake news was large enough to impact the incredibly close outcomes in the three states that mattered most in the election: Wisconsin, Michigan, and Pennsylvania.

The question quickly becomes what effect did the Google Search algorithm have in the distribution of fake news. If we pay attention to the logic of how the search algorithm works, however, it is in fact doubtful that most of the impact from fake news came through Google searches for information about Hillary Clinton. From our empirical results, we know that many of the sources Google returned with information on ballot measures were national news organizations, and that most users only click highly ranked links. One hope is that Google users will not encounter fake news because its algorithm will down-rank the newly created sites with few inbound links that were created for this effort. However, when someone is able to have their manufactured news go "viral" (i.e., the *Christian Times* "story" about Ohio voting precincts with closets full of ballots completed for Hillary Clinton well in advance of Election Day [Shane 2017]), we have jumped out of the Google Search algorithm and into social media. This means when someone searches for fake news stories they encounter on social media the actual primary source of the misinformation is social media. Google searches would not be the origination of the fake news in this case. Manipulated, hacked accounts or bots that spread misinformation through social media are much more likely to be the source of fake news. To combat fake news, scholars should focus on sources of information within social media that have generated and disseminated fake news.

Google searches—if anything—would work as a corrective to fake news, if the fake news item is widespread enough to have mainstream media or other well-known, well-respected news sources comment on it. This is because any newly created website will not have very many inbound links. If a major news organization or well-respected blog comments on the story, more than likely it will be to debunk the fake news. The only situation in which the Google Search algorithm will fail to debunk the fake news by directing the user to a mainstream source, is the previously mentioned scenario where no mainstream media has commented on this exact fake news topic. In aggregate, the Google Search algorithm should work as a corrective to most fake news attacks. This again shows the power of analyzing the search algorithm, because it shows that the distribution of news including fake news is determined by what the algorithm chooses. At this point, these are merely suppositions, so further research should be directed in analyzing the algorithms of social media to determine how and why they allow fake news to be distributed to their users.

Direct Democracy Information Online

At its core, this book it is about direct democracy. We have argued repeatedly in this book—as have others we cite in previous chapters—that direct democracy is difficult for citizens. Citizens have to directly decide on policy, and these decisions are fraught with all sorts of difficulties of cognition. Our goal was to consider whether the Internet helps citizens determine how to vote in direct democracy. The Internet seems an optimal place for citizens to research the potential outcomes of these difficult policy decisions. Internet research allows citizens to have access to information that they would never be able to obtain on their own. Furthermore, there are often specific websites about the ballot measure with information created by both sides and easily distributed by Google to users. The convenience of the Internet allows citizens to research these topics conveniently. It enables them to know more about the ballot measure than would have been possible before the Internet. The potential for direct democracy has been openly debated for 2,500 years, and this very important new resource to create educated voters needs much further investigation by scholars and researchers.

We show in this book across three samples, three elections, and three topics that citizens are able to gain valuable information by doing a few minutes of research. Most of the participants in our experiments spent less than five minutes researching these topics, and yet most were able to gain a significant information advantage over those who did not do the research. Perhaps most interesting is that even the adult sample that researched charter schools, which had no participant who was a college student or an Internet worker—and was therefore reflective of everyday citizens—was still able to gain beneficial information by doing Internet searches. This shows that the average person is able to use the Internet successfully to gain information. Of course, we cannot show that this information will be used wisely. Nonetheless, *a priori*, it is clear that we would prefer an educated voter to an uneducated one if the cost of education is low. The cost of becoming educated now about direct democracy ballot measures is trivial because almost 85% of population has Internet access (Perrin and Duggan 2015), and this number is growing, so it is easier to assume that citizens have access to all the information they need to make the correct decision.

Additionally, using survey data from the 2012 ANES, we note the characteristics that make it likely someone will use the Internet to do research on ballot measures and show that Internet research on ballot measures correlates with ease of understanding, enjoyment from voting, and decreases the number of ballots on which respondents report rolling-off. These two sets of empirical analyses— experiments and nationally representative survey data—create a robust test of the impact of the Internet, Google, and how citizens become more competent in this complex area of politics.

If we were to use formal models that predict what is needed for people to make rational decisions, we see that heuristics plays a large and important role. Google searches allow access to valuable heuristics. Before the Internet, access to heuristics would have to come through personal recommendations or perhaps seeing advertising on the subject. We found empirical evidence that Internet search results often lead to interest group websites which are easily recognizable heuristics. If one knows their relationship to the NRA, the Chamber of Commerce, and the Sierra Club—and those websites all state clearly their opinion on the ballot measure—it is fairly easily to discern how to vote. Meanwhile, all Google does is merely connect quickly, easily, and efficiently the voter to the heuristic, which should facilitate better voting decisions (see Lupia 1994 for how this works in direct democracy).

Citizens having access to the Internet and using research to buttress their voting decisions is becoming extremely important as more and more citizens move to voting by mail. The states that most often used to direct democracy are also the ones that most often use vote by mail. This is not a coincidence. One of the chief arguments in favor of voting by mail was that citizens could conduct thorough and deliberate research and have the time to think about direct democracy at home in ways that they could never do in a voting booth (Richey 2008). This is because vote by mail distributes the ballots about three weeks ahead of time of Election Day. This gives most voters plenty of time to research the aspects of the policy on which they are about to vote. More to the point, we already know the main source of information research for those who vote by mail is online searches (Mossberger, Tolbert, and McNeal 2007). This phenomenon is expected to grow as states adopt vote by mail, and we can expect that there will be more users searching for information about ballot measures on Google. This book provides useful empirical evidence that we can expect Google to provide valuable information for these future voters who are looking for better information on the ballot measures on which they are voting. As mobile phone penetration increases, including smartphone penetration, the ability to conduct Internet searches on ballot measures will be near 100% in a very short time. All of this taken together demonstrates the urgent nature of the empirical realities we discuss in this book. Google is a net positive for direct democracy.

Google and Mass Media

It is important to note that the fundamental beneficial effect of Google is simply connecting users to mass media and other mainstream information sources. There are, however, increasingly large financial pressures on mainstream media and we have seen the collapse of several large newspapers in America. There have been decreasing profits from broadcast media and some well-known print media has moved entirely online, such as the *Christian Science Monitor*. Several famous news magazines have gone out of business. Many other news sources are mere shells of their former selves and have greatly reduced their investigating and reporting staffs. The Nielsen ratings for broadcast media have greatly decreased in the last twenty years, combined with demographic trends that suggest what viewers that are left are greatly aging. Younger viewers are turning more and more to social media to gain news, which is placing large financial pressures on mainstream media outlets.

The beneficial effect in using Google is thus dependent on the financial survival of mainstream media. Since America does not engage in sponsored national broadcast media which is common in other media systems, we can only rely on for-profit mass media to provide correct information and do investigative journalism. While the benefits of having a sponsored national broadcast media have been clearly documented in providing citizen knowledge due to its public affairs focus and lack of sensationalism driven by a profit motive (Iyengar 2015), this new-media environment provides further incentive for the creation of sponsored national broadcast media. Although a national sponsored media has the potential to be manipulated by those who control its budgets, other such systems such as available in Great Britain and France have not had these pressures even after almost 100 years of existence. Thus, since Google and the Internet require high-quality content providers, and the current advertising system is not profitable to provide that through online advertising, this is a clear justification for public financing of media.

The Google Search algorithm in and of itself provides no actual content. Content providers are not currently making enough money through online advertising to support large staffs of reporters which were critical to the great investigative reporting of the twentieth century. As the new-media business model has not yet generated a system whereby profits will be great enough to allow the needed public service that was provided by traditional media in America, it is clear some other dissemination system must be created. An alternative to public financing is for the advertising rates to adjust to the new-media environment at such a level that will provide profitability. However, due to the balkanization of the media market going from three or four television channels in the 1970s to dozens of channels in the '80s and '90s through cable, and now with hundreds of channels with digital cable in the '00s, we have been left with a new situation whereby there are literally millions of content providers online. This effectively breaks up the profits into millions of pieces that were concentrated in a few hands previously.

Yet, we know that many of these online content providers are often not professional and do not have the norms of objectivity that prevailed during the twentieth century. In many ways, the twentieth century was a golden age for investigative reporting and the provision of high-quality content through mass media. This was due to a specific combination of factors such as the concentration of profits, a highly literate public, and a well-protected public sphere which guaranteed journalistic rights. Without the key piece of the puzzle of profits, this model for the dissemination of quality information will not hold.

The results of our book are therefore dependent on the solvency of mainstream mass media or the creation of alternative information dissemination mediums that are of similar quality. Without these content providers, Google searches will not provide high-quality information, and therefore the results of our book will not hold in the future.

Note

1 See the previous citations for Google's treatment of Holocaust denial websites for more information.

References

Chokkattu, Julian. 2016. "New Google Algorithm Lowers Search Rankings for Holocaust Denial Sites." *Digital Trends*. December 25. www.digitaltrends.com/web/google-search-holocaust/.

Davis, Julie Hirschfeld and Maggie Haberman. 2017. "Donald Trump Concedes Russia's Interference in Election." *The New York Times*. January 12. www.nytimes.com/2017/01/11/us/politics/trumps-press-conference-highlights-russia.html.

Epstein, Robert. 2016. "Subtle New Forms of Internet Influence Are Putting Democracy at Risk Worldwide." In *Google It: Total Information Awareness*, edited by Newton Lee, 253–60. New York, NY: Springer.

Epstein, Robert and Ronald E. Robertson. 2015. "The Search Engine Manipulation Effect (SEME) and Its Possible Impact on the Outcomes of Elections." *Proceedings of the National Academy of Sciences* 112 (33): E4512–21. doi:10.1073/pnas.1419828112.

Graber, Doris. 2004. "Mediated Politics and Citizenship in the Twenty-First Century." *Annual Review of Psychology* 55: 545–71.

Habermas, Jurgen. 2006. "Political Communication in Media Society: Does Democracy Still Enjoy an Epistemic Dimension? The Impact of Normative Theory on Empirical Research." *Communication Theory* 16: 411–26.

Iyengar, Shanto. 2015. *Media Politics: A Citizen's Guide*. 3rd Edition. New York: W. W. Norton & Company.

Kennedy, Kevin. 2015. "Google to Penalize Non-Mobile Sites Starting in April | Digital Marketing Insights | The Marketpath Web Digest." *Marketpath.com*. www.marketpath.com/digital-marketing-insights.

Lee, Newton. 2016. "To Google or Not to Google." In *Google It: Total Information Awareness*, edited by Newton Lee, 3–53. New York, NY: Springer.

Lupia, Arthur. 1994. "Shortcuts Versus Encyclopedias: Information and Voting Behavior in California Insurance Reform Elections." *American Political Science Review* 88 (1): 63–76. doi:10.2307/2944882.

McCombs, Maxwell E. 2014. *Setting the Agenda: Mass Media and Public Opinion*. 2nd Edition. Oxford, UK: Wiley. http://public.eblib.com/choice/publicfullrecord.aspx?p=1631739.

Manduric, Aylin. 2016. "Social Media as a Tool for Information Warfare." In *Google It: Total Information Awareness*, edited by Newton Lee, 261–4. New York, NY: Springer.

Mossberger, Karen, Caroline J. Tolbert, and Ramona S. McNeal. 2007. *Digital Citizenship: The Internet, Society, and Participation*. Cambridge, MA: MIT Press.

Mutz, Diana C. 1998. *Impersonal Influence: How Perceptions of Mass Collectives Affect Political Attitudes*. Cambridge, UK: Cambridge University Press.

Pearce, Katy E. and Ronald E. Rice. 2013. "Digital Divides From Access to Activities: Comparing Mobile and Personal Computer Internet Users." *Journal of Communication* 63 (4): 721–44. doi:10.1111/jcom.12045.

Perrin, Andrew and Maeve Duggan. 2015. "Americans' Internet Access: 2000–2015." Information Blog. *Pew Research Center: Internet, Science & Tech*. June 26. www.pewinternet.org/2015/06/26/americans-internet-access-2000-2015/.

Peyser, Eve. 2016. "Google Won't Alter the Holocaust-Denying Results for 'Did the Holocaust Happen.'" *Gizmodo*. December 12. http://gizmodo.com/google-wont-alter-the-holocaust-denying-results-for-di-1790025043.

Richey, Sean. 2008. "Voting by Mail: Turnout and Institutional Reform in Oregon." *Social Science Quarterly* 89 (4): 902–15. doi:10.1111/j.1540–6237.2008.00590.x.

Sanger, David E. and Scott Shane. 2016. "Russian Hackers Acted to Aid Trump in Election, U.S. Says." *The New York Times*. December 9. www.nytimes.com/2016/12/09/us/obama-russia-election-hack.html.

Shane, Scott. 2017. "From Headline to Photograph, a Fake News Masterpiece." *The New York Times*. January 18. www.nytimes.com/2017/01/18/us/fake-news-hillary-clinton-cameron-harris.html.

Appendix to Chapter 4

A List of Ballot Measures From the ANES 2012 Direct Democracy Study

(This list is from ANES 2015, 10–17).

State	Data Item	Item Description
AZ (86)	1	**Proposition 114** protects crime victims from having to pay damages to a person who was injured while that person committed or attempted to commit a felony against the victim.
AR (71)	1	**Issue No. 1** authorizes a temporary one-half cent sales and use tax for state highways and bridges and county and city roads, bridges, and other surface transportation with state revenues securing four-lane highway construction and improvement bonds.
CA (93)	1	**Proposition 30** increases taxes on earnings over $250,000 for seven years and sales taxes by ¼ cent for four years, to fund schools. It guarantees public safety realignment funding.
CO (84)	1	**Amendment 64** provides for the regulation of marijuana; permitting a person twenty-one years of age or older to consume or possess limited amounts of marijuana; providing for the licensing of cultivation facilities, product manufacturing facilities, testing facilities, and retail stores; permitting local governments to regulate or prohibit such facilities; requiring the general assembly to enact an excise

State	Data Item	Item Description
		tax to be levied upon wholesale sales of marijuana; requiring that the first $40 million in revenue raised annually by such tax be credited to the public school capital construction assistance fund; and requiring the general assembly to enact legislation governing the cultivation, processing, and sale of industrial hemp.
FL (59)	1	**Amendment 1** proposes a constitutional amendment to prohibit laws from compelling any person or employer to purchase, obtain or provide health care coverage. This would allow a person/employer to purchase services directly from a health care provider and allow a health care provider to accept direct payment for services if a patient chooses to pay out of pocket.
MA (14)	1	**Question 1** would require motor vehicle manufacturers to allow vehicle owners and independent repair facilities in Massachusetts to have access to the same vehicle diagnostic and repair information made available to the manufacturers' Massachusetts dealers and authorized repair facilities.
MI (34)	1	**Proposal 12–1, the Emergency Manager Law,** would expand the powers of emergency managers and the ability of the Governor to appoint emergency managers.
MO (43)	1	**Amendment 3** will change the current nonpartisan selection of supreme court and court of appeals judges to a process that gives the governor increased authority to appoint a majority of the commission that selects these court nominees. This measure also allows the governor to appoint all lawyers to the commission by removing the requirement that the governor's appointees be nonlawyers.
ND (44)	1	**Constitutional Measure No. 1** would remove the constitutional provision the legislative assembly to levy an annual poll tax of not more than one dollar and fifty cents on every male inhabitant of this state over twenty-one and under fifty years of age, except paupers, idiots, insane persons, and Indians are not taxed.
OH (31)	1	**State Issue 1** would create a convention to revise, alter or amend the state constitution.
OR (92)	1	**Measure 77** grants the Governor constitutional authority to declare a "catastrophic disaster" (defined); requires legislative session; legislature may suspend specific constitutional spending restrictions to aid response, recovery.

State	*Data Item*	*Item Description*
SD (45)	1	**Constitutional Amendment M** removes restrictions on the Legislature's authority to enact laws regarding corporations. It allows the Legislature to: (1) authorize alternative methods of voting in elections for corporate directors; (2) expand the types of contributions a corporation may receive for the issuance of stock or bonds; and (3) establish procedures governing the increase of corporate stock or debt.
WA (91)	1	**Initiative Measure No. 1185** would restate existing statutory requirements that legislative actions raising taxes must be approved by two-thirds legislative majorities or receive voter approval, and that new or increased fees require majority legislative approval.
AZ (86)	2	**Proposition 115** increases term length and raises the retirement age for justices and judges; modifies membership of court appointment commissions; requires publishing court decisions online and transmitting a copy of judicial performance reviews of each judge up for retention to the state legislature.
AR (71)	2	**Issue No. 2** authorizes cities and counties to create districts where sales tax receipts would be used to pay off bonds issued for infrastructure improvements; issue bonds to retire unfunded liabilities for closed police and fire pension plans; and to allow cities and counties to use money from sources other than the general fund to pay off short-term loan debt.
CA (93)	2	**Proposition 31** establishes a two-year state budget that sets rules for offsetting new expenditures, and Governor budget cuts in fiscal emergencies.
FL (59)	2	**Amendment 2** would allow for property tax discounts for disabled veterans. It explicitly extends the rights to ad valorem tax discounts, made available in 2010 to all veterans who were residents of Florida prior to their service, to all combat disabled veterans currently living in Florida whether they were residents prior to their service or not.
MA (14)	2	**Question 2** would allow a physician licensed in Massachusetts to prescribe medication, at the request of a terminally-ill patient meeting certain conditions, to end that person's life.
MI (34)	2	**Proposal 12–2, regarding collective bargaining,** would grant public and private employees the constitutional right to organize and bargain collectively through labor

State	Data Item	Item Description
		unions. It would also invalidate existing or future state or local laws that limit the ability to join unions and bargain collectively, and to negotiate and enforce collective bargaining agreements, including employees' financial support of their labor unions.
MO (43)	2	**Proposition A** will allow any city not within a county (the City of St. Louis) the option of establishing a municipal police force by transferring certain obligations and control of the city's police force from the board of police commissioners currently appointed by the governor to the city. This amendment also establishes certain procedures and requirements for governing such a municipal police force including residency, rank, salary, benefits, insurance, and pension. The amendment further prohibits retaliation against any employee of such municipal police force who reports conduct believed to be illegal to a superior, government agency, or the press.
ND (44)	2	**Constitutional Measure No. 2** would require the governor and other executive officials to take an oath of office to support the Constitution of the US and of North Dakota.
OH (31)	2	**State Issue 2** would remove the authority of elected representatives and grant new authority to appointed officials to establish congressional and state legislative district lines. It would create a state funded commission of appointed officials including members from each party to draw district boundaries.
OR (92)	2	**Measure 78** changes constitutional language describing separation of powers to refer to three "branches" (instead of three "departments") of government; makes other grammatical, spelling changes.
SD (45)	2	**Constitutional Amendment N** repeals the constitutional requirement that the mileage reimbursement rate for legislators is fixed at five cents per mile for legislators' travel to and from a legislative session. It repeals this limitation allowing legislator travel reimbursement to be set by the Legislature.
WA (91)	2	**Initiative Measure No. 1240** would authorize up to forty publicly-funded charter schools open to all students, operated through approved, nonreligious, nonprofit organizations, with government oversight; and modify certain laws applicable to them as public schools.

State	Data Item	Item Description
AZ (86)	3	**Proposition 116** would set the amount exempt from annual property taxes on business equipment and machinery purchased after 2012 to an amount equal to the combined earnings of 50 Arizona workers.
AR (71)	3	**Issue No. 3** would amend the Arkansas state constitution to allow Nancy Todd's Poker Palace and Entertainment Venues, LLC to own and operate four casino gaming establishments, one each in Pulaski, Miller, Franklin and Crittenden counties.
CA (93)	3	**Proposition 32** restricts unions from using payroll-deducted funds for political purposes and applies same use restrictions to payroll deductions, if any, by corporations or government contractors. It also restricts union and corporate contributions to elected officers or their committees and limits government contractor contributions to candidates and their committees.
CO (84)	3	**Amendment 66** would extend rights to all human beings at any stage of development the protections for life provided for in the state constitution applying equally to all innocent persons.
FL (59)	3	**Amendment 3** replaces the existing state revenue limits with a new limitation based on inflation and population changes. Any funds that exceed the revenue limits would be placed in the state's "rainy day fund." Once the fund reaches 10% of the prior year's total budget the Florida State Legislature would be required to vote to either provide tax relief or reduce property taxes.
MA (14)	3	**Question 3** would eliminate state criminal and civil penalties related to the medial use of marijuana allowing patients meeting certain conditions to obtain marijuana produced and distributed by new state-regulated centers or, in specific hardship cases, to grow marijuana for their own use.
MI (34)	3	**Proposal 12–3, the Renewable Energy Amendment,** would require utilities to obtain at least 25% of their electricity from clean renewable energy sources which are wind, solar, biomass, and hydropower, by 2025.
MO (43)	3	**Proposition B** will create the Health and Education Trust Fund with proceeds from a tax on cigarettes and other tobacco products. The amount of the tax is $0.0365 per cigarette and 25% of the manufacturer's invoice price for roll-your-own tobacco and 15% for other tobacco products. The Fund proceeds will be used to reduce and

State	*Data Item*	*Item Description*
		prevent tobacco use and for elementary, secondary, college, and university public school funding. This amendment also increases the amount that certain tobacco product manufacturers must maintain in their escrow accounts, to pay judgments or settlements, before any funds in escrow can be refunded to the tobacco product manufacturer and creates bonding requirements for these manufacturers.
ND (44)	3	**Initiated Constitutional Measure No. 3** would amend the constitution to guarantee the right of farmers and ranchers to engage in modern farming and ranching practices and states that "No law shall be enacted which abridges the right of farmers and ranchers to employ agricultural technology, modern livestock production and ranching practices."
OR (92)	3	**Measure 79** prohibits state/local governments from imposing taxes, fees, assessments on transfer of any interest in real property, except those operative December 31, 2009.
SD (45)	3	**Constitutional Amendment O** replaces the existing method for cement trust fund distributions. The amendment would require a yearly transfer of 4% of the market value of the cement plant trust fund to the state general fund for the support of education.
WA (91)	3	**Engrossed Substitute Senate Bill 6239** would allow same-sex couples to marry, preserve domestic partnerships only for seniors, and preserve the right of clergy or religious organizations to refuse to perform, recognize, or accommodate any marriage ceremony.
AZ (86)	4	**Proposition 117** sets a limit on the annual percentage increase in property values used to determine property taxes to no more than 5% above the previous year, and establishes a single limited property value as the basis for determining all property taxes on real property, beginning in 2014.
AR (71)	4	**Issue No. 4** would amend the Arkansas state constitution to allow Arkansas Hotels and Entertainment, Inc. to own and operate seven casino gaming establishments, one each in Sebastian, Pulaski, Garland, Miller, Crittenden, Boone and Jefferson counties.

State	*Data Item*	*Item Description*
CA (93)	4	**Proposition 33** changes current law to allow insurance companies to set prices based on whether the driver previously carried auto insurance with any insurance company. It also allows proportional discount for drivers with some prior coverage and increased cost for drivers without history of continuous coverage.
CO (84)	4	**Amendment S** would implement certain testing methods for job applicants, restrict the number of finalists for a particular job or position, place limits on the hiring of temporary workers and require that applicants be residents.
FL (59)	4	**Amendment 4** would prohibit increases in the assessed value of homestead property if the fair market value of the property decreases; reduces the limitation on annual assessment increases to non-homestead property; and provides an additional homestead exemption.
MI (34)	4	**Proposal 12–4, the Home Health Care Amendment,** would establish the quality Home Council, provide certain information to consumers, require training of providers, create a registry of workers who pass background checks, provide financial services to patients, and provide collective bargaining rights for in-home care workers.
MO (43)	4	**Proposition E** will deny individuals, families, and small businesses the ability to access affordable health care plans through a state-based health benefit exchange unless authorized by statute, initiative or referendum or through an exchange operated by the federal government as required by the federal health care act.
ND (44)	4	**Initiated Statutory Measure No. 4** would amend the North Dakota Century Code to prohibit smoking, including the use of electronic smoking devices, in public places and most places of employment in this state, including certain outdoor areas.
OR (92)	4	**Measure 80** allows commercial marijuana (cannabis) cultivation/sale to adults through state-licensed stores; allows unlicensed adult personal cultivation/use; prohibits restrictions on hemp.
SD (45)	4	**Constitutional Amendment P** requires the Governor to propose a balanced budget. In addition, it prohibits legislative appropriations from exceeding anticipated revenues and existing available funds.

State	Data Item	Item Description
WA (91)	4	**Initiative Measure No. 502** would license and regulate marijuana production, distribution, and possession for persons over twenty-one; remove state-law criminal and civil penalties for activities that it authorizes; tax marijuana sales; and earmark marijuana-related revenues.
AZ (86)	5	**Proposition 118** changes the distribution formula for the State Land Trust Permanent Endowment Fund, which funds various public institutions, including schools, to be 2.5% of the average monthly market values of the Fund for the immediately preceding five calendar years.
AR	1	**Issue No. 5, the Arkansas Medical Marijuana Act,** would make the medical use of marijuana legal under Arkansas state law; non-medical marijuana would remain illegal.
CA	5	**Proposition 34** repeals the death penalty and replaces it with life imprisonment without possibility of parole. It applies retroactively to existing death sentences. It also directs $100 million to law enforcement agencies for investigations of homicide and rape cases.
CO (84)	5	**Amendment 5** proposes that three justices be added to the seven-member court. Additionally, two divisions—civil and criminal—would be created within the high court with five justices each. The governor would be in charge of appointing the chief justices for each division and two would alternate as chief justice of the entire court. Appointees would have to be confirmed by the Senate. The proposed legislation also grants the House access to investigative files of the Judicial Qualifications Commission and sets aside at least 2.25 percent of the state's general revenue to fund the judicial branch.
FL (59)	5	**Proposal 12–5, the limit on enactment of new taxes by state government,** would require a 2/3 majority vote of the State House and the State Senate, or a statewide vote of the people at a November election, in order for the State of Michigan to impose new or additional taxes on taxpayers or expand the base of taxation or increasing the rate of taxation.
ND (44)	5	**Initiated Statutory Measure No. 5** would make it a class C felony to maliciously and intentionally harm a living dog, cat or horse. It would not apply to production agriculture, or to lawful activities of hunters and trappers,

State	Data Item	Item Description
		licensed veterinarians, scientific researchers, or to individuals engaged in lawful defense of life or property.
OR (92)	5	**Measure 81** changes commercial non-tribal fishing in Oregon "inland waters" by banning gillnets, adopting other regulatory changes; recreational salmon fishers ensured their share.
SD (45)	5	**Referred Law 14** establishes the "Large Project Development Fund." Beginning January 1, 2013, 22% of contractors' excise tax revenues would be transferred from the state general fund to the Large Project Development Fund. The South Dakota Board of Economic Development would use Large Project Development Fund monies to provide grants for the construction of large economic development projects within the state.
WA	5	**Engrossed Senate Joint Resolution 8221**
AZ (86)	6	**Proposition 119** authorizes the exchange of state trust lands if the exchange is related to either protecting military facilities or improving the management of state trust lands; outlines the process for exchanges, including independent appraisals and analyses, public hearings, and approval by public vote.
CA (93)	6	**Proposition 35** increases prison sentences and fines for human trafficking convictions. It requires convicted human traffickers to register as sex offenders. It also requires registered sex offenders to disclose internet activities and identities.
FL (59)	6	**Amendment 6** prohibits public dollars from funding abortions. It would prohibit the State Constitution from being interpreted to create broader rights than those contained in the U.S. Constitution. Exempts federal law requirements, physician certified physical danger to the mother and instances of rape or incest.
MI (34)	6	**Proposal 12–6, regarding international bridges and tunnels,** would require the approval of a majority of voters at a statewide election and in each municipality where "new international bridges or tunnels for motor vehicles" are to be located before the State of Michigan may expend state funds or resources for acquiring land, designing, soliciting bids for, constructing, financing, or promoting new international bridges or tunnels.

State	Data Item	Item Description
OR (92)	6	**Measure 82** authorizes privately owned casinos; requires such casinos to give percentage of monthly revenue to State Lottery for specified purposes.
SD (45)	6	**Referred Law 16** would establish a teacher scholarship program; create a program for math and science teacher bonuses; create a program for teacher merit bonuses; mandate a uniform teacher and principal evaluation system; and eliminate state requirements for teacher tenure.
WA (91)	6	**Senate Joint Resolution 8223** would create an exception to constitutional restrictions on investing public funds by allowing the University of Washington and Washington State University to invest specified public funds as authorized by the legislature, including in private companies or stock.
AZ (86)	7	**Proposition 120** repeals Arizona's disclaimer of all right and title to federal public lands within the state and declaring Arizona's sovereignty over public lands and all natural resources within its boundaries.
CA (93)	7	**Proposition 36** revises law to impose life sentence only when new felony conviction is serious or violent. It may authorize re-sentencing if third strike conviction was not serious or violent.
FL (59)	7	**Amendment 8** removes a prohibition on revenues from public treasury being used to aid any church, sect or religious denomination in aid of a sectarian institution. This would insure that no individual/entity can be denied any government benefit, funding or support based on religious identity or belief.
OR (92)	7	**Measure 83** authorizes a single privately-owned casino in Wood village; requires casino to give percentage of monthly revenue to State Lottery for specified purposes.
SD (45)	7	**Measure 15** would increase state general sales and use taxes from 4% to 5% for additional K-12 public education and Medicaid funding.
AZ (86)	8	**Proposition 204** permanently increases the state sales tax by one cent per dollar for the purpose of funding educational programs, public transportation infrastructure projects, and human services. It forbids reductions to current K-12 and university funding levels and forbids reductions to the current state sales tax base.
CA (93)	8	**Proposition 37** requires labeling of food sold to consumers made from plants or animals with genetic material changed in specific ways. It prohibits marketing

State	*Data Item*	*Item Description*
		such food, or other processed food, as "natural" and provides exemptions.
FL	8	**Amendment 9** would authorize the legislature to totally or partially exempt surviving spouses of military veterans or first responders who died in the line of duty from paying property taxes.
OR (92)	8	**Measure 84** phases out existing inheritance/estate taxes on large estates, death-related property transfers, and taxes on certain intra-family property transfers; reduces state revenue.
CA (93)	9	**Proposition 38** increases taxes on earnings using sliding scale, for twelve years. Revenues go to K-12 schools and early childhood programs, and for four years to repaying state debt.
FL (59)	9	**Amendment 10** would provide an exemption from ad valorem taxes levied by local governments on tangible personal property that's value is greater than $25,000 but less than $50,000.
OR	9	**Measure 85** allocates the corporate income and excise tax "kicker" refund to the (92) General Fund to provide additional funding for K through 12 education.
CA (93)	10	**Proposition 39** requires multistate businesses to pay income taxes based on the percentage of their sales in California. It dedicates revenues for five years to clean/efficient energy projects.
FL (59)	10	**Amendment 11** would enable the state legislature to authorize counties and municipalities to offer additional tax exemptions on the homes of low-income seniors. It will also provide an additional exemption to low-income seniors if counties and municipalities choose to offer it.
CA (93)	11	**Proposition 40.** A "Yes" vote approves and a "No" vote rejects, new State Senate districts drawn by the Citizens Redistricting Commission. If rejected, districts will be adjusted by officials supervised by the California Supreme Court.
FL (59)	11	**Amendment 12** would replace the president of the Florida Student Association with the chair of the council of state university student body presidents as the student member of the Board of Governors of the State University System. The amendment also requires that the Board of Governors create a council of state university student body presidents.

APPENDIX TABLE 4.1 Number of Clicks by Website Type on Three Ballot Measures

Type	Transportation	Charter Schools	Minimum Wage
Blog	1586	1071	588
Information	1586	969	476
Interest Group	3662	204	838
Irrelevant	—	—	58
Newspaper	1220	2142	726
Television	—	459	105
Government	1952	153	64
YouTube	732	255	39
Google	122	—	9
Ads	1220	102	—

APPENDIX TABLE 4.2 Summary Statistics for Transportation

	Control		Treatment	
	Mean	S.D.	Mean	S.D.
Gender	0.36	0.48	0.40	0.49
Black	0.53	0.50	0.37*	0.48
White	0.24	0.43	0.30	0.46
Hispanic	0.006	0.24	0.07	0.26
Age	23.74	7.25	25.22	9.81
Education	2.39	1.17	2.41	1.12
Party ID	2.14	1.55	2.22	1.53
Ideology	4.49	1.55	4.25	1.56
Internet Usage	0.56	0.75	0.58	0.74
Pre-Test Political Knowledge	4	1.66	4.04	1.86
Observations	118		123	

Note: Difference between treatment and control groups on a variable is significant as noted where † $p < 0.10$, *$p < 0.05$, **$p < 0.010$, ***$p < 0.001$. 'Pre-Test Political Knowledge' is a measure of general, civics-based political knowledge captured in the pre-test.

APPENDIX TABLE 4.3 Summary Statistics for Charter Schools

	Control		Treatment	
	Mean	*S.D.*	*Mean*	*S.D.*
Gender	0.41	0.50	0.25†	0.44
Black	0.35	0.48	0.39	0.49
White	0.49	0.50	0.47	0.50
Hispanic	0.00	0.00	0.02	0.14
Age	40.76	12.62	33.75*	11.64
Education	5.19	1.57	4.52	0.98
Party ID	2.12	1.61	1.84	1.28
Ideology	4.46	1.95	4.69	1.62
Internet Usage	0.76	0.81	0.76	0.86
Pre-Test Political Knowledge	−0.18	1.49	0.17	1.87
Observations	51		51	

Note: Difference between treatment and control groups on a variable is significant as noted where † $p < 0.10$, *$p < 0.05$, **$p < 0.010$, ***$p < 0.001$. 'Pre-Test' Political Knowledge' is a measure of general, civics-based political knowledge captured in the pre-test.

APPENDIX TABLE 4.4 Summary Statistics for Minimum Wage

	Control		Treatment	
	Mean	*S.D.*	*Mean*	*S.D.*
Gender	0.48	0.50	0.32*	0.47
Black	0.68	0.47	0.60	0.49
White	0.20	0.40	0.27	0.45
Hispanic	0.07	0.25	0.13	0.34
Age	32.88	10.81	30.76	10.28
Education	4.20	1.39	4.48	1.18
Party ID	2.20	0.72	2.18	0.76
Ideology	4.54	1.63	4.82	1.68
Internet Usage	4.71	1.85	4.58	1.88
Pre-Test Political Knowledge	0.91	0.29	0.89	0.32
Observations	169		62	

Note: Difference between treatment and control groups on a variable is significant as noted where † $p < 0.10$, *$p < 0.05$, **$p < 0.010$, ***$p < 0.001$. 'Pre-Test' Political Knowledge' is a measure of general, civics-based political knowledge captured in the pre-test.

APPENDIX: EXPERIMENTAL QUESTIONNAIRES

T-SPLOST: Summer 2012

Charter School Amendment: Fall 2012

NJ Minimum Wage: Fall 2013

Subject #: _____   *Questionnaire*   Researcher ID: _____

Please answer all pages of information, and follow any instructions listed inside. *IF* you are instructed to use the computer, please do so.

Personal Information: (Please Circle or Write Answers)

Name: _____,   _____
                    Last   **First**

Who is your 1101 instructor? Instructor's name _____
Your instructor WILL NOT be sent the information in this form. They will only be told that you participated in this activity.
****

Please mark your answer choice for each question below.

Gender:

☐ Male
☐ Female

Race:

☐ African American/Black
☐ Asian
☐ Multi-Racial
☐ White
☐ Other

Hispanic: Do you consider yourself to be Hispanic or Latino?

☐ Yes
☐ No

Age: Indicate what year you were born: _____

Education:

☐ Freshman
☐ Sophomore
☐ Junior
☐ Senior

Party Identification: Which political party do you usually support?

☐ Democratic Party
☐ Republican Party
☐ Other: _____
☐ Independent
☐ Don't know

Ideology: Do you consider yourself politically conservative or liberal?
- ☐ Strong conservative
- ☐ Moderate conservative
- ☐ Leaning conservative
- ☐ Neither
- ☐ Leaning liberal
- ☐ Moderate liberal
- ☐ Strong liberal

Voting: Have you ever voted? If so, please mark which all the years that you did vote:

☐ 2004	☐ 2005
☐ 2006	☐ 2007
☐ 2008	☐ 2009
☐ 2010	☐ 2011

Activities: Please mark how often you have done the following political activities.

1. Signed a petition

- ☐ Never
- ☐ Once or twice
- ☐ More than twice

2. Sent an email or letter to politician

- ☐ Never
- ☐ Once or twice
- ☐ More than twice

3. Commented on a website about politics

- ☐ Never
- ☐ Once or twice
- ☐ More than twice

4. Discussed politics with friend or family

- ☐ Never
- ☐ Once or twice
- ☐ More

5. Volunteered for a campaign

- ☐ Never
- ☐ Once or twice
- ☐ More than twice

6. Donated money to a campaign

☐ Never
☐ Once or twice
☐ More than twice

7. Attended a meeting/event on a political issue

☐ Never
☐ Once or twice
☐ More than twice

Political questions: (Fill in the answers on the blanks below)

1. What job or political office is now held by Joseph Biden?
   _____

2. Whose responsibility is it to determine if a law is constitutional or not. . . . Is it the President, the Congress, or the Supreme Court? _____
   _____

3. How much of a majority is required for the U.S. Senate and House to override a presidential veto? _____
   _____

4. Do you happen to know which party currently has the most members in the House of Representatives in Washington? _____
   _____

5. Would you say that one of the parties is more conservative than the other at the national level? Which party is more conservative? _____
   _____

6. Who is the current Chief Justice of the Supreme Court?
   _____

7. Who is the Mayor of Atlanta? _____
   _____

Issue Importance

Of the following issues, mark the answer that best describes how important that issue is to you personally.

Traffic and Transportation

☐ Not important
☐ Somewhat important
☐ Very important

Please give this completed form to the person who signed you in up front, and you will receive your instructions and packet

Subject #: _____   *Questionnaire*   Researcher ID: _____

Please Answer All Pages of Information, and Follow Any Instructions Listed Inside

Amendment No. 1: Indicate how you would vote on the following Amendment 1 on the Atlanta Regional Transportation Referendum (also known as the T-SPLOST), if you were in a voting booth on Election Day.

"Shall the transportation system and the transportation network in this region and the state be improved by providing for a 1 percent special district transportation sales and use tax for the purpose of transportation projects and programs for a period of ten years?"

☐ Yes
☐ No
☐ I would not vote

Please Continue on Next Page

1. How much additional percent in sales taxes will you pay if Amendment No. 1 passes? _____

2. How long will the tax be paid if Amendment No. 1 passes? _____

3. Approximately how much money is expected to be generated by this additional sales tax? _____

4. Which areas will get a new Marta train line if Amendment No. 1 passes? (list as many as you know)_____

5. Which highways will get a new intersection if Amendment No. 1 passes? (list as many as you know)_____

6. Will Atlanta get money for the Beltline line if Amendment No. 1 passes?

   ☐ Yes
   ☐ No
   ☐ I don't know

7. Will Peachtree City get money for the Ropeway line if Amendment No. 1 passes?

   a. Yes
   b. No
   c. I don't know

8. Will you personally benefit if Amendment No. 1 passes?

   a. Yes
   b. Maybe
   c. No
   d. I don't know

9. Thinking about your vote choice on Amendment No. 1, how confident are you that you choose the correct answer for yourself?

   a. Not at all confident
   b. Somewhat confident
   c. Confident
   d. Very confident

Continue on Next Page. . .

10. Thinking about your vote choice on Amendment No. 1, did you have enough information so that you chose the correct answer for yourself?

   a. Not at all
   b. Somewhat
   c. Mostly
   d. Very much so

11. How interested are you in question Amendment No. 1 on traffic and transportation issues?

   a. Not at all interested
   b. Somewhat interested
   c. Interested
   d. Very interested

12. On a scale of 1 to 10, with 1 least likely and 10 being most likely, how likely are you to discuss Amendment No. 1 with friends or family? Please circle your answer.

1	2	3	4	5	6	7	8	9	10
Not likely									Very likely

13. If you like, we will email an information packet on the **Amendment No. 1** transportation ballot measure to your friends or family if they would like more information on it. We will not email them about any other issue or use their email in any other way. Please write up to five names and email addresses below.

Name	Email Address
1._____	1._____
2._____	2._____
3._____	3._____
4._____	4._____
5._____	5._____

Continue on Next Page. . .

14. Would you like a form for help writing a letter to send to politicians and policy makers for your position on this issue?

    Please check the appropriate box below and submit an email address where the form may be sent.

    ☐ Yes
    ☐ No

Email for letter assistance: _____

Instructions

Please Follow These Instructions

Please fill out the questionnaire below on the Atlanta Regional Transportation Referendum (also known as the T-SPLOST), which is a ballot question about a sales tax for transportation projects. Voters will vote in July on whether or not to increase taxes to raise money for traffic and transportation.

Do NOT use a mobile phone or a computer to assist you in answering the questions.

When you are done, please give this questionnaire to the person who signed you in.

Subject #: _____   *Questionnaire*   Researcher ID: _____

Please Answer All Pages of Information, and Follow Any Instructions Listed Inside

Amendment No. 1
Indicate how you would vote on the following Amendment, if you were in a voting booth on Election Day.

"Shall the transportation system and the transportation network in this region and the state be improved by providing for a 1 percent special district transportation sales and use tax for the purpose of transportation projects and programs for a period of ten years?"

☐ Yes
☐ No
☐ I would not vote

Please Continue on Next Page

1. How much additional percent in sales taxes will you pay if Amendment No. 1 passes? _____

2. How long will the tax be paid if Amendment No. 1 passes? _____

3. Approximately how much money is expected to be generated by this additional sales tax? _____

4. Which areas will get a new Marta train line if Amendment No. 1 passes? (list as many as you know)_____

5. Which highways will get a new intersection if Amendment No. 1 passes? (list as many as you know)_____

6. Will Atlanta get money for the Beltline line if Amendment No. 1 passes?

    ☐ Yes
    ☐ No
    ☐ I don't know

7. Will Peachtree City get money for the Ropeway line if Amendment No. 1 passes?

    a. Yes
    b. No
    c. I don't know

8. Will you personally benefit if Amendment No. 1 passes?

    a. Yes
    b. Maybe
    c. No
    d. I don't know

9. Thinking about your vote choice on Amendment No. 1, how confident are you that you choose the correct answer for yourself?

    a. Not at all confident
    b. Somewhat confident
    c. Confident
    d. Very confident

Continue on Next Page. . .

10. Thinking about your vote choice on Amendment No. 1, did you have enough information so that you chose the correct answer for yourself?

    a. Not at all
    b. Somewhat
    c. Mostly
    d. Very much so

11. How interested are you in question Amendment No. 1 on traffic and transportation issues?

    a. Not at all interested
    b. Somewhat interested
    c. Interested
    d. Very interested

12. On a scale of 1 to 10, with 1 least likely and 10 being most likely, how likely are you to discuss Amendment No. 1 with friends or family? Please circle your answer.

1	2	3	4	5	6	7	8	9	10
Not likely									Very likely

13. If you like, we will email an information packet on the **Amendment No. 1** transportation ballot measure to your friends or family if they would like more information on it. We will not email them about any other issue or use their email in any other way. Please write up to five names and email addresses below.

Name	Email Address
1._____	1._____
2._____	2._____
3._____	3._____
4._____	4._____
5._____	5._____

Continue on Next Page. . .

14. Would you like a form for help writing a letter to send to politicians and policy makers for your position on this issue?
    Please check the appropriate box below and submit an email address where the form may be sent.

    ☐ Yes
    ☐ No

Email for letter assistance: _____

Name _____, _____
                                  Last   **First**

Zip Code of primary residence: _____

Recalling the research study you participated in, and the ballot question you were asked, please answer the following questions. . . .

15. How much additional percent in sales taxes will you pay if Amendment No. 1 passes? _____
16. How long will the tax be paid if Amendment No. 1 passes? _____
17. Which areas will get a new Marta train line if Amendment No. 1 passes? (list as many as you know)_____
18. Which highways will get a new intersection if Amendment No. 1 passes? (list as many as you know)_____
19. Will Atlanta get money for the Beltline line if Amendment No. 1 passes?

    ☐ Yes
    ☐ No
    ☐ I don't know

20. Will Peachtree City get money for the Ropeway line if Amendment No. 1 passes?

    a. Yes
    b. No
    c. I don't know

21. Will you personally benefit if Amendment No. 1 passes?

    a. Yes
    b. Maybe
    c. No
    d. I don't know

22. Thinking about your vote choice on Amendment No. 1, how confident are you that you choose the correct answer for yourself?

    a. Not at all confident
    b. Somewhat confident
    c. Confident
    d. Very confident

23. Thinking about your vote choice on Amendment No. 1, did you have enough information so that you chose the correct answer for yourself?

    a. Not at all
    b. Somewhat

    c.   Mostly

    d.   Very much so

24. How interested are you in question Amendment No. 1 on traffic and transportation issues?

    a.   Not at all interested

    b.   Somewhat interested

    c.   Interested

    d.   Very interested

25. On a scale of 1 to 10, with 1 least likely and 10 being most likely, how likely are you to discuss Amendment No. 1 with friends or family? Please circle your answer.

1	2	3	4	5	6	7	8	9	10
Not likely									Very likely

Subject #: _____   *Questionnaire*   Researcher ID: _____

Please Answer All Pages of Information, and Follow Any Instructions Listed Inside. If You are Instructed to Use the Computer, Please Do So.
****

Please mark your answer choice for each question below.

Gender:

☐ Male   1
☐ Female 0

Race:

☐ African American/Black 1
☐ Asian 2
☐ Multi-Racial 3
☐ White 4
☐ Other 5

Hispanic: Do you consider yourself to be Hispanic or Latino?

☐ Yes 1
☐ No 0

Age: Indicate what year you were born: _____

Occupation: Please write your job or occupation _____

Party Identification: Which political party do you usually support?

☐ Democratic Party 1
☐ Republican Party 2
☐ Other: _____ 3
☐ Independent 4
☐ Don't know 5

Ideology: Do you consider yourself politically conservative or liberal?

☐ Strong conservative 1
☐ Moderate conservative 2
☐ Leaning conservative 3
☐ Neither 4
☐ Leaning liberal 5
☐ Moderate liberal 6
☐ Strong liberal 7

ZIP Code: What is your ZIP Code _____

Voting: Have you ever voted? If so, please mark which all the years that you did vote:

☐ 2004   ☐ 2005
☐ 2006   ☐ 2007
☐ 2008   ☐ 2009
☐ 2010   ☐ 2011

Education: What is the highest level of education you have completed?

☐ Less than high school   ☐ College degree
☐ Some high school   ☐ Some graduate school
☐ High school diploma   ☐ Graduate degree
☐ Some college

Activities: Please mark how often you have done the following political activities.

8. Signed a petition

    ☐ Never 0
    ☐ Once or twice 1
    ☐ More than twice 2

9. Sent an email or letter to politician

    ☐ Never 0
    ☐ Once or twice 1
    ☐ More than twice 2

10. Commented on a website about politics

    ☐ Never 0
    ☐ Once or twice 1
    ☐ More than twice 2

11. Discussed politics with friend or family

    ☐ Never 0
    ☐ Once or twice 1
    ☐ More 2

12. Volunteered for a campaign

    ☐ Never 0
    ☐ Once or twice 1
    ☐ More than twice 2

13. Donated money to a campaign

    ☐ Never 0
    ☐ Once or twice 1
    ☐ More than twice 2

14. Attended a meeting/event on a political issue

    ☐ Never 0
    ☐ Once or twice 1
    ☐ More than twice 2

Political questions: (Fill in the answers on the blanks below)

8. What job or political office is now held by Joseph Biden? _____
9. Whose responsibility is it to determine if a law is constitutional or not. . . .
   Is it the President, the Congress, or the Supreme Court? _____
   _____
10. How much of a majority is required for the U.S. Senate and House to over-
    ride a presidential veto? _____
11. Do you happen to know which party currently has the most members in the
    House of Representatives in Washington? _____
    _____
12. Would you say that one of the parties is more conservative than the other at
    the national level? Which party is more conservative? _____
    _____
13. Who is the current Chief Justice of the Supreme Court? _____
14. Who is the Mayor of Atlanta? _____
    _____
15. Should the state of Georgia be able to override the decisions of local school
    systems to establish charter schools?

    ☐ Yes 1
    ☐ No 0

16. Of the following issues, mark the answer that best describes how important
    that issue is to you personally.

    Traffic and Transportation

    ☐ Not important 0
    ☐ Somewhat important 1
    ☐ Very important 2

    Jobs and the Economy

    ☐ Not important
    ☐ Somewhat important
    ☐ Very important

Education

☐ Not important
☐ Somewhat important
☐ Very important

War in Afghanistan

☐ Not important
☐ Somewhat important
☐ Very important

Please give this completed form to the person who signed you in, and you will receive your instructions and packet.

Subject #: _____   *Questionnaire*   Researcher ID: _____

Please Follow These Instructions

Please use the computer in front of you. Use Google to research information about the Georgia Charter Schools Amendment for AT LEAST THE NEXT 15 MINUTES.

This is a ballot question about possible changes to the way Georgia implements charter schools. You will need this information to answer questions later.

When you are done do NOT turn off your browser.

Do NOT use a mobile phone to assist you in answering the questions.

When you are done, please alert the person who is gave you this document. They will come and give you another questionnaire.

STOP HERE

DO NOT PROCEED UNTIL DIRECTED TO DO SO

Please Answer All Pages of Information, and Follow Any Instructions Listed Inside

Amendment No. 1: Indicate how you would vote on the following Amendment 1 on the Georgia Charter Schools Amendment.

"Shall the Constitution of Georgia be amended to allow state or local approval of public charter schools upon the request of local communities?"

- ☐ Yes
- ☐ No
- ☐ I would not vote

Please Continue on Next Page

1. If the amendment passes, if a local school system does not want to establish a charter school within their system, can the state approve a charter school anyway?

   ☐ Yes
   ☐ No
   ☐ Don't know

2. As proposed in the Amendment, are the charter schools established going to be public or private schools?

   ☐ Public
   ☐ Private

3. Under current law, who has the legal right to establish charter schools?

   ☐ State
   ☐ Local school systems
   ☐ Private citizens

4. If the amendment passes, who will have the legal right to establish charter schools?

   ☐ State
   ☐ Local school systems
   ☐ Private citizens

5. Under the amendment, will the state, local school systems or private citizens be responsible for funding the charter schools?

   ☐ State
   ☐ Local school systems
   ☐ Private citizens

Continue on Next Page. . .

1. Will you personally benefit if Amendment 1 passes?

   a. Yes
   b. Maybe
   c. No
   d. I don't know

2. Thinking about your vote choice on Amendment 1, how confident are you that you choose the correct answer for yourself?

   a. Not at all confident
   b. Somewhat confident
   c. Confident
   d. Very confident

3. Thinking about your vote choice on Amendment 1, did you have enough information so that you chose the correct answer for yourself?

   a. Not at all
   b. Somewhat
   c. Mostly
   d. Very much so

4. How interested are you in question Amendment 1 or on school issues generally?

   a. Not at all interested
   b. Somewhat interested
   c. Interested
   d. Very interested

5. On a scale of 1 to 10, with 1 least likely and 10 being most likely, how likely are you to discuss Amendment 1 with friends or family? Please circle your answer.

1	2	3	4	5	6	7	8	9	10
Not likely									Very likely

6. If you'd like, write the names and email addresses of anyone you know—including yourself—who you think may be interested in learning more information about the charter schools amendment.

Name	*Email Address*
1. _____	1. _____
2. _____	2. _____
3. _____	3. _____
4. _____	4. _____
5. _____	5. _____

Continue on Next Page. . .

7. Would you like a form for help writing a letter to send to politicians and policy makers for your position on this issue?

    Please check the appropriate box below and submit an email address where the form may be sent.

    ☐ Yes
    ☐ No

Email for letter assistance: _____

Subject #: _____   *Questionnaire*   Researcher ID: _____

Please answer all pages of information, and follow any instructions listed inside.

Amendment No. 1: Indicate how you would vote on the following Amendment 1 on the Georgia Charter Schools Amendment.

"Shall the Constitution of Georgia be amended to allow state or local approval of public charter schools upon the request of local communities?"

- ☐ Yes
- ☐ No
- ☐ I would not vote

Please Continue on Next Page

1. If the amendment passes, if a local school system does not want to establish a charter school within their system, can the state approve a charter school anyway?

    ☐ Yes
    ☐ No
    ☐ Don't know

2. As proposed in the Amendment, are the charter schools established going to be public or private schools?

    ☐ Public
    ☐ Private

3. Under current law, who has the legal right to establish charter schools?

    ☐ State
    ☐ Local school systems
    ☐ Private citizens

4. If the amendment passes, who will have the legal right to establish charter schools?

    ☐ State
    ☐ Local school systems
    ☐ Private citizens

5. Under the amendment, will the state, local school systems or private citizens be responsible for funding the charter schools?

    ☐ State
    ☐ Local school systems
    ☐ Private citizens

Continue on Next Page. . .

1. Will you personally benefit if Amendment 1 passes?

   a. Yes
   b. Maybe
   c. No
   d. I don't know

2. Thinking about your vote choice on Amendment 1, how confident are you that you choose the correct answer for yourself?

   a. Not at all confident
   b. Somewhat confident
   c. Confident
   d. Very confident

3. Thinking about your vote choice on Amendment 1, did you have enough information so that you chose the correct answer for yourself?

   a. Not at all
   b. Somewhat
   c. Mostly
   d. Very much so

4. How interested are you in question Amendment 1 or on school issues generally?

   a. Not at all interested
   b. Somewhat interested
   c. Interested
   d. Very interested

5. On a scale of 1 to 10, with 1 least likely and 10 being most likely, how likely are you to discuss Amendment 1 with friends or family? Please circle your answer.

1	2	3	4	5	6	7	8	9	10
Not likely									Very likely

6. If you'd like, write the names and email addresses of anyone you know—including yourself—who you think may be interested in learning more information about the charter schools amendment.

Name	Email Address
1. _____	1. _____
2. _____	2. _____
3. _____	3. _____
4. _____	4. _____
5. _____	5. _____

Continue on Next Page. . .

7. Would you like a form for help writing a letter to send to politicians and policy makers for your position on this issue?

Please check the appropriate box below and submit an email address where the form may be sent.

☐ Yes
☐ No

Email for letter assistance: _____

Amazon MTurk HIT Advertisement

Heading: Answer a one-question survey!!

Description: Answer this one-question survey for $0.01—it takes 5 seconds!

Question:

1. In which state do you currently live?

    a.   [Dropdown menu with all 50 states]

***We used the "re-contact" protocol written by Thomas Leeper for R and MTurk to give MTurkers the option of continuing in the project.

Pre-Test

MTurk Pre-Treatment Questionnaire for New Jersey Minimum Wage Ballot Measure

****

Please select the most appropriate answer for each question. You will be paid $0.10 upon completion of this survey. If you are re-contacted, we will contact you within two weeks.

Gender:

☐ Male
☐ Female

Race:

☐ African American/Black
☐ Asian
☐ Multi-Racial
☐ White
☐ Other

Hispanic: Do you consider yourself to be Hispanic or Latino?

☐ Yes
☐ No

Age: Indicate what year you were born: _____
Education:

☐ Some High School
☐ High School Diploma
☐ Some College
☐ College Degree
☐ Some Graduate School
☐ Graduate or Professional Degree

Party Identification: Which political party do you usually support?

☐ Democratic Party
☐ Republican Party
☐ Other: _____
☐ Independent
☐ Don't know

Ideology: Do you consider yourself politically conservative or liberal?

☐ Strong conservative
☐ Moderate conservative

☐ Leaning conservative
☐ Neither
☐ Leaning liberal
☐ Moderate liberal
☐ Strong liberal

Internet Usage: How often do you use the Internet to research information about society or politics?

☐ Rarely
☐ Once a month
☐ Once a week
☐ Everyday
☐ Multiple times a day

Political questions: (Fill in the answers on the blanks below)

17. What job or political office is now held by Joseph Biden? _____
18. Whose responsibility is it to determine if a law is constitutional or not. . . . Is it the President, the Congress, or the Supreme Court? _____
_____
19. How much of a majority is required for the U.S. Senate and House to override a presidential veto? _____
20. Do you happen to know which party currently has the most members in the House of Representatives in Washington? _____
21. Would you say that one of the parties is more conservative than the other at the national level? Which party is more conservative? _____
_____
22. Who is the current Chief Justice of the Supreme Court? _____

MTurk Google Search Instructions

Please take the next 15 to 20 minutes researching information regarding New Jersey's upcoming amendment to increase the minimum wage. You may follow the link below or you may search on your own.

1. Research for 15–20 minutes.
2. When you are finished, please copy and save your search history from only the portion of time you spent researching the amendment as a Word or RTF file.
3. Upload that file to the MTurk website.
4. You will be paid $0.50 upon the completion of this HIT.

MTurk Post-Treatment Questionnaire

To the best of your ability, please answer the following questions without looking up the answers. Questions will appear one-at-the-time, and are on a timer that will automatically forward to the next question. You will be compensated $0.05 for this HIT.

1. What will be the new minimum wage in NJ if it passes?
2. What is the current minimum wage in NJ?
3. Why will there be annual increases in the new minimum wage?
4. If the federal minimum wage increases, will NJ's minimum wage also increase?
5. Does NJ Governor Chris Christie support raising the minimum wage?

INDEX

For Product Safety Concerns and Information please contact our EU
representative GPSR@taylorandfrancis.com
Taylor & Francis Verlag GmbH, Kaufingerstraße 24, 80331 München, Germany